The Revolutionary War in
Bergen County

Gabrielle Wright of the Fourth Battalion New Jersey Volunteers cooking at Fort Lee Historic Park, with George Washington Bridge in background, during the 225TH anniversary of the Fort Lee blockhouse battle, 2006. *Courtesy of Susan Braisted.*

The Revolutionary War in
Bergen County
The Times that Tried Men's Souls

Edited by Carol Karels

Published by The History Press
Charleston, SC 29403
www.historypress.net

Copyright © 2007 by Carol Karels
All rights reserved

Cover image: George Washington on the Palisades, by H. Willard Ortlip, circa 1930s. *Restored by Paul Ortlip, 2003. Photo credit Donna Brennan. Courtesy of the Ortlip family.*

First published 2007
Second printing 2008
Third printing 2008

ISBN 978.1.54023.428.5

Library of Congress Cataloging-in-Publication Data

The Revolutionary War in Bergen County : the times that tried men's souls /
[edited by] Carol Karels.
p. cm.
Includes bibliographical references and index.
ISBN-13: 978.1.54023.428.5
1. Bergen County (N.J.)--History--Revolution, 1775-1783. 2. New Jersey--History--
Revolution, 1775-1783. I. Karels, Carol.
F142.B4R48 2007
973.309749'21--dc22
2007027616

Notice: The information in this book is true and complete to the best of our knowledge. It is offered without guarantee on the part of the author or The History Press. The author and The History Press disclaim all liability in connection with the use of this book.

All rights reserved. No part of this book may be reproduced or transmitted in any form whatsoever without prior written permission from the publisher except in the case of brief quotations embodied in critical articles and reviews.

Contents

Foreword: Revolutionary Bergen, by Kevin Tremble	7
Introduction, by Carol Karels	9
British and Hessian Accounts of the Invasion of 1776, by Lieutenant Colonel Donald M. Londahl-Smidt, USAF-Retired	17
The Invasion and the Myths Surrounding It, by John Spring	25
The Retreat to Victory, by Barbara Z. Marchant	32
Thomas Paine and "The Times That Tried Men's Souls," by Thomas Meyers	38
Preserving the Hudson River Battlefield, by Kevin Tremble	46
New Bridge: History at the Crossroads, by Kevin Wright	53
Bergen's Loyalists, by Todd W. Braisted	65
Daniel's Tale: The Career of One Bergen County Militiaman, by Eric Nelsen	77
Major General Lafayette: A Passion for Liberty, by Arthur Aranda	85
The Significance of the Hopper House, by Joan Dater	90
A Resourceful Woman in Revolutionary Bergen County: Theodosia Prevost at the Hermitage, by Dr. Henry Bischoff	92
General George Washington and His Command of the Revolution. From Letters Written in July 1778 While Headquartered at the Hermitage, by Dr. Henry Bischoff	97

Contents

General Charles Lee: A Disobedient Servant,
  by Barbara Z. Marchant — 105

"The Enemy…will have no Mercey upon our Loaded Barns":
  British Foraging at Hackensack, September and October 1778,
  by John U. Rees — 112

The Baylor Massacre, by Edmund A. Moderacki — 118

The Hard Winter of 1779–80, by Robert Griffin — 124

Thomas Ward and the Woodcutters of Bergen,
  by Todd W. Braisted — 130

The Hanging of Major André, by Steve Kelman — 142

W3R: The March to Win a War, by Carol W. Greene — 147

Black Loyalists in Bergen County and "The Book of Negroes,"
  by Arnold E. Brown — 162

George Washington: First of the Big-time Spenders,
  by Marvin Kitman — 169

Military Actions in Bergen County and Vicinity, 1776–1781:
  A Timetable, by Dr. Henry Bischoff — 175

Bibliography — 181

Index — 187

Foreword
Revolutionary Bergen

As I travel across our state, I am constantly reminded of the Revolutionary War events and the people who won our freedom. In almost every town, you will find a street named for Washington, Hamilton or Lafayette. In Bergen County, we also have towns themselves bearing their names: Fort Lee, Leonia, Washington Township. The *stories* behind these names, however, are still mysteries to many.

Our eighteenth-century ancestors, a remarkably diverse group, here in Bergen County and throughout New Jersey, live on among us in the sites, scenes and stories of the American Revolution. We need to continue to preserve, protect and promote them all with as much creativity as we can muster. Their relevance to the present and future residents of New Jersey, and the nation, is essential to our continued strength as the place of "out of many, one."

As president of the Crossroads of the American Revolution Association, I am pleased to be a contributor to this book, which is a gathering of those stories that have been written from the local perspective. As I have learned of the often untold, I have marveled at the way stories of the American Revolution, so numerous in Bergen County and all over our state, are little known by scholars. Our high school and college students seem to be even less aware.

Many of these essays highlight stories, people, places and events of Revolutionary New Jersey as experienced in eighteenth-century Bergen County. Today we find monuments, memorials and markers to be the wayside icons to help us discover these stories. This book is also designed to be an icon into a deeper appreciation of the struggle and sacrifice to create this country.

Crossroads Association is now a partner with the National Park Service and, in a cooperative fashion, responsible for the protection and support of these historic sites and their stories in the newly created Crossroads of the American Revolution National Heritage Area. More connections to the many stories throughout New Jersey can be found at www.revolutionarynj.org.

Kevin Tremble
President, Crossroads of the American Revolution Association

Introduction

Hidden history. That's what I call Bergen County's, as it's a county filled with history hidden below high-rises and cliffs, between housing developments, in the basements of malls and behind auto junkyards.

The most hidden history of all is the story of the Revolutionary War in Bergen County. Were it not for knowledgeable friends and historically minded coworkers who grew up in Bergen County, I still might not know that it played a major role in the Revolutionary War. I learned bits and pieces while pushing a stroller up and down the streets of Leonia. Every few blocks, I'd come across a historic marker to a place or person that piqued my interest.

From these markers I learned, for example, that Leonia was once known as "English Neighborhood," that Grand Avenue was once called King's Highway and that Fort Lee Road was named for a Revolutionary War fort at the top of the hill. I discovered that the Marquis de Lafayette's encampment had been across the street from the Leonia Public Library, and that a colonial-era tavern named Day's had been situated down by the present-day railroad tracks. A slave cemetery had been established at the north end of town, just up the block from the historic Vreeland house. Learning of the cemetery surprised me; I'd never realized slavery existed this far north. A sign on Hillside Avenue informed me that the first church in Leonia, a Dutch Reformed congregation, had been abandoned shortly after the war began, when the Loyalist minister fled, taking all of the church records with him. I learned about the treachery of Loyalist Sam Cole toward his Patriot neighbors from the historic plaque in front of the Cole-Boyd House on Prospect Street. Van Horne's gristmill, on the banks of the Overpeck Creek, was perhaps where General Nathanael Greene had made his headquarters in the fall of 1776. And George Washington's famous retreat through New Jersey is memorialized on a bronze plaque in front of the Leonia Presbyterian Church on Fort Lee Road; it was created by Leonia resident Mahonri Young, the grandson of Brigham Young, in 1916. A few years later, while listening to concerts

Introduction

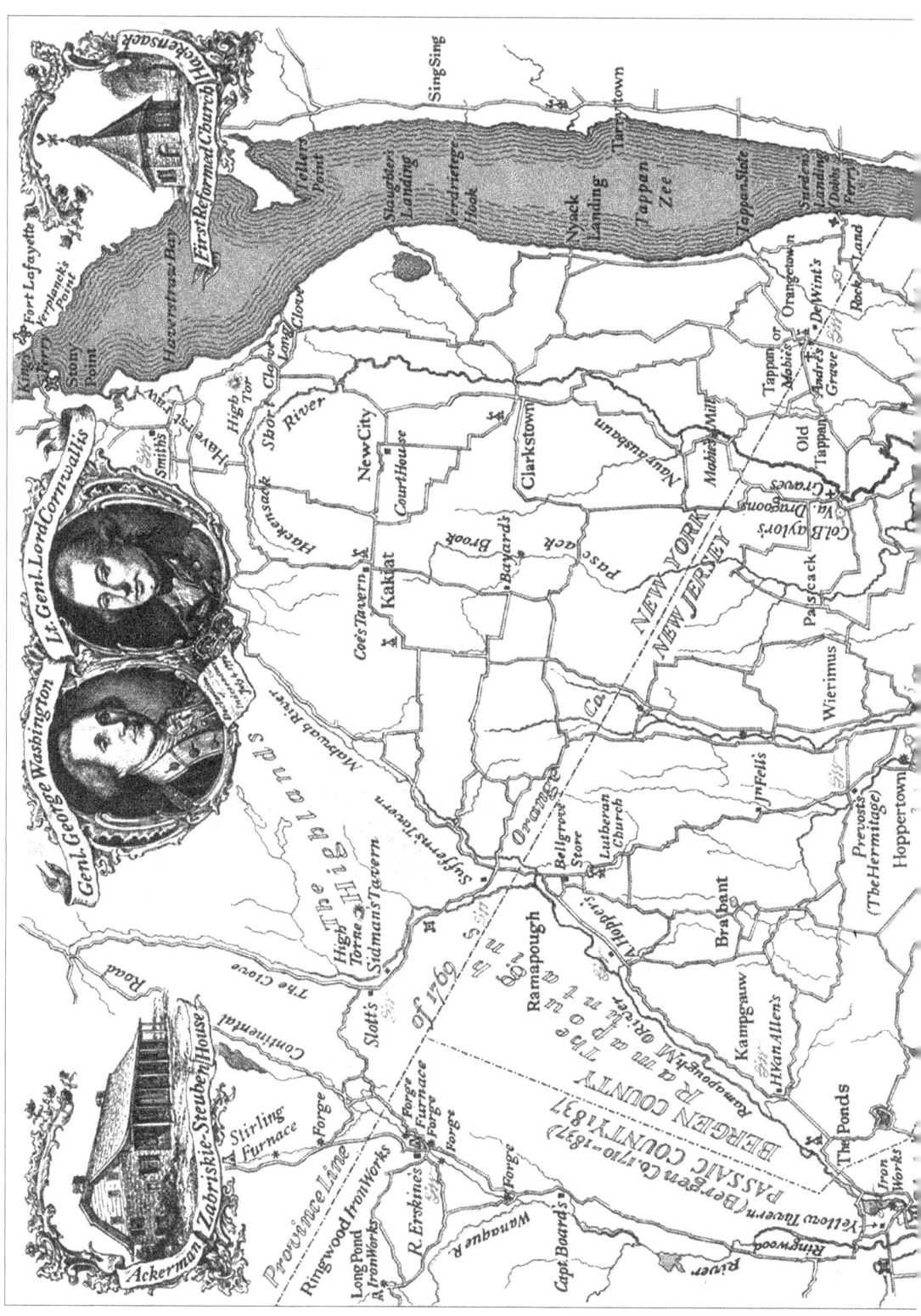

Introduction

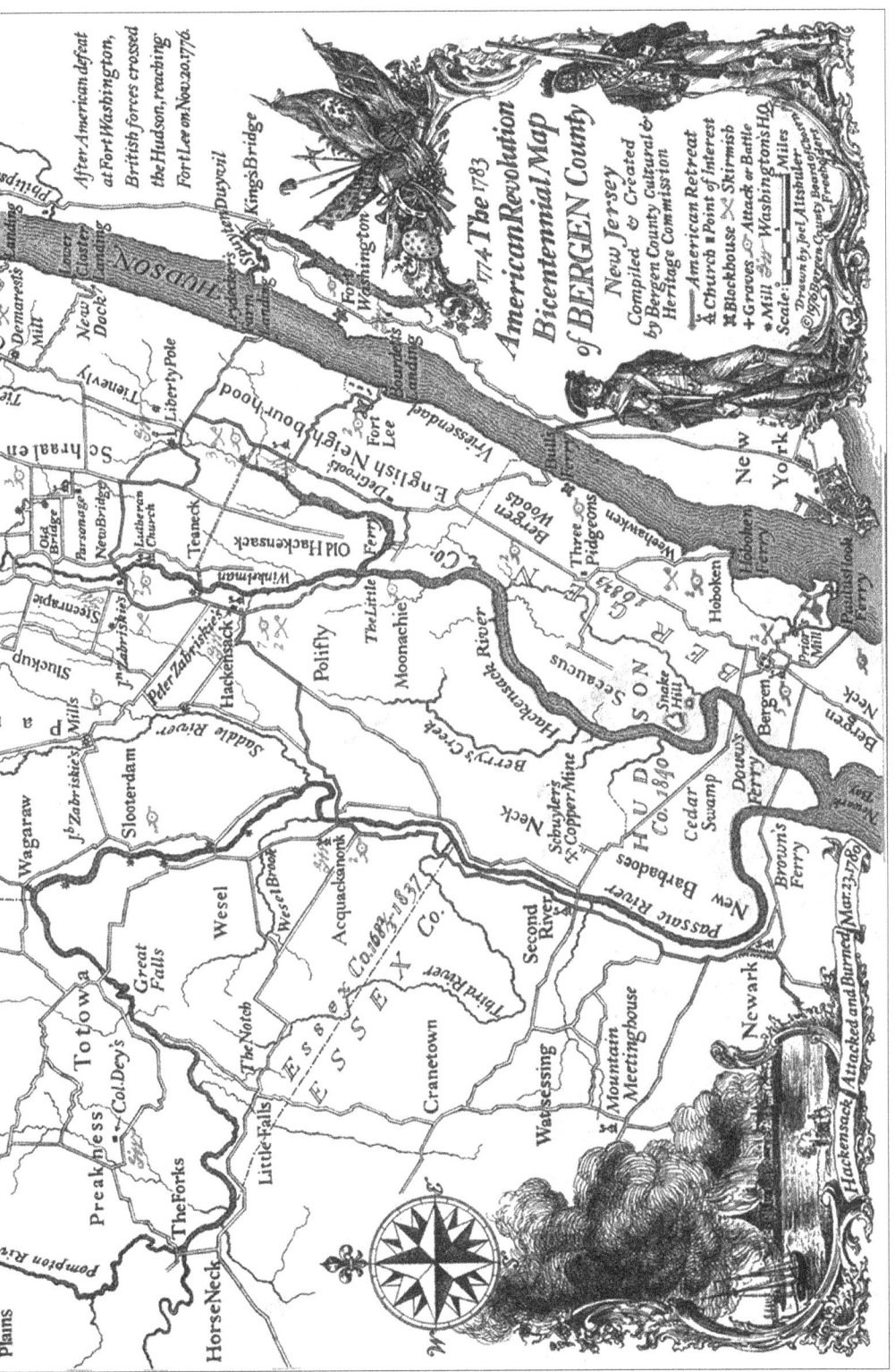

Bicentennial map of the Revolutionary War in Bergen County, 1774–83. *Courtesy of Bergen County Division of Cultural and Historic Affairs.*

Introduction

in the grammar school, I saw another reminder of the historic retreat on the wall of the school auditorium—an idealized life-size painting of George Washington on horseback leading his improbably well-dressed soldiers down Fort Lee Road. Leonia artist Howard McCormick had painted it as part of a WPA arts project in 1936.

Had it not been for these historic markers, paintings and sculptures, I would only have known Leonia as a charming suburb close to New York City, one with easy access to major highways and proximity to major airports—which was the primary reason I moved there from my native Chicago in 1985. Ten years later, that insatiably curious Chicago transplant had become the borough historian!

Over time, I found both the well-hidden Fort Lee Historic Park and the even better hidden Kearney House at the base of the Palisades in the Palisades Interstate Park. A few years later, I attended a Christmas concert at the historic Steuben House at New Bridge Landing; the place lay behind an auto junkyard, and without explicit directions I would never have found it on my own—or have learned of its importance in the history of our country.

When a flurry of books on the Revolution and our Founding Fathers was published after 2000, I read all with great interest, for these books made the Revolution, and the men and their ideas behind it, come alive. I learned that Thomas Paine's famous words, "These are the times that try men's souls," were conceived as he retreated with Washington's army through Bergen County. I then read Adrian Leiby's *The Revolutionary War in the Hackensack Valley* and had a much better understanding of the important role Bergen County played than I could have gleaned from the sentence or two it received in most books.

Leiby wrote of the constant terror that residents of Bergen County, both Patriots and Loyalists, endured throughout the war, in a place "where neither army dared to place itself, a country that was far too dangerous for any but desperate men, spies, marauders and foragers." The war came to New York and New Jersey in the summer of 1776, when hundreds of British ships bearing thirty thousand well-trained British and Hessian soldiers reached New York Harbor to squelch the drive for independence. A few months later, after squelching Washington's army on Long Island (Brooklyn) and then Harlem Heights, the British invaded New Jersey one early morning. For the next seven years, life in bucolic Bergen County became anything but, as the war there was fought with unimaginable viciousness. British, Hessian and Continental troops helped themselves to Bergen County farmers' crops to feed their hungry troops. Troops from both sides cut down trees and fences for fuel and warmth. They pillaged and plundered homes. Residents lived in constant fear of being ambushed, having their property seized, their houses burned down, their fields stripped and their men hauled off to prison for their political beliefs. Although it was known as "the neutral ground" because it was located between the American troops in the New Jersey Highlands and the British troops in Manhattan, few in Bergen County were politically neutral. Families, neighborhoods and churches were divided over loyalty to the king or to the United States, leading to lifelong animosity.

Leiby's book has long been considered the definitive history of the war in Bergen County. But much new information has come to light since its publication,

Introduction

Historic marker in Leonia, off Grand Avenue on Hillside Avenue. *Courtesy of Ira Lieblich.*

information that expands on his work and dispels some of the myths and folklore that have been passed down. Much of this new information is included in this book.

The essays that follow were contributed by writers who share, *at least*, a strong curiosity about local history, and *at most*, a lifelong passion for the world-altering events that took place in our own backyards during the Revolutionary War. The contributors include academics, reenactors, archivists, historic preservationists, museum curators, historic interpreters, historic book publishers, journalists, local historians, members of historic preservation societies, and entrepreneurs. Their contributions will make you realize that we who find ourselves in this area are living, working and playing on hallowed ground.

The essays examine the events from the perspective of all who were involved in the conflict—the military commanders on both sides, the foreign volunteers, the patriots and loyalists, the militiamen and the New Jersey Volunteers, the Jersey Dutch farmers, the women left alone to defend their homes, blacks both free and enslaved, the British and Hessian troops, the opportunistic London traders and the outlaws.

Much of the information comes from primary sources—letters, diaries, pension records, muster rolls, ship logs, bills of sale, military after-action reports and George Washington's handwritten expense reports. Some essays were written expressly for this

Introduction

book; others were adapted or excerpted from previous work. All focus on events or people who spent time in or around Bergen County during the Revolutionary War. The essays are arranged in chronological order.

Many serendipitous events occurred during the preparation of this book, including my search for the "perfect cover." I hoped to find one that had not been overused. While visiting the Building Department at Fort Lee Borough Hall, I was literally stopped in my tracks by a painting I'd never seen, one of George Washington atop the Palisades, overlooking the Hudson River. The artist was H. Willard Ortlip, a notable twentieth-century Fort Lee artist. I learned that the painting had been in storage for years, and had been restored only recently by his son, Paul Ortlip. More hidden history! I also discovered that an exhibit of Ortlip's paintings was on display at both the Fort Lee Public Library and the Fort Lee Museum that month, and that a reception for Paul Ortlip would be held later that week! I contacted the Ortlip family's studio on Cape Cod, asked for and was given enthusiastic support for using the painting for the cover of this book. I also met Paul Ortlip. Just in time to meet the deadline, borough photographer Donna Brennan photographed the painting for this book.

I thank all the contributors for their enthusiasm, for making tight deadlines, and for entrusting me with their efforts. Thanks to the Bergen County Historical Society for permission to reprint images and selected essays from their *1976 Annual*. Thanks to the Bergen County Division of Cultural and Historic Affairs for supporting and acknowledging the efforts of local historians. Thanks to my colleague and employer Kevin Tremble, the president of the Crossroads of the American Revolution Association, for suggesting I undertake this project. Thanks also go to both Kevin and Robert Griffin for their guidance in selecting the stories and those who could best tell them. Thanks to all those who keep history alive in Bergen County: the members of the Bergen County Historical Society, the local historical societies, the local historians, the curators, the webmasters, the newsletter editors, and those who meticulously and lovingly restore historic homes and buildings.

Also important to acknowledge are the members of various historical reenactment groups, including the Brigade of the American Revolution (BAR), Outwater's Company and the Continental Line. Members of the BAR represent elements of all the armies then involved: Continental, militia, British, Loyalist, German, French, Spanish and Native American forces, plus civilian men, women and children. Many photos of reenactments are included in this book.

Finally, many thanks to my coworker Robert Gerber for his assistance in preparing the images for publication and my friend Barbara Marchant for her assistance with last minute proofreading. Thanks to Josh Sommers for his assistance in obtaining approval to use the Ortlip painting as a cover, and to Donna Brennan for photographing the painting. For more on the Ortlips, visit www.Fourgenerationsart.com. Thanks to friends Martha and Ira Lieblich for photographing historic markers throughout Bergen County, for these are the visible reminders that keep history alive in our communities.

Introduction

All proceeds from the sale of this book in retail bookstores will go to the Bergen County Historical Society, a nonprofit volunteer organization whose museum collections are displayed at the Steuben House, a State Historic Site, and the Campbell-Christie House, a County Historic Site. The Steuben House sustained substantial damage from the "flood of the century" in April 2007, during the production of this book. Please consider making a donation to assist them in their efforts to keep history alive with their museum exhibits, monthly lectures, educational events and library collection. Online donations can be made at www.bergencountyhistory.org.

Carol Karels, a native Chicagoan, is the Leonia, New Jersey borough historian. She has published four books on Leonia history, including Images of America: Leonia *in 2001. She received a Bergen County Historic Preservation Commendation in 2007 for her efforts to preserve the Vreeland Papers, a large collection of eighteenth-century documents found in a Leonia attic in 2001. Her book* Cooked: An Inner City Nursing Memoir, *about Chicago's historic Cook County Hospital, received an American Journal of Nursing Book of the Year award in 2005. She has a BA in history from the University of Illinois.*

British and Hessian Accounts of the Invasion of 1776

Lieutenant Colonel Donald M. Londahl-Smidt, USAF-Retired

Donald Londahl-Smidt spent years seeking and translating the diaries, journals and letters of the British and Hessians involved in the invasion of Bergen County. What follows are excerpts from an essay he wrote for Bergen County History—1976 Annual.

On November 19, 1776, General William Howe, commander in chief of the British and German forces employed in the North American colonies lying along the Atlantic Ocean, issued the following general order from his headquarters at De Lancey's Mill:

> *The following Corps are to Strike their Tents Load their Waggons & be in reddiness to March with their Blanketts & Provision this Night at Nine O'Clock. Two Compy Chassuiers 1st & 2d Lt. Infantry 1st & 2d Battn of Guards 100 Men of Rogers's Corps without Arms two Engineers with twelve Carpenters & three Guides. They will receive their Orders from Lt. Gl. Ld. Cornwallis.*

This order set in motion the invasion of Bergen County.

The sequence of events as gathered from the accounts gives us the following overview of the invasion: Sometime after nine o'clock on the night of November 19, 1776, a force of about 2,500 British and Hessians under Lieutenant General Earl Cornwallis embarked aboard fifty large flatboats and an undetermined number of bateaux at Spuyten Duyvil. Their intention was to diagonally cross the Hudson and land "about 5 miles further up the River" at the foot of the Palisades "beyond the usual landing place and considered as inaccessible for any body of troops." This division was supposed to go ashore at midnight, but Lord Cornwallis could not believe that the landing place selected by the guides was the correct site and lost time exploring two or three miles farther along on the river in a heavy rain. After Cornwallis returned to the original site, the troops, led by a detachment of British light infantry and the Hessian Jägers, went ashore in the early morning hours of November 20 and scrambled up a

Hessian Jägers from the Brigade of the American Revolution taking part in the 225th anniversary of the 1776 British invasion of Bergen County. Tenafly, 2001. *Courtesy of Ira Lieblich.*

path that was scarcely four feet wide. Reaching the top, which they found unguarded, they formed a semicircular defensive perimeter. Gradually as the main body of the first division joined them on the summit, the perimeter was expanded.

After unloading this division, the boats crossed over to the east shore to fetch the second division of Cornwallis's force, which was composed of approximately 2,500 more men. These troops embarked at eight o'clock in the morning from the present Ludlow area, proceeded directly across to the same landing used by the first division, disembarked and climbed to the top. Eight light artillery pieces were also dragged up the rugged path by seamen and soldiers. On the heights, Lord Cornwallis then formed his corps into two columns and at about two o'clock in the afternoon, started to move southward toward Fort Lee, which was defended by about 936 Americans. At four o'clock the British and Hessian advanced guard approached the fort, which the Patriots had hastily abandoned. Large quantities of stores, provisions and ordnance, which the Americans had not been able to send off to safety, were captured.

On November 21, at least part of the Hessian grenadiers and light infantry and one company of Hessian Jägers advanced and captured New Bridge on the Hackensack River. A detachment of the Sixteenth Regiment of Light Dragoons was sent directly across the Hudson from New York to join Cornwallis. Cornwallis halted in the English Neighborhood (Leonia) until November 25. The reason may lie in the fact that an American force of over nine thousand men under Major General Charles Lee was posted at, and near, North Castle in Westchester County and another five thousand men were stationed in the Highlands under Major General William Heath. Until General William Howe, the British commander in chief, was reasonably certain that these forces did not intend to move southward against his lines above Kingsbridge, he probably did not feel justified in weakening that position by detaching additional troops to reinforce Cornwallis. Finally, on the afternoon of November 25, after it had become clear that the Americans did not intend to attack the British lines in force, Howe sent the greater part of the Second Brigade, the entire Fourth Brigade and one battalion of the Seventy-first Regiment of Foot across the Hudson to New Jersey.

The Second Brigade and the battalion of the Seventy-first remained at Fort Lee to remove the stores and to demolish the works. The Fourth Brigade advanced to New Bridge while Cornwallis's main force took post on the western side of Hackensack. On November 26, Cornwallis's body of troops crossed the Passaic River near the city of Passaic, then called Acquackanonk. The Fourth Brigade joined Cornwallis's force the next day. On November 28, Colonel Johann Rall's brigade of Hessians crossed the Hudson from New York to Fort Lee and the following day took up quarters in Hackensack. They remained there until December 3, when they marched to Newark.

The Second Brigade remained at Fort Lee until December 19, when it embarked and sailed down the Hudson to New York. The battalion of the Seventy-first Regiment of Foot remained in Bergen County until December 6.

This, then, is a synopsis of what happened in our country in 1776. Let the participants now speak for themselves.

The Revolutionary War in Bergen County

The British Invasion, by Thomas Davies. *Courtesy of New York Public Library.*

In his narrative, ANDREW SNAPE HAMOND, captain of his Majesty's ship *Roebuck*, which was anchored in the Hudson River, wrote that:

> *After the reduction of this Post* [Fort Washington] *which the Rebels had looked upon as almost impregnable, the General* [Howe] *lost no time in pursuing his success, and immediately sent my Lord Cornwallis with 5. Thousand Men into the Jerseys to attack the Fort on the opposite side of the River. They embarked in the Flat Boats early in the Evening, intending to land at midnight at a place about 5 Miles further up the River: but when his Lordship came to see the place, the path seemed so narrow, & difficult of access, that he could not be persuaded that it was the right spot, and went along shore 2 or 3 miles further to look for a better: by which delay the Enemy got apprized of their being landed and had just time enough to make their escape before the Army appeared in sight, and had drawn out of the Fort some of their Cannon & Mortars, but as My Lord Cornwallis was immediately reinforced to 10 Thousand Men he marched into the Country where the Rebels flew every where before him, and all their Cannon & Military Stores fell into his hands, among which were the Mortars that had been taken in the Nancy ordnance Brig the last winter, and every thing else of any consequence that they had taken from us.*

The following extracts from returns submitted to Lord George Germain by GENERAL HOWE on December 3, 1776, show the American losses in men and ordnance during the Bergen County campaign:

British and Hessian Accounts of the Invasion of 1776

Return of prisoners taken during the Campaign, 1776.
November 20, Fort Lee
Commissioned Officers, 1 Lieutenant, 1 Ensign
Staff. 1 Quarter-Master, 3 Surgeons
Privates, 99.
(Signed) Jos. Loring, Commissary of Prisoners.

Return of Ordnance and Stores taken by His Majesty's Troops in the Redoubts and Lines of the Enemy, from their Landing in Frog's Neck, West Chester County, from the 12th of October to the 20th of November 1776.
Fort Lee, the Rock, Redoubt, and Batteries, in the Jerseys.
  Iron Ordnance: 5 Thirty-two Pounders, 3 Twenty-four ditto, 2 Six ditto, 2 Three ditto. 1 Thirteen Inch Brass Mortar, 1 Ten Inch ditto. 2 Thirteen Inch Mortars, 1 Ten Inch ditto, 1 Eight Inch ditto.
  On the road leading to Hackinsack in the Jerseys.
  Iron Ordnance: 2 Twenty-four Pounders, 2 Eighteen ditto, 4 Twelve ditto, mounted on traveling Carriages, 4 Six pounders.
(Signed) Sam. Cleaveland, B. Gen. Royal Artillery.

Orderly books, which contain the orders issued at various levels of command, are of particular significance to the military historian because they provide information concerning the organization and intended movements of an army and its component parts. The New York Historical Society has in its magnificent collections an ORDERLY BOOK OF THE FIRST BATTALION OF THE BRIGADE OF GUARDS, a unit that participated in the invasion of New Jersey. For our period of interest, this orderly book contains the orders of Lord Cornwallis, as well as the brigade orders of Brigadier General Edward Mathew and the regimental orders of the First Battalion of the brigade. Excerpts follow:

HeadQuarters English Neighbourhood 21st Novr. 1776
The Brigade of Guards take the posts now occupied by the 2nd. Battn. Lt. Infantry. Genl. Mathew will post such Guards on the Stores & Magazines as he shall Judge proper & Necessary. As the Inhabitants in General are well Affected to Government, Earl Cornwallis expects that the Commanders of Brigades & Corps will exert themselves to prevent their being plunder'd. All the Cattle that were taken on the march Yesterday to be sent to the Field opposite the Wheat Magazine where a Commissary will attend to receive them. An Immediate Distribution of Fresh Provisions will be made to the Troops as a Gratuity for they fatigue they have Undergone.

HeadQuarters English Neighbourhood Nov. 22nd, 1776
The troops that have not receiv'd their provision will receive it to Morrow morg. At day break at the mill [probably the gristmill of Lawrence Van Horne on the Overpeck Creek] *opposite head quarters. Vizt. Four days bread & Rum 3 days fresh & one salt.*
Headquarters English Neighbourhood Nov. 23rd 1776

The Revolutionary War in Bergen County

Historic marker in Leonia, Grand and Lakeview Avenues. *Courtesy of Ira Lieblich.*

> *The Commr. In Chief desires to Return his thanks to Lt. Genl. Earl Cornwallis, Majr. Genl. Vaughan, Brigr. Genl. Mathew Command for the Meritorious service perform'd by the Corps on the 20th. Inst. Accomplish'd with Immence Fatigue to the troops. Commg. Officers of Corps will be Responsible to the Commr. In Chief the Regulation of Horses is Strictly Complied with, No Follower of the Army except the sutlers of Each Regt. Can be Allow'd a horse.*

Colonel Earl Emilius von Donop was the commander of the Hesse Cassel grenadier brigade and the two Jäger companies, which were the elite troops of the Hessian contingent. Donop was mortally wounded and captured at the unsuccessful assault on Fort Redbank on October 22, 1777 and died on the 29th of that same month. His reports to Lt. General Leopold von Heister, commander of the Hesse Cassel forces in America, shed much light on the events that occurred in Bergen County in November 1776. After the fall of Fort Lee Donop reported:

> *About two o'clock in the afternoon the corps started its march in two columns. At 4 o'clock in the afternoon our advanced guards, without losing a man, were already on the summits of both Forts Lee and Constitution which the Rebels had hastily left for fear of being entirely cut off and captured. At the foot of the mountain an important storehouse for corn was found, and in almost all the houses large quantities of provisions were stored. At the summit of the forts themselves there were huts and tents for more than 6000 men and quantities of all sorts*

British and Hessian Accounts of the Invasion of 1776

of provisions and a large amount of ammunition. The number of prisoners is not large and amounts to only 50 or so.

The local area seems to be very fertile and is well cultivated and I hope that this expedition will contribute greatly to our better subsistence in the upcoming winter quarters so that the infamous plundering, which the English are again uncommonly engaged in in spite of orders to the contrary, will be entirely eliminated. Up to this time the Hessian grenadiers cannot be charged with anything on this account and it actually gives me much satisfaction that our chief here, Lt. Genl. Cornwallis, personally declared to me this morning that he had had a number of marauders arrested but there were no Hessians among them.

An ORDERLY BOOK OF THE SEVENTEENTH REGIMENT OF FOOT supplies information concerning the movement of that unit and the 4th brigade, to which it belonged, into and through Bergen County.

Orders 7 OClock in the Evening 24th Novr. 1776.
Tents to be Struck tomorrow morning at 5 oclock and ye Waggons loaded immediately afterwed. Wagon to each Divison no Women Will be allow'd with ye Regt. Corpl. Radfor Corpl [blank] and 8 Germans for ye Baggage Guard…The Sick to be left under the care of Westgarth who will convey them to ye Hospatel as soon as possible. They will be put upon the wagons and go with ye Regt. as far as fort Kniphausen. Offrs. Commanding Grand Divisions to be answerable that ye Waggons are not loaded with any thing but the mens Tents and Offrs. Necessaries Baggage and Beding. The men to Carry their Tent poles and Camp Kettles. The prisoners to be march'd in the rear of ye Regt. by the Qr. Guard.

JOHANN EMANUEL WAGNER was a first lieutenant in the grenadier company of the von Ditfurth regiment. Although his company was part of the von Minnigerode grenadier battalion, he was serving on detached duty as Colonel von Donop's adjutant. During the attack on Fort Redbank on October 22, 1777, Wagner was seriously wounded and captured. In a letter to Lieutenant General Wilhelm von Ditfurth, chief of his regiment, who remained behind in Hess, Wagner wrote,

In Camp at Neighborhood below Fort Lee, in the Province of Jersey, November 22, 1776
On the 20th instant Lieutenant General Cornwallis crossed over to New Jersey with a corps, to which Colonel Donop and his brigade now belong, and took possession of the other two forts belonging to the Rebels, namely Lee and Constitution, in addition to their camp and all the store houses, as they had retired in haste and left many things behind them. Our disembarkation appeared terrible and impracticable as we landed at the foot of a rocky height and had to go up a very steep and narrow path. Fifty men would have sufficed to hold back the entire corps if they had only hurled stones down on us.

I prefer this province to any other I have seen in America so far. It is not very mountainous; the coast is [not] high and steep except near the North River. It is well cultivated and I find excellent fruits everywhere and very many cattle. This expedition must compensate us for our future winter quarters. The autumn has been extremely pleasant up to now but now and then the nights are very cold. It has been rainy since the day before yesterday but otherwise we have almost always had clear good weather and the days have often been very warm…General Washington is said to have gone to Philadelphia. Should the season permit it, it is not at all impossible that we shall follow him there this month with our corps. The hope is now indulged in that most of the Rebels will return to their homes because they had pinned their faith on Forts Washington and Lee. Huts and barracks have been built for more than 6,000 men near the latter fort as winter quarters.

The British army pursued the retreating Americans through New Jersey and then established winter quarters in New York City and New Jersey, including a few along the Delaware River, for what they mistakenly thought would be a quiet season of repose.

Donald M. Londahl-Smidt, a retired Air Force and commercial bank officer, lives in Montvale. He holds an MA in history from the University of Delaware. A fellow of the Company of Military Historians, he has been awarded that organization's Distinguished Service Award. Lieutenant Colonel Londahl-Smidt is a member of the board of directors and editorial committee and the director of military research for the Johannes Schwalm Historical Association, a society dedicated to researching the history of the Hessian and other German troops that fought on the British side during the Revolutionary War. He has coauthored one book, written numerous published articles and given many lectures to various audiences on Revolutionary War history.

The Invasion and the Myths Surrounding It

John Spring

Many of the stories passed on about the Revolution in Bergen County were based on myths, family lore and legend. Unfortunately, sometimes that information makes its way into well-meaning award-winning books and onto local historic markers. John Spring has spent much of his life trying to correct some of the misinformation about the British invasion of November 20, 1776.

The events of November 20, 1776, the British invasion and the American retreat, are among the most thoroughly researched and written about of all the episodes of the American Revolution in Bergen County. Yet myths and inaccurate information continue to be promulgated, despite evidence to the contrary. A reexamination of original documents relating to the event indicates that historical facts previously accepted became distorted in the twentieth century into stories that cannot be substantiated. This misinformation continues to be passed on, in classrooms, newspaper articles and in award-winning books such as David Fischer's *Washington's Crossing*. The misinformation is over where the invasion actually occurred, who notified the troops at Fort Lee of the invasion, and why the British missed the opportunity to end the war that very day.

What we know for certain is that immediately after the fall of Fort Washington on November 16, 1776, General William Howe gave orders to Lieutenant General Lord Charles Earl Cornwallis to "bring some fifty large, flat-bottomed boats and bateaux up the Hudson River at night, and to hide them on the shores of Spuyten Duyvil." This Cornwallis accomplished without detection by American forces, despite the fact that American General Nathanael Greene had about five hundred out guards posted in anticipation of such an invasion.

Three days later, on the rainy evening of November 19, Cornwallis began the famous invasion of New Jersey. The first wave was an assortment of light infantry, grenadiers, Jägers and Rogers Rangers totaling about 2,500 men. These men

The Revolutionary War in Bergen County

British reenactors from the Brigade of the American Revolution scaling the Palisades at Huyler's Landing during the 225th anniversary of the 1776 British invasion of Bergen County. Alpine, 2001. *Courtesy of Anthony G. Taranto Jr., Palisades Interstate Park.*

embarked and rowed diagonally, about five miles up river, to the Jersey shore, with the intention of going ashore around midnight, scaling the Hudson River Palisades and hiking south to capture Fort Lee.

General Cornwallis, who didn't know the area, had three local guides to help him determine the best place to scale the Palisades, thirty miles of sheer rock wall rising in places some five hundred feet from the water's edge. Cornwallis doubted the trail his guides led him to, and he spent hours exploring the riverbank in search of a more suitable trail to ascend. His three guides knew, no doubt, what Cornwallis could not know in the dark: the trail to the top of the Palisades passed through a seismic break in the cliffs, making them lower and easier to climb near the top.

Who were his guides? One of them was certainly John Aldington, a Loyalist who owned twenty acres and a brewery in the English Neighborhood (Leonia) before Patriots seized his property and converted his brewery into a storehouse. He fled with his family to Manhattan and joined a Loyalist brigade. In 1964, Dr. Richard P. McCormick of Rutgers University traveled to England and found Aldington's application for compensation in the British Records office from 1784, along with a note signed by Cornwallis stating that, "I hereby certify that Major John Aldington was a zealous Loyalist and that he guided the troops under my command when I landed in the Province of New Jersey in the year 1776."

The second guide was probably William Bayard, who ran the Hoboken ferry and for some time had recruited Loyalists to fight in the British Provincial army. He knew

The Invasion and the Myths Surrounding It

Aldington and had "brought him as a guide to Sir William Howe the first evening of Howe's arrival." The third guide would have been John Ackerson, who owned the property that included the New Dock.

Once they found it, the first wave of British and Hessians struggled in the dark up the four-foot-wide trail and were surprised to find no resistance at the top. The troop carriers then returned to the opposite shore to load the cannons and the remaining 2,500 troops. General Greene's army, meanwhile, had received word of the attack and, on Washington's orders, evacuated the fort and crossed the Hackensack River at New Bridge, beginning the retreat that took them across New Jersey and the Delaware River.

It appears that, for at least a century, no one thought the Cornwallis landing had been made anywhere but the Lower (New) Dock. A.H. Walker in the *1876 Atlas of Bergen County*, the first history of the area, states, "Huyler's Landing on the Hudson River was formerly known as Lower Closter, and was the place at which the British crossed when on their raid to Fort Lee." The 1882 *History of Bergen and Passaic County* says the same thing.

One of the maps of the Northern Valley (map 24, part 3) made by Robert Erskine, geographer and surveyor general to the American army for General Washington, showed the Lower (New) Dock as the site of the invasion. The 1778 map had a notation: "Road to the New Dock where the Enemy landed the latter end of the Campaign of 1776." Bear in mind that the New Dock was the Lower Landing leading to present-day Cresskill.

A few years later, in 1780, Generals Wayne and Erskine surveyed the road at New Dock in preparation for an attack on the Bull's Ferry Blockhouse. They reported that the grade was one foot in five, or about $11\frac{1}{2}$ degrees, whereas the road at the Upper Dock was "impracticable for wagons part of the way forming an angle of near 20 degrees descent."

Further indication that the Lower Landing was the one used in the 1776 invasion is contained in the *Diary of the American War 1776–1784*, written by Captain Johann Ewald, a Hessian officer who was with Cornwallis that day and throughout much of the war. The diary was translated and annotated by Joseph P. Tustin of Tuckerton, New Jersey, and published by Yale University Press in 1979. In describing the events of the day, Captain Ewald says the troops, after coming ashore at daybreak, "scaled the rocky and bush heights as quickly as possible." Ewald says further that, at the top, they found some plantations in a district called Dunnefledt (Tenafly), two hours distant (five miles) from Fort Lee. The location and distances mentioned would certainly seem to refer to the closer of the two landings—the New Dock, or Lower Landing. That site later became Huyler's Landing, and the road to the valley became the Huyler Landing Road. In later years, however, especially after the formation of the Palisades Interstate Park, Huyler Landing Road became an almost forgotten, little-used hiking trail.

Ewald also wrote that he saw some troops retreating from Fort Lee en route to New Bridge. He skirmished with them and sent a Jäger back to Cornwallis for more men. Ewald could not possibly have seen and skirmished with the American troops retreating from the fort if the British had landed at the Closter Dock Landing at present Alpine, which is a distance of six or seven miles from the fort. Ewald's testimony supports the theory that the landing place was the Lower New Dock and not the Upper Closter Dock landing.

The Revolutionary War in Bergen County

A FLAW IN THE MAP

It was almost a century before any account claimed the invasion came by way of the old Closter Dock Road. That claim was made by someone who knew little to nothing about nineteenth-century roads through the Palisades. In 1920, some diligent researchers at the Bergen County Historical Society (BCHS) decided to compose a wall map showing all of the roads in Bergen County, which General Erskine's staff had mapped during the American Revolution. I stood in awe when my parents showed me this composite map at a friend's house. But in later years I found that the map had a flaw that caused much mischief in the 1950s and the years following.

In August 1778, Captain John Watkins, a Paramus schoolteacher, was making a map of what is now County Road and what was then referred to as "Map of the road from 15 mile stone near Suffren's to Fort Lee." At the point where a crude wagon trail branched off to the east, a local militiaman, possibly Major John Mauritius Goetschius or even Captain John Huyler, both of whom lived and fought locally, gave Watkins some information of military significance that he recorded in a fine hand. The inscription written under the road to the river was, "Road to the New Dock where the enemy landed the latter end of the campaign of 1776."

However, Captain Watkins's handwriting was too fine for the elderly gentleman making the map. They read it as "Road to New York," which of course, it was not! A 1957 pamphlet entitled *Washington in Bergen County* included the section of the BCHS map with the mistaken road labeled Closter Dock Road and with a Yonkers ferry boat at its end.

Since it was known that Cornwallis had landed at Closter, it was assumed to have been at the foot of Closter Dock Road, where a busy ferry dock and boat basin existed in the twentieth century. It was then that the Daughters of the American Revolution placed a well-meant but badly mistaken marker on the upper trail. The New Jersey Federation of Women's Clubs, which had done heroic work halting quarrying of the Palisades at the turn of the century, placed a "Cornwallis House" marker on the Rachel Kearney House. This marker has recently been removed.

By 1962, when Adrian Leiby completed his fine work *The Revolutionary War in the Hackensack Valley*, the notion that the British had used the Upper Landing was so widespread that even he did not question it. However, upon reexamination a year later, he decided that the evidence clearly pointed to the Lower Landing.

It wasn't until 1964 that the Bergen County Historical Society agreed that Erskine's maps indicated that the November 1776 invasion came by way of Lower Closter Landing. After the BCHS made their conclusion, an official roadside marker was installed at the intersection of County Road (the earlier Closter Road) and Madison Avenue in Cresskill (formerly Lower Closter). Adrian Leiby and I wrote the words for it, after discovering that an 1816 Road Return for Madison Avenue from Schraalenburgh (now Dumont) indicated that the continuation of Madison Avenue was labeled "Road to the New Closter Dock."

The BCHS received further confirmation of their decision in 1975 when the *New York Times* published a story about the upcoming bicentennial reenactment of the invasion as a "Closter" event. When I questioned the story, they sent the same writer,

Huyler's Landing marker. *Courtesy of Ira Lieblich.*

The Revolutionary War in Bergen County

Joseph Sullivan, to hear Cresskill's viewpoint. Sullivan had received a letter from Joseph Tustin, a military historian who had purchased the diary of Captain Ewald. Tustin, who was fluent in German, had spent twenty years translating and annotating the diary as well as locating a missing volume. This was like a voice from the distant past speaking to us and confirming our research.

Several Bergen County historians, including Adrian Leiby, Claire Tholl, Lieutenant Colonel Donald Londahl-Smidt and myself, invited Tustin to address the Bergen County Historical Society. Tustin, upon examining the Alpine Boat Basin and the trail leading from there to the Closter Dock Road, had agreed that the trail was too steep and unlike the painting illustrating the invasion to be the historically accurate place. He also said that the distance from the top of the trail to Fort Lee did not agree with Ewald's diary; the distance was about five miles, not seven, by way of Closter Dock Road.

Today the consensus of opinion among recognized local historians and researchers is that the Lower Landing is where the invasion took place.

There has probably been even greater speculation about how the Continental forces were notified of the landing. Was it slave girl Polly Wyckoff, the mysterious Closter horseman or a Patriot sentry? A famous "Closter horseman" painting has a home in the Fort Lee Museum. Thomas Paine was at Fort Lee on the morning of the twentieth and he recorded that "an officer" was their informant. In his best-selling book *Washington's Crossing*, published in 2005, Fischer writes, "The British infantry quickly established a perimeter and began to send out patrols. At last they were observed, not by the American army but by a slave girl named Polly Wyckoff, who was working in the kitchen of Matthew Bogert's farm and saw the British approaching across the fields. She ran into the parlor and cried, 'Bogert's fields are full of red coats.'" Fischer cites Lefkowitz's book *The Long Retreat*.

This is a very interesting passage for several reasons. A Bergen County slave might have been named "Polly," but if she had a last name she would have been the only Bergen County slave with one. If that last name was "Wyckoff," she was the only Wyckoff in the county then, according to the Wyckoff genealogy published in 1935.

During the bicentennial of the Revolution, the *North Jersey Suburbanite* ran a series of articles about the Revolution written by local historians. On November 12, 1975, an article entitled "The Mystery of Polly Wyckoff," written by Tenafly historian and DAR leader Virginia Mosley, claims that Polly and her mother might have been visiting Bogert relatives from Allentown, New Jersey. However, even Mrs. Mosley admitted she was just conjecturing.

Arthur Lefkowitz continued to spread this legend about Polly Wyckoff in his book *The Long Retreat*. This was mystifying to me, for while he was writing the book, we visited the invasion site and discussed Polly Wyckoff, who made a transition from a nameless slave in one early twentieth-century publication to the Polly Wyckoff who lived in Fort Lee and had a chapter of the Daughters of the American Revolution named after her. Even more mystifying is his preface in his book, where he writes, "I want to give special thanks to Bergen County historian John Spring, who generously

The Invasion and the Myths Surrounding It

shared his considerable knowledge about the British army's entry into and march through Bergen County *and especially the legend of Polly Wyckoff.*"

It is conceivable that several people did see the British and set off to warn the fort, but were not the first to reach there.

A third point of considerable conjecture regarding the events of November 20, 1776, has dealt with why the British troops did not make a dash cross country to New Bridge or to the Liberty Pole to cut off the American retreat. As Leiby has indicated, the sole intent of Lord Cornwallis appears to have been to take Fort Lee, which in the British eyes was a major fortification as well as a thorn in their side.

This analysis is borne out in Captain Ewald's diary. He says that upon leaving the invasion road (probably in the Tenafly/Englewood area) to talk to a farmer, he spied the Americans retreating from Fort Lee. Ewald had the opportunity to skirmish with the retreating Americans. When he asked for more troops, he was called off by an order from Cornwallis to let the Americans go and proceed toward Fort Lee. He wrote, "Now I perceived what was afoot. We wanted to spare the King's subjects and hoped to terminate the war amicably, in which assumption I was strengthened the next day by several English officers."

Whether or not this was so is open to serious question, but there seems little doubt that the British objective that day was the taking of Fort Lee and herding the Americans away from the area, rather than intercepting Washington's army.

If enough searching is done, new evidence such as the Aldington documents and the Ewald diary may turn up from time to time. If so, our understanding of the events of November 20, 1776, will be increased. It is almost certain, however, that additional romanticized versions of what happened that day will be produced. It will continue to be necessary to cut through the confusion created by such stories, if we are to have a reasonably accurate picture of what happened that day.

John Spring has researched, lectured and photographed Bergen County history for almost half a century. His findings in the 1960s proved that even Adrian Leiby, author of The Revolutionary War in the Hackensack Valley, *had erred in locating the site of the British 1776 invasion. But Spring didn't stop there. Working with hikers, he persuaded Palisades Interstate Park authorities to blaze and clear the invasion road so anyone can use it year-round. He became a leader of the Bergen County Historical Society and was president from 1983 to 1986. He played a leading role in the county bicentennial, doing the British invasion the right way. He wrote about Skunk Hollow and did a series of slide talks, hikes and visits to historic sites in the Northern Valley for the McGuire Senior Center in Northvale. In 1988, he was given the New Jersey Local Historian's Award as Cresskill's town historian. He is responsible for five historic markers in his hometown.*

The Retreat to Victory

Barbara Z. Marchant

*M*any military historians consider the British invasion of November 20, 1776, to be one of the greatest blunders, and the American retreat as the greatest withdrawal in military history. The British could easily have won the war that day, but instead of aggressively pursuing the retreating army, British General William Howe gave orders to wait, giving the Americans ample time to retreat and regroup. Some historians believed that Howe didn't want to annihilate the Rebel army, but instead just wanted to overwhelm it, hoping that the Americans would become both physically and mentally exhausted, and reconcile with the mother country.

When studying the War of Independence in school in Brooklyn, I was primarily taught about the two Georges (Washington and King George III), Bunker Hill, Paul Revere and Lexington and Concord. Briefly mentioned in passing was the Battle of Long Island; New Jersey was never even mentioned! Perhaps the author of my history textbook was from New England. It was not until I was a young adult that I discovered, for instance, that the Battle of Long Island (now sometimes known as the Battle of Brooklyn) was fought within spitting distance from where I grew up and that George Washington had spent time in Brooklyn. When the Battle of Long Island was mentioned, I assumed it was near Mineola, not right through Prospect Park where I spent winters ice skating. All that I was taught regarding the American Revolution in the local area was that there was a battle on Long Island, and that the Americans who survived escaped north. They eventually rallied and routed out the British and because of this victory, we wound up speaking the English of King's County instead of the King's English.

It was not until I moved into Bergen County in 1985 that I discovered the mind-boggling history that took place both literally and figuratively outside my front door. George Washington once again passed by near where I currently live, not once, but several times, in the autumn of 1776, as he traveled between his headquarters at the Peter Zabriskie House in Hackensack and the headquarters of his commandant of Fort Lee, General Nathanael Greene, in the English Neighborhood, near current

The Retreat to Victory

The Retreat, by Howard McCormick, 1936. *Courtesy of Leonia Board of Education.*

Grand Avenue in Leonia. Washington also rode near present-day Fort Lee Road to inspect Fort Lee and observe the activities in Fort Washington across the North (Hudson) River. On hearing the facts of what transpired in Bergen County, New Jersey, in late autumn of 1776, how can only the most jaded of us fail to be impressed? Our fledgling nation almost came to a heart-rending halt in that November. If the Americans at Fort Lee had not been warned that the British were indeed coming, and left camp with their breakfast still cooking on the open fires; if the enemy troops had better information about New Bridge Landing on their maps, the Americans might have been halted before crossing the river into Hackensack; if the enemy forces had traveled farther south into Englewood instead of marching west on the border of present-day Englewood and Tenafly; if the British had moved faster to intercept the retreating Rebels…So many ifs, and so many instances in which the cause of independence could have been lost in the span of a few hours, not just a few days! However, as Adrian Leiby pointed out in *The Revolutionary War in the Hackensack Valley*, "British Regulars did not scramble after a frightened and disorganized rabble, they marched in formation to the roll of drums; no provincial who saw that force would ever again doubt Britain's power to deal with rebels."

The Americans were forced from Brooklyn (Long Island) at the end of August 1776. After several other battles, Manhattan was totally lost when Fort Washington was surrendered to the British on November 16, 1776. The British and Hessian forces numbered twenty thousand strong. According to Lefkowitz in *The Long Retreat*, Greene had sent additional troops from Fort Lee to assist Colonel Robert Magaw's (the commandant of Fort Washington) forces at Fort Washington. Those unfortunate reinforcements had either been killed while defending the fort or had been taken captive. Even though Fort Washington had some natural defenses, in *The Battle of New York*, Schecter advises that "the vaunted pentagonal fortress, enclosing four acres of ground, was in fact nothing more than a large, crude earthwork, open to the sky and without proper barracks or magazines for ammunition; water had to be drawn from the Hudson, 230 feet below, because the fort had no well."

Even though Washington felt that Greene and Magaw were incorrect in their assumption that Fort Washington could be defended, he did not overrule and reluctantly agreed with them. Washington had accepted the responsibility for this major disaster and Greene knew that it was on his bad advice that defending Fort Washington had been done. However, in keeping Greene on his staff, Washington knew that the young general had other skills, such as organization, which would be important in the future. As Terry Golway notes in *Washington's General*, "Anticipating the worst, a march through the state toward the capital [at that time, the capital was Philadelphia], he [Greene] organized supply depots in several towns, including Princeton and Trenton, along a possible line of retreat. This was precisely the kind of foresight and organization that so impressed Washington." Greene was also instrumental in reorganizing the army's hospitals in New Jersey, as he realized that healthy soldiers could be demoralized by the suffering of the injured troops.

At Fort Lee, in addition to also having some impressive physical barricades, the American troops had constructed an abatis, which were long wooden spikes carved

The Retreat to Victory

An abatis in Fort Lee Historic Park. *Courtesy of Carol Karels.*

from trees to repel the enemy. According to Leiby in *The Revolutionary War in the Hackensack Valley*, once Fort Washington fell, Washington and Greene had both decided to abandon Fort Lee and move the provisions at the fort to Bound Brook, Springfield, Princeton and Acquackanonk Bridge, "places that will not be subject to sudden danger in case the enemy should pass the river." Unfortunately, November 20 was a cold, rainy day and not a good day for moving the supplies from Fort Lee. On this same day, the British and Hessian forces crossed the Hudson (North) River to try to capture Fort Lee. There are several accounts of how the troops at Fort Lee were notified, but suffice it to say, most of the Americans escaped following a route through the current towns of Fort Lee, Leonia, Englewood (at Liberty Pole in Englewood, George Washington met them and traveled with them through to Hackensack), Teaneck, New Milford, River Edge and crossed the New Bridge until they came to an exhausted stop for the night in Hackensack.

Some of the other American troops split from the main escaping army at the present-day intersection of Fort Lee Road and Grand Avenue (then known as the King's Highway) in Leonia and traveled southwest on foot and then by small boats at Little Ferry over to Hackensack. Finally, another small group separated close to current Lakeview Avenue in Leonia and crossed the Overpeck near current Cedar Lane in Teaneck. This group eventually arrived in Hackensack and also joined with

Historic marker in Leonia, Grand Avenue and Fort Lee Road. *Courtesy of Ira Lieblich.*

Continental troops from the Brigade of the American Revolution on Fort Lee Road en route to New Bridge during the 225th anniversary of the British invasion of Bergen County. Leonia, 2001. *Courtesy of Ira Lieblich.*

The Retreat to Victory

the main body of troops. Since the British map that may have been used was slightly inaccurate (New Bridge is shown located where Little Ferry is located and does not show any bridge at the actual New Bridge), this may have assisted the Americans from being annihilated. As Leiby stated in *The Revolutionary War in the Hackensack Valley*, "The Tories who guided the invaders were so overweening and self-confident that they had not thought it necessary to cut off Greene's line of retreat; the Tories, for their part, like as not spent the day in damning the self-confident British officers for not listening to their pleas that the New Bridge was the key to the peninsula between the Hackensack and the Hudson." According to McCullough in *1776*, future president James Monroe estimated that there were approximately three thousand troops that were retreating on November 21.

After fleeing Fort Lee, the weary American army spent their first night in retreat on the cold, wet grounds surrounding the Mansion House in Hackensack. Most had no tents or blankets, having left them behind in their rush to flee Fort Lee. The Mansion House was the home of Peter Zabriskie, a passionate Patriot; his brother, John Zabriskie Jr., was an equally passionate Loyalist. The "broken and dispirited" Patriot army continued their humiliating retreat down Main Street Hackensack up the Polifly Road to Acquackanonck Bridge (in present-day Passaic), Newark, New Brunswick and ultimately Trenton. Many men deserted along the way. Those whose military terms were up during the retreat, including the New Jersey unit of the Flying Camp, could not be persuaded to stay on. When Governor Livingston ordered the New Jersey Militia to assist the Continental army for six weeks, few responded. Washington was disappointed with them, calling them "stubborn individualists" who returned to the warmth of their homes instead of helping his army. He felt they lacked an "ardor for the cause." General Greene wrote at the time, "The people of New Jersey behave scurvily and don't deserve the freedom for which the army was fighting." On December 8, they crossed the Delaware River into Pennsylvania and the rest was history.

As Lefkowitz points out in *The Long Retreat*, the main goal for the enemy forces on November 20 was the capture of Fort Lee and not the American army. In that, the British succeeded admirably.

Barbara Z. Marchant is a member of the Leonia Historic Preservation Commission and the Brooklyn Historical Society. She was the Leonia liaison on the Retreat to Victory Committee in 2001 and she also served on the Grand Forage Committee in 2003 (both 225th commemorative events of the Revolutionary War in Bergen County, New Jersey). She is also on the Board of Directors for the Ridgewood Historical Society.

THOMAS PAINE AND "THE TIMES THAT TRIED MEN'S SOULS"

Thomas Meyers

Thomas Paine believed that the American Revolution was the greatest cause in the history of mankind; he saw America as the only place in the world that was not overrun with oppression. The Fort Lee Office of Cultural and Heritage Affairs, the Fort Lee Historic Site, Structural, Cultural & Landmark Committee and the Fort Lee Historical Society plan to erect a statue to Thomas Paine in Monument Park to be unveiled in November 2008 to commemorate the centennial of Monument Park. This will be only the sixth statue of Paine in the world and the fourth statue of Paine in the United States. What he observed at Fort Lee and during the subsequent retreat formed the basis of the words he would write to stir a young nation to action.

"These are the times that try men's souls...The summer soldier and the sunshine patriot will, in this crisis, shrink from the service of their country; but he that stands it now deserves the love and thanks of man and woman." Those immortal words, written by Thomas Paine, were written about the "retreat to victory" that began on November 20, 1776, in Fort Lee, New Jersey. The retreat was a decisive event considered by many historians to be the greatest military withdrawal in the history of warfare. Similarly, Paine's words, as written in his *American Crisis* pamphlets, were considered words that had merit equal to that of the sword in the pursuit of independence.

As I write this essay not far from the bluffs of Fort Lee's Palisades, I try to picture what it was like here, in the summer and fall of 1776, when General George Washington's army of three thousand men gathered in this cliff town. In September of that year Paine was imbedded with the American troops and serving as aide-de-camp to General Nathanael Greene, whose troops held this rocky precipice on the west side of the Hudson River, overlooking Harlem Heights.

Paine was a working-class Englishman by birth who had immigrated to the colonies in 1774 on the advice of Benjamin Franklin, a kindred spirit he had met in London. Franklin encouraged Paine, who he considered his political son, to move to America, and he provided him with a letter of introduction.

Thomas Paine and "The Times That Tried Men's Souls"

Thomas Paine. *Courtesy of National Archives and Records Administration.*

Paine repaid Franklin in full for his kindness and faith through his publication of *Common Sense* on January 10, 1776. It was a clearly written, persuasive pamphlet that espoused two central themes. The first was that republican government was superior to hereditary monarchy and second, that equality of rights was a birthright of humanity. He also criticized those who wanted reconciliation.

Paine's pamphlet breathed new life into the Revolution and set fire to the colonies. For the first time the debate switched from that of injustice from Britain to the matter of independence for the thirteen colonies. Printing presses couldn't keep up with the demand. In the first three months, 120,000 copies of the forty-seven-page pamphlet were sold; half a million were distributed by the end of the war. Although it sold for two shillings, Paine made nothing on the pamphlet; he donated all profits to the struggling army.

Less than a year later, Paine would write the first of his *Crisis Papers*, which served a different but no less important purpose—to give the newly born American nation faith in the darkest days of the Revolution and to prevent that nation from being stillborn. Those dark days began here, in Bergen County, with the Retreat to Victory on November 20, 1776, just a few months after the signing of the Declaration of Independence on July 4 of that year.

In July, Paine joined the military and was assigned to a militia unit, where he served as personal secretary to General Daniel Roberdeau. Fortuitously, Paine transferred to the Continental army in September of 1776 and began his service as an aide to General Greene in Fort Lee, New Jersey. In this capacity, he also served as a war correspondent sending reports via couriers to newspapers in Philadelphia.

There was much to write about in the summer of 1776. In August, the British pushed the Americans north into Manhattan after the Battle of Long Island. A few weeks later, on September 16, the American forces won the Battle of Harlem Heights, which greatly improved the morale of Washington's troops. This was followed by a decisive victory for the British in White Plains under British General William Howe, a victory that forced Washington to divide his forces and retreat across the Hudson into Bergen County.

General Howe then positioned his British forces at Fort Washington, directly across the Hudson from Fort Lee. On November 16, George Washington and Nathanael Greene watched in horror from Fort Lee as the British captured, and later imprisoned, some two thousand men.

Less than a week later, under cover of darkness and rain, the British invaded New Jersey with the intention of capturing Fort Lee. Washington ordered his army to retreat. The American army, led by General Greene, retreated down the hill through present-day Leonia, to Liberty Pole in Englewood, across the New Bridge and then south to the city of Hackensack. Paine continued the retreat with Washington's army southward, leaving northern New Jersey to the British. Washington retreated successfully across the Delaware River at Trenton by December 8. The British on the other side of the Delaware were well equipped and numbered ten thousand strong.

Washington's army was much fewer in number and the troops were short on both supplies and hope. In addition to the men lost at Fort Washington, General

COMMON SENSE;

ADDRESSED TO THE

INHABITANTS

OF

AMERICA,

On the following interesting

SUBJECTS.

I. Of the Origin and Design of Government in general, with concise Remarks on the English Constitution.

II. Of Monarchy and Hereditary Succession.

III. Thoughts on the present State of American Affairs.

IV. Of the present Ability of America, with some miscellaneous Reflections.

Man knows no Master save creating HEAVEN,
Or those whom choice and common good ordain.
                                    THOMSON.

PHILADELPHIA;
Printed, and Sold, by R. BELL, in Third-Street.

MDCCLXXVI.

Common Sense, written by Thomas Paine. *Courtesy of Fort Lee Historic Museum.*

Washington worried about losing another two thousand men when their enlistments ran out in December. Washington wrote, "If this fails, I think the game will be pretty well up." Something was needed to save the fledgling nation at this time of crisis.

Paine was determined to keep the game going, and here was where the famous imagery of Paine writing on drumhead by campfire came into play. The fate of this fledgling nation rested on Paine's pen and his ability to wrap this retreat in a blanket of nobility, purpose and cause—cause for the continuation of a struggle larger than any single military engagement. Paine spoke not of defeat but of hope when he wrote in *The Crisis Papers*, "The harder the conflict, the more glorious the triumph."

General Greene, understanding the importance of Paine's mission, allowed Paine to leave camp so he could finish the work and have it printed in Philadelphia. *The American Crisis* was published on December 19, 1776, and the author's signature was Common Sense. The tide was about to turn for General Washington and his men and for the cause of liberty.

Immediately, General Washington realized the power of Paine's words. He ordered that his officers read *The Crisis Papers* to the troops prior to their Christmas night crossing of the Delaware to attack British forces occupying Trenton. The result was a successful engagement in Trenton and a subsequent victory for American forces in Princeton. Washington also used the pamphlet as a selling tool to encourage soldiers to reenlist. The stirring words had enormous impact and resulted in an infusion of new recruits. The return of former enlisted militiamen bolstered Washington's forces.

The American Crisis was read throughout the colonies, despite the difficulty of getting it printed. In the winter of 1776–77, many presses closed due to fear of the British, the high cost of paper and newspaper subscriptions and the scarcity of post riders (due to ever-present danger).

Paine's writings literally resuscitated the American Revolution. He continued to be an integral part of this Revolutionary cause through his service as aide-de-camp to General Greene (1777–78), secretary to the Committee on Foreign Affairs (1777–79), clerk of the Pennsylvania Assembly (1779–81) and a member of the diplomatic mission to France (1781). Paine published sixteen *American Crisis* papers between 1776 and 1783. All were read in the homes and pulpits of all thirteen states. *The Crisis* truly became the Bible of the American Revolution.

Americans today forget the radical nature of our Founding Fathers. No less than Thomas Jefferson used these words to explain revolution in reference to Shays' Rebellion:

> *God forbid we should ever be twenty years without such a rebellion…We have had thirteen states independent eleven years. There has been one rebellion. That comes to one rebellion in a century and a half for each state. What country before ever existed a century and a half without a rebellion? And what country can preserve its liberties if their rulers are not warned from time to time that their people preserve the spirit of resistance? Let them take arms. The remedy is to set them right as to the facts, pardon and pacify them. What signify a few lives lost in a century or two? The tree of liberty must be refreshed from time to time with the blood of patriots and tyrants. It is its natural manure.*

Thomas Paine and "The Times That Tried Men's Souls"

The *American* CRISIS.

NUMBER I.

By the Author of COMMON SENSE.

THESE are the times that try men's souls: The summer soldier and the sunshine patriot will, in this crisis, shrink from the service of his country; but he that stands it NOW, deserves the love and thanks of man and woman. Tyranny, like hell, is not easily conquered; yet we have this consolation with us, that the harder the conflict, the more glorious the triumph. What we obtain too cheap, we esteem too lightly:---'Tis dearness only that gives every thing its value. Heaven knows how to set a proper price upon its goods; and it would be strange indeed, if so celestial an article as FREEDOM should not be highly rated. Britain, with an army to enforce her tyranny, has declared, that she has a right (*not only to* TAX, but) "*to* BIND *us in* ALL CASES WHATSOEVER," and if being *bound in that manner* is not slavery, then is there not such a thing as slavery upon earth. Even the expression is impious, for so unlimited a power can belong only to GOD.

WHETHER the Independence of the Continent was declared too soon, or delayed too long, I will not now enter into as an argument; my own simple opinion is, that had it been eight months earlier, it would have been much better. We did not make a proper use of last winter, neither could we, while we were in a dependent state. However, the fault, if it were one, was all our own; we have none to blame but ourselves*. But no great deal is lost yet; all that Howe has been doing for this month past is rather a ravage than a conquest, which the spirit of the Jersies a year ago would have quickly repulsed, and which time and a little resolution will soon recover.

I have as little superstition in me as any man living, but
my

* "The present winter" (meaning the last) "is worth an "age, if rightly employed, but if lost, or neglected, the whole "Continent will partake of the evil; and there is no punish- "ment that man does not deserve, be he who, or what, or "where he will, that may be the means of sacrificing a season "so precious and useful." COMMON SENSE.

The Crisis Papers, written by Thomas Paine during the 1776 retreat. *Courtesy of Fort Lee History Museum.*

The Revolutionary War in Bergen County

Rebelmen, in Fort Lee. Placed by the Borough of Fort Lee, State of New Jersey and the Palisades Interstate Park Commission in 1908. *Courtesy of Carol Karels.*

Paine's *Crisis XIII* was issued on April 19, 1783, following the signing of the Treaty of Paris. Paine wrote, "The times that try men's souls are over and the greatest and completest revolution the world ever knew, gloriously and happily accomplished." A remarkable man in most respects, Paine did not realize that the impact of his work in *The Crisis* would be relevant for future generations of Americans and offer hope, encouragement and fortitude in times of darkness and struggle. Our nation will always look to Paine in every crisis we face and through Paine we will be united in cause with the generation of our American Revolution.

Bergen County and Fort Lee can validly lay claim to being the birthplace of *The American Crisis*. Fort Lee's Monument Park, dedicated in 1908, includes a unique statue entitled *Rebelmen* that honors the foot soldiers of Washington's army. The plaque at the base of the monument, written by Dan Mahoney, reads, "These trap rocks, aged two hundred million years, stand eternally, natural monuments towering high for the rebels and their cause for rebels without a cause can quickly fall. See to it now your voices rise in peace for the ears of generations yet to learn they have the power to abolish wars."

The Borough of Fort Lee rededicated this monument for the 225th anniversary of the Retreat to Victory in 2001. The plaque placed on the monument reads:

Thomas Paine and "The Times That Tried Men's Souls"

225 years ago patriot Thomas Paine wrote about his experience in Fort Lee in "The Crisis." He spoke of summer soldiers and sunshine patriots. Those were the times that tried men's souls. At that, the darkest hour of the American Revolution, Paine, General Washington and the troops of the American Army turned retreat into victory. The retreat road out of Fort Lee led to the establishment of our America. The world was turned upside down by these brave patriots. We rededicate this monument to their cause, American liberty.

Thomas Meyers is the administrator of Cultural Affairs for the Borough of Fort Lee and executive director of the Fort Lee Film Commission. He is a fourth-generation resident of the borough of Fort Lee and founder of the Fort Lee Museum and Fort Lee Film Commission. Meyers served three terms as a councilman for the borough of Fort Lee and has been an active member of the Fort Lee Historical Society for eighteen years. Presently Meyers is vice-chair of the Common Sense Society of Fort Lee, which is at work on the placement of a statue of Tom Paine in Fort Lee's Monument Park for that park's centennial in 2008.

Preserving the Hudson River Battlefield

Kevin Tremble

"Why should we include or document Fort Lee....? No battles happened there...nothing...just a retreat." Kevin Tremble, president of the Crossroads of the American Revolution, set out to refute this misconception with this speech he gave at the American Battlefield Protection Program Conference in Nashville, Tennessee, in 2004.

Telling the story of actions at Fort Lee, New Jersey, and Fort Washington, New York, is the story of the Hudson River Battlefield. The engagements included some of the newest frigates of the Royal Navy; the heaviest cannon the Continental artillery could muster; the aggressive naval forces using fire ships, row galleys and a submarine; and novel underwater obstacles. These elements are mostly missing or misunderstood from recent studies of the land engagements in the New York area. The Hudson River Battlefield lies between lower Manhattan and the Tappan Zee, a length of twenty-five miles. The main engagements were conducted between Fort Washington and Fort Lee over the period of July through November 1776.

Having a physical feature for telling this story would help the public understand the nature of these battlefield actions. Having half a fortified site (Fort Washington is obscured) and no vessels or underwater obstructions make the story difficult to tell. Practically though, the use of ships and boats for interpretation of battle actions is not likely here. Nor will the high-rise apartments between the river and Fort Washington disappear soon. In order to ensure the preservation of this battlefield, the story must include clear, well-researched information.

In the following brief recounting of battlefield actions, there are three areas of significance: 1) the naval engagements of July–November 1776; 2) the crisis—the British and Hessian invasion of November 20, 1776; and 3) divided loyalties—our first Civil War.

Preserving the Hudson River Battlefield

NAVAL ENGAGEMENTS

The summer of 1776 in New York saw the Declaration of Independence publicly read just after the first major elements of the Royal Navy arrived in New York. On July 9, the statue of King George was reportedly torn down in Bowling Green, in lower Manhattan. On July 12, a two-frigate squadron consisting of the HMS *Phoenix* and the HMS *Rose* sailed north and were cannonaded as they passed Fort Washington, New York, on their way to the Tappan Zee, seventeen miles farther upriver. Fort Constitution, later called Fort Lee, on the New Jersey shore, was just beginning to be constructed. Washington and his chief engineer, Colonel Rufus Putnam, outlined the batteries on the top of the Palisades at Burdett's Ferry. They also located the site of a field fortification and blockhouse to protect the flank of the batteries on the Palisades. There was also a need to protect the passage through the Palisades to and from the ferry. It was another ten miles north before the high rock walls of the Palisades could be easily passed.

The *Phoenix* and the *Rose* were attacked by row galleys at the Tappan Zee near Nyack, New York, on August 3, 1776. They were partially damaged with one killed and four wounded. They were again attacked on August 16 by two fire ships. This

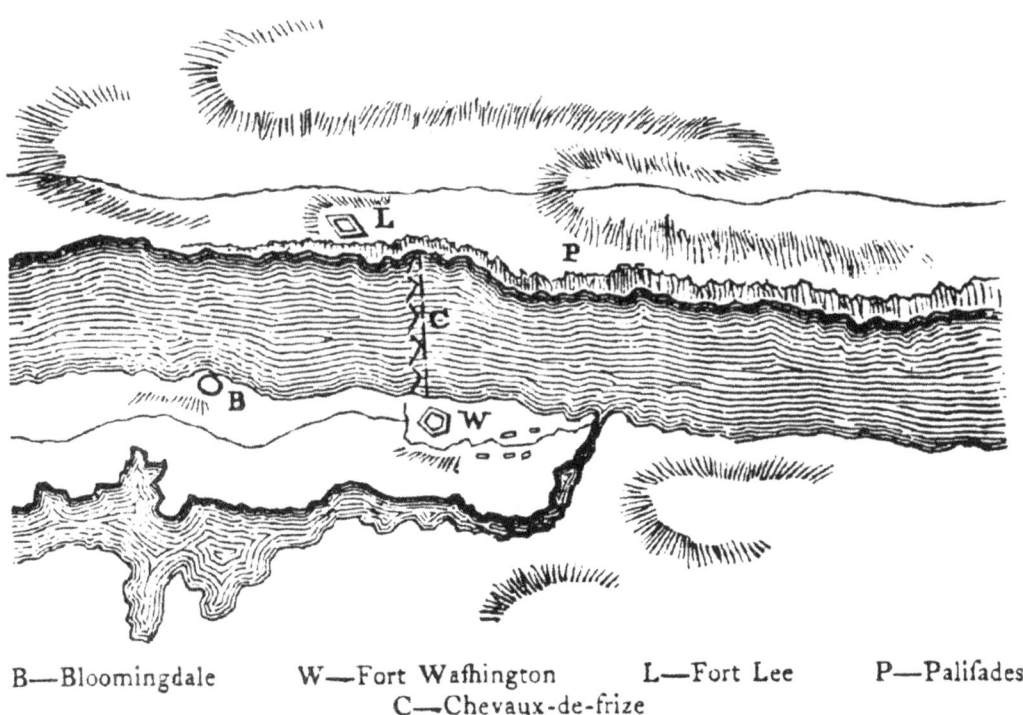

B—Bloomingdale   W—Fort Waſhington   L—Fort Lee   P—Paliſades
C—Chevaux-de-frize

1860 map showing chevaux-de-frise obstructing the Hudson.

The Revolutionary War in Bergen County

A reenactor from the Brigade of the American Revolution firing a thirty-two-pound artillery piece during the annual Fort Lee reenactment, 2006. *Courtesy of Ira Lieblich.*

engagement occurred four miles north of the Spuyten Duyvil, a creek at the northern tip of Manhattan, along the lee of the Palisades.

A tender to the HMS *Rose* was burned to the waterline. The ships returned south on August 18 and were then fired upon by both Fort Washington and Fort Constitution, with one wounded.

Throughout the summer construction continued and a plan to block the river channel was developed. The scheme involved creating an underwater blockade using a line of sunken ships and stone-filled wooden cribs with iron-tipped logs projecting from them. A ship hitting such a barrier would be slowed or stuck and then be at the mercy of the forts' cannons. The location of this barrier, called a chevaux-de-frise, was between the two forts.

The plan went awry when the channel proved deeper than thought and the current swifter than anticipated. There were reports that some of the sunken vessels drifted upriver and downriver from their intended locations. In addition, some of the wooden cribbing also floated away. A substantial number of iron-tipped, cross-spiked obstacles were also reported as being constructed in northern New Jersey and supplied for placement in the river.

An attempt was made in September, as desperation grew, to try a naval attack—a secret underwater ship designed by David Bushnell of Connecticut was launched from Manhattan to attack the Royal Navy. Unsuccessful on its first attempt, the *Turtle*, as it was known, was again launched just off Fort Washington for a second attack on October 5. This time the target was the HMS *Phoenix*, laying about two to three miles south. With this attack also unsuccessful, the *Turtle* was abandoned in an engagement on October 9 and later recovered by Bushnell.

Preserving the Hudson River Battlefield

The British command sent another squadron north on October 9, 1776. The forty-four-gun frigate HMS *Phoenix* led the HMS *Roebuck* and HMS *Tartar* with their tenders into the chevaux-de-frise and the cannonades from the two forts.

The two forts did much damage. Nine sailors and officers were killed and eighteen wounded; the Fort Lee gunners had found the range. During this action, six American row galleys were engaged at the chevaux-de-frise and were later chased up to Dobb's Ferry, several miles north, by the British squadron. The British captain of the *Phoenix*, Hyde Parker, was knighted for his gallantry in this action. The squadron remained at station in the Tappan Zee until returning after the assault on Fort Washington.

THE CRISIS—BRITISH AND HESSIAN INVASION, NOVEMBER 1776

November 16 was a disastrous day for the American cause. Fort Washington was attacked and overwhelmed within a few hours by Hessian-led land forces. The Royal Navy stationed the HMS *Pearl* north of Fort Washington in the Hudson to offer fire support. She retreated back north after being heavily fired upon from the shore.

Washington observed the loss from Fort Lee with General Nathanael Greene and his adjutant Thomas Paine. Washington was reportedly overwhelmed with grief. Fort Washington's commander, Colonel Robert Magaw, surrendered over 2,700 of the Continental army's best troops and much equipment. Washington and Greene knew Fort Lee could no longer be of use and began to prepare to abandon it. The British quickly developed an invasion plan to remove any future Fort Lee threat. Two divisions were assembled in northern Manhattan and Riverdale. Under cover of darkness on November 19, 1776, they were ferried in row galleys and landing craft across the Hudson at a point about seven miles north of Fort Lee. Here they scaled the three-hundred-foot-high cliffs of the Palisades and began their march south. In his book *Washington's Crossing*, Professor Fischer refers to this as a brilliant amphibious assault.

As news reached them on the morning of November 20, Washington and Greene immediately ordered the retreat. A brief skirmish occurred between some of the Continental rear guard and the Hessian Jägers at Liberty Pole, a few miles northwest of the fort. Lord Cornwallis directed the Hessians not to pursue the Continentals; his mission was to capture Fort Lee.

A British officer reported upon the capture: stores, tents, heavy guns, blankets, food, ammunition, about one hundred sickly prisoners and some of that "Common Sense" man's papers.

Thomas Paine wrote an eyewitness account of the retreat from Fort Lee and the total loss of New York, "These are the times that try men's souls." He worked on his paper as the army made its way across New Jersey into safety in Pennsylvania, just north of Trenton. He published it as his *American Crisis* in December, shortly before Washington's crossing of the Delaware on Christmas night, 1776. In late December we find a militia report that the British had dismantled Fort Lee. Fort Lee was the last major post lost as New York City fell to the British.

The Revolutionary War in Bergen County

DIVIDED LOYALTIES—OUR FIRST CIVIL WAR

Perhaps the least understood action related to this key location was the engagement of the Bergen County Militia with refugee Loyalist troops in May of 1781. Documents researched thus far tell of civil strife and a determination to rid the area of those remaining loyal to the King. The mostly Dutch farmers had been tormented by both sides raiding and foraging over the past five years. In a combined effort, several Bergen County Militia companies swept the Tory fighters from Fort Lee's walls. This action too has much missing. There is little published on local militia actions. Loyalist reports, such as Royal Navy After Action Reports, were not studied. We know it lasted several days. We know of some who were involved. We know there were casualties. Leiby first reports the scope of the civil war in the area in 1964, well prior to the date of exhibit design and construction at Fort Lee.

We can now examine the evolution of the protection of the battlefield area. Existing programs at Fort Lee Historic Park contribute much to the public understanding of the Hudson River Battlefield events. The economics of land development and municipal zoning in the latter part of the twentieth century need to be recognized as a threat to the protection of remaining battlefield resources.

PARK PROGRAMS

The Fort Lee Historic Museum focus is the retreat of November 1776. It contains a theater with a twelve-minute film on the retreat, displays, graphic panels, models and a retreat diorama. The exhibits depict, through historical paintings, the fire ship action with the *Phoenix* and *Rose* on August 16 and "Forcing the Hudson Passage… October 9, 1776," the *Roebuck*, *Phoenix* and *Tartar* engagement without explanation. Mention is not made of the militia/refugee engagement.

Shortly after the bicentennial and the construction of the museum, a school program was developed for fifth grade students. The program, run by site manager and curator John Muller, is a 5½-hour immersion in the daily life of the Fort Lee garrison. The program involves having the students assigned rank, organizing into units and completing a series of "details" that include foraging, food preparation, cooking, close order drill, camp making, clothing care and musket and artillery practice, using the park's three-pounder. The students bring their own food for lunch, which the cooking detail prepares onsite, in addition to churning the butter for their bread.

The program runs three days per week from mid-September to mid-December and resumes again from mid-March to June. The busiest months are October and May and the program has a 1½- to 2-year waiting list. Recently the park employed expert carpenter Roland Cadle to help rebuild the replica soldiers' hut that had been destroyed by arson.

The other commemorative events that occur are the annual reenactment of the British and Hessian invasion and Continental retreat in November. Participants from

Preserving the Hudson River Battlefield

Fort Lee educational programs, with curator John Muller. *Courtesy of Anthony G. Taranto Jr., Palisades Interstate Park.*

the Brigade of the American Revolution usually present public demonstrations of military and camp life in the American Revolution.

AFTERMATH

The residents of Fort Lee and Bergen County would periodically find remnants of activity at Fort Lee. In 1908, the American Scenic and Historic Preservation Society mapped much of the remaining features of the field fortification. The New Jersey Legislature provided funds to the Palisades Interstate Park Commission (PIPC) and Fort Lee Boro to construct a monument near the field fortification site. The *Rebelman* statue was reportedly dedicated in 1908 with a battleship salute on the Hudson, arranged by President Theodore Roosevelt.

As area development occurred and acquisition of parklands continued throughout the early twentieth century, commercial and residential use was made of the unprotected battery and fort site. In 1963, the PIPC sought justification for protecting some of the battlefield area. Dr. Jacob Judd of Sleepy Hollow Restorations researched what was widely believed to be the significant event at Fort Lee, the British and Hessian invasion of November 20, 1776. Dr. Judd found that Fort Washington and Fort Lee were unable to protect the Hudson River Valley. He based this primarily on

Burdette's Landing Historic Marker. *Courtesy of Ira Lieblich.*

the communication of Colonel Tench Tilghman, who reported to Washington that the forts had been ineffectual in their fire upon the British squadrons.

By comparing the Fort Washington experience with that of Fort Lee, we have seen that limitations of earlier research can deeply affect the outcome of battlefield protection efforts. Opportunities may still exist at Fort Lee, along the Palisades shore and under the Hudson's surface to better understand our nation's earliest struggles. "These are the times…"

Kevin Tremble is a preservation/conservationist who is president of the Crossroads of the American Revolution Association; a former National Park Service Planner; a founding member of the Tenafly, New Jersey Historic Preservation Commission; chair of the Palisades Interstate Park Citizens Advisory Council; a member of the Bergen County Historic Preservation Advisory Board; a former board member and treasurer of Preservation New Jersey; a founding member and advisor of the National Alliance of Preservation Commissions; a representative of the New Jersey Historical Commission; and the owner of a National Register–listed pre–Revolutionary War Dutch sandstone house.

NEW BRIDGE: HISTORY AT THE CROSSROADS

KEVIN WRIGHT

In 1995, the Historic New Bridge Landing Park Commission was formed to protect the historic Steuben House and New Bridge Landing. The commission created a partnership between the Division of Parks and Forestry, the County of Bergen, the Bergen County Historical Society, the Blauvelt-Demarest Foundation, the Borough of New Milford and the Township of Teaneck. Kevin Wright's essay is an excerpt from a paper he wrote for the Bergen County Historical Society in 2007.

Strategically located at the narrows of the Hackensack River, New Bridge is steeped in Revolutionary War legend and lore. Set in a no man's land between the two opposing armies, it served as a fort, military headquarters, intelligence-gathering post, encampment ground and battleground throughout the long war. New Bridge Landing was the business center of the upper Hackensack Valley—the shopping mall of its day. Iron made in stone furnaces along the Ramapough Mountains was carried in ox carts to New Bridge Landing, where it was loaded onto boats for shipment to market. Flour and animal feed were shipped from the mill. All kinds of wares came in from boats returning from the city.

New Bridge spans the narrows of the Hackensack River, fifteen miles inland from Newark Bay. In the eighteenth century, the Hackensack River was navigable to a public landing at the head of the tides in present-day Oradell, to which "boats of seven or eight Cords frequently come up for Wood and other Produce." Pettiaugers and canoes were the principal transport to market.

The first recorded visit by a tourist came in the summer of 1888, when a granddaughter of Hackensack's Revolutionary War tavern keeper Archibald Campbell drove up in her carriage and asked to be shown the vaulted root cellar where her grandfather had hidden to escape his British captors in 1780. Writing about the old Zabriskie-Steuben House in 1909, one correspondent noted:

The Revolutionary War in Bergen County

It is certain that one or more skirmishes occurred around this house during the War for Independence, for when the roof was removed some years ago, to be replaced with a new one, the rafters were found with bullets imbedded in them, and there were marks of many others. There is a dungeon in the cellar and any number of old nooks and passages which might have been useful in those times, when it was unsafe to venture abroad much or when the possession of valuables might have worked injury to the owner. The front side of the building is of dressed stone, but the back is rough and appears like the original buildings. The gables are of brick, but whether these bricks were made on the place it is impossible to say.

Much has changed and evidence of the past is much harder to come by these days. It is possible, however, with a careful search of the historic record and some imagination to revisit New Bridge in the times that tried men's souls.

The name New Bridge didn't come into use until Michael Cornelisse established the Paulus Hook Ferry in July 1764, making the overland route via New Bridge of considerable use to travelers going to and from Manhattan. A "new road or highway, which leads from New Bridge Easterly to Teaneck"—in other words, present-day New Bridge Road—was laid out on the line dividing the farms of Peter Demarest, deceased, to the north and Lawrence P. Van Buskirk, deceased, in 1767. On June 9, 1767, Peter P. Demarest Jr. applied to the Court of the General Quarter Session of the Peace and was granted a license to keep a tavern for the term of one year. The stage stop, therefore, was popularly designated "New Bridge."

THE JERSEY DUTCH

New Jersey was the most culturally diverse colony on the Atlantic seaboard, bringing different cultures and ethnicities into community throughout its complicated settlement history. By the time of the American Revolution, only one-third of the population of Bergen County could claim Netherlandish descent. Africans composed one-fifth of the population; Germans composed another fifth; while English, French and Scotch-Irish formed the remainder. Through intermarriage and the convenient adoption of a hybrid language rooted in Dutch, this varied stock blended to form the Jersey or Bergen Dutch. The process of creolization commenced immediately on the frontiers of settlement. By October 1751, the Lutheran Pietist preacher Reverend Henry M. Muhlenberg offered this description of the congregation at New Bridge:

The inhabitants of Hackensack are natives of this country. Most of them are descendants from three or four ancestors who came from Holland and purchased this tract [that is, the New Hackensack tract at Teaneck] *from the Indians about 80 or 90 years ago and settled here. Hence, almost all of them are inter-related and bear the original family names, such as van Buskirk, van Horn, van Orden, etc. The old folks had a certain natural honesty and artlessness. They did not use documents, seals, signatures, bonds and other such contracts. A man's word and handshake was his bond. The older folks at the present times are shrewd; they are still good as their word; they are sociable and command great respect in their families.*

New Bridge: History at the Crossroads

Drawing of an eighteenth-century Jersey Dutch kitchen depicting a jambless fireplace. Source unknown. *Courtesy of Bergen County Historical Society.*

Like all other nationalities, they have a special love for their mother tongue. The young people are gradually degenerating because they receive no instruction in God's Word and are mixing with other nationalities.

The process of creolization was particularly evident at New Bridge, which, as the gateway into the upper valley of the Hackensack, seems to have attracted certain ethnicities from among the general population of New Netherlands who wished to preserve their cultural identity: the Van Buskirks who settled northern Teaneck were Holstein (Danish) Lutherans; Cornelis Mattysen, first owner of the lands in River Edge whereon the Steuben House stands, was a Swede and Lutheran; Albert Zabriskie, first owner of a neighboring tract in River Edge, was Polish Silesian and a Lutheran; and the Demarests who established the French Patent (now New Milford) were French Huguenots who established a French Reformed congregation.

The Great Awakening fractured Jersey Dutch society into competing conservative (Conferentie) and liberal (Coetus) factions, often dividing families. Conservatives wanted all their ministers trained in Holland, conducting services in Dutch. Espousing the value of the conversion experience and religious "enthusiasm," the liberals were

The Dutch Reformed Church in Hackensack, 1696, by Dick Belcher. *Courtesy of Bergenfield Public Library.*

eager to Americanize their church and to appeal to a younger generation. This split widened during the American Revolution, taking on an often violent political dimension. The success of the Whig rebellion and the attainment of American independence drove away many Loyalists or diminished (at least briefly) their social standing. It is interesting to note how the genealogical entries in many Jersey Dutch Bibles change from Dutch to English after 1783, indicating the emergence of a larger and more nearly national sense of cultural identity. In a journal of his travels through

New Bridge: History at the Crossroads

this vicinity in 1797-99, the Polish Patriot and poet Julian Ursyn Niemcewicz noted, "The whole countryside is inhabited by old Dutch colonists. I recognized them by their favorite bent for navigation. They were all busy constructing or refitting boats. They are said to be ignorant, avaricious and inhospitable. They love to work and to hoard. They have kept until now their mother tongue; however, nearly all speak and understand English."

Their favorite bent for navigation is understandable. The typical eighteenth-century farm in the Hackensack valley depended upon the river for the transport of bulk commodities and therefore was most advantageously situated near a public dock. It might contain upward of 150 acres, half of which would be cleared land "neatly divided into Tillage, Meadow, and Pasture." Livestock included hogs, cattle, oxen and horses. The principal crops were rye, wheat, corn, buckwheat, turnips, melons, potatoes, salad greens and fresh and salt hay. A domicile, preferably a good stone house, and a large barn serving as a granary would be situated on the upland or terraces above the river, close to the public highways that generally maintained a somewhat level gradient by following the contour of the ridges. Horseback, wagons and sleighs conducted overland transportation. The upland bordering the river was cultivated in orchards, a sufficiency of meadow for pasturage and grain fields, interspersed with woodlots supplying enough timber for fuel and fences. As apples provided cider, long the common beverage, large orchards might contain as many as 120 trees, together with other fruit trees, particularly pear and plum, set on well-drained slopes. The upland would also have to provide sources of good water.

Since most Bergen Dutch farms were oriented to the production of cereal grains, gristmills were conveniently located for the conversion of kernel to flour and feed. In

New Bridge Landing, by B. Spence Newman. *Courtesy of Bergen County Historical Society.*

August, many farmers went to city market. Their produce was carried in ox carts and farm wagons over rutted, dirt roads. Most heavy goods were carried on sleds after snow and ice provided a smoother road surface. Those who waited for the early morning trade of the city grocers and hucksters went to a nearby lodging house and turned in for an hour or two before business commenced. Others attempted to make themselves as comfortable as possible on their market wagons and sleep until daybreak.

The Hackensack River long remained the principal artery of commerce and travel through the cultivated heartland of Bergen County. By 1748, the river was considered "navigable for Vessels of about 50 Tons" as far inland as New Bridge. When visiting the Lutheran Church at New Bridge in October 1751, Reverend Henry Muhlenberg noted that local farmers and merchants "bring the products they raise to the market in New York in little ships or vessels, and take back whatever is necessary for subsistence."

As an inland port and trading center, New Bridge grew to include the stone mansion of a prominent river merchant and miller, with its attendant outbuildings, a gristmill and a wharf. On the east side of the river, there was a commercial bakery, a stage wagon and drovers' inn and a classical academy. Stores, workshops and several farmhouses lined the riverside roads leading to the bridge. Tidal navigation remained an important activity through the end of the nineteenth century, as evidenced by the installation of an extant iron swing bridge in 1889, which is now listed on the New Jersey and National Registers of Historic Places as the oldest highway swing bridge in the state.

NEW HACKENSACK

Lawrence Pieterse Van Buskirk inherited his father's portion of the New Hackensack Patent on the east side of the river at New Bridge in 1738. Construction of the New Bridge in 1744–45 clearly encouraged commercial development in the neighborhood. While the deed record is incomplete, county records covering the maintenance of the bridge refer to Lawrence Van Buskirk's ownership of these lands. In 1765, the Freeholders ordered "that Lawrence Van Buskirk, Esq., and John Zabriskie do take the chains that are now on the New Bridge & dispose of them to the best advantage for the benefit of the county and ordered that they shall buy good Pitched Ropes & fix upon the Draw Bridge & have said Bridge put in good repair." Again in 1768, the Freeholders ordered "that the Bridge commonly called the New Bridge between Lawrence Van Buskirk's, Esq. and John Zabriskie shall be repaired." Lawrence Van Buskirk's real estate was divided among his heirs in 1767. Again, the records are incomplete, but we know that Lawrence Pieterse Van Buskirk had at least four children: Jacobus, Abraham, Andrew and Elizabeth (wife of Isaac Vroom, Vroomen or Roome). Lawrence Van Buskirk's three sons—Captain Jacobus Van Buskirk, Dr. Abraham Van Buskirk and Andrew Van Buskirk—were to play important roles at New Bridge in the years leading up to the American Revolution.

Abraham Van Buskirk, of New Bridge, a "Physician, Surgeon and apothecary" with a "considerable Practice," is the best-known Loyalist of military rank from

New Bridge: History at the Crossroads

Bergen County. By his own admission, he signed the first association drawn up by Major Daniel Isaac Brown, but never took any oath to support Congress. At the outbreak of war in 1775, Dr. Van Buskirk was chosen to represent Bergen County in the Provincial Congress. He did this with the advice and consent of British agents and sympathizers. He resigned his office and was tried for opposing Congressional measures and for preventing arms from being carried out of Bergen County. Lord Percy described him as "being very active in furnishing Intelligence and assisting Loyalists to join the British Arm, before he himself joined the Army." In 1776, he was obliged to hide in the woods to avoid capture, but "he joined the British army when they came into his house and has remained with the Army ever since." On November 16, 1776, Sir William Howe commissioned Dr. Van Buskirk lieutenant colonel commandant of a battalion in the Fourth Battalion, New Jersey Volunteers, bringing "100 Men with him when he joined." After the war, Lord Cornwallis testified that he "rendered very essential services to the British Forces being a Loyalist of the greatest merit and served the whole war with Zeal and Fidelity."

The State of New Jersey confiscated Dr. Van Buskirk's properties and his claim for compensation from the Crown, written at Halifax on March 31, 1786, states, "At the commencement of the troubles he was settled at New Bridge on the Hackensack River." He produced a copy of his father's will, dated December 6, 1774, "by which it appears that the Property here Claimed is devised to Claimant, burdened with certain Legacies, which he declares are discharged or Property to more than the amount of his Share is in the hands of his Brother John Van Buskerk, who is in New Jersey." His confiscated lands included "a dwelling house, Grist Mill and other Outhouses laying on the Hackensack River," valued at £2,000.

Archaeological explorations, paint and mortar analysis and careful detective work conclusively demonstrate that the oldest part of the Zabriskie-Steuben House at New Bridge was a stone saltbox, forty-five feet front and thirty-five feet, ten inches deep, with front rooms flanking a center hall and three narrow rooms at the back of the house. In its original form, this house resembles the description of a contemporary house in Hackensack that David W. Provost offered for sale in 1746. It was described as "Forty-eight Foot in Length and Twenty-four Foot Broad, with a large Cellar-Kitchen, a Dairy and Store Cellar all joyn'd together, the said Dwelling House has two large Rooms, and an Entry [hall], with a large flush Garret." According to this floor plan, the front door opened into a wide center hall, which also served as a breezeway. The room on the north side of the hall was a parlor, holding the family's best bed, used only for wedding nights, births and wakes. The large room on the south side of the hall was the dwelling room—here the family ate, worked and slept around the largest fireplace in the house. Three narrow rooms at the back of the house were used for a kitchen, a milk room and a root cellar, where food could be kept cold, much like in a modern refrigerator. A winding staircase led from the back of the hall into the garret.

This five-room house grew to its present size by a single enlargement, whereby the three-bay north block, twenty-one feet, three inches by thirty-five feet, ten inches, and the second floor along the rear (or west elevation) were added at the same time. We know that the Zabriskie mansion reached its present size by 1784, according to a

The Revolutionary War in Bergen County

The Retreat at New Bridge Landing, by B. Spence Newman. *Courtesy of Bergen County Historical Society.*

compensation claim filed on January 24, 1784, by John J. Zabriskie, "now a refugee in the City of New York" for his former homestead at New Bridge. Mr. Zabriskie described his estate as "One large Mansion House, seventy feet long and forty feet wide, containing twelve rooms built with stone, with Outhouses consisting of a bake House, Smoke House, Coach House, and two large Barns, and a Garden, situated at a place called New Bridge (value £850)." It is most improbable that the Zabriskies undertook such a substantial construction project during the Revolutionary War. Since the family grew wealthy from increased trade during the French and Indian War (1756–63), it is most likely that the house was enlarged about the time of Jan Zabriskie's marriage to Jannetje Goelett on November 21, 1764, in order to create a double house with separate quarters for two generations of the family.

The tidal gristmills at New Bridge were of vital interest to farmers who wished to sell their grain at the best possible price. Grinding kernels into flour or animal feed tripled the value. Two heavy stone wheels, called *millstones*, did the work of grinding. The bottom or *nether* stone was fixed in the floor of the mill while the top or *runner* stone turned above it. The grain trickled from a large wooden holder or *hopper* through an *eye* or hole in the center of the runner stone.

John Zabriskie, third generation of that name to inhabit the sandstone mansion at New Bridge, was born September 30, 1767, the son of John and Jane (Goelet) Zabriskie. When his grandfather, John the first, died in September 1774, he assumed the title of Junior. We can imagine the wide eyes of this nine-year-old boy, face pressed against the pane, as he counted the ragtag garrison of Fort Lee, General Washington at their head, passing his threshold and vanishing southward in a cold drizzle. Continental troops used his home as a fort to defend their passage. We don't know what he overheard of his father's political whisperings, but on July 14, 1777, he may have watched approaching bateaux, loaded with soldiers under command of Major Samuel Hayes, as they landed alongside the gristmill. They arrested his father as a "disaffected person" and imprisoned him at Morristown. Once on parole, John Sr. abandoned the family homestead, fleeing to New York City where his family found refuge with their cousins, the Seamans. Whatever bitterness the Zabriskies felt at the British evacuation of Manhattan was compounded when the victorious Revolutionary officers of the State of New Jersey confiscated their properties.

Discouraged in his hopes of returning to a profitable station in Europe, Major General Frederick William Baron Von Steuben informed the New Jersey Legislature that he was "anxiously desirous to become a citizen of the State of New Jersey." In recognition of his "many and signal services to the United States of America," state legislators responded on December 23, 1783, by presenting him with the use and emoluments of the confiscated estate of Jan Zabriskie at New Bridge, provided that the Baron would "hold, occupy and enjoy the said estate in person, and not by tenant." Accordingly, General Philemon Dickinson of the New Jersey Militia informed the Baron of this legislative gift and related his knowledge of the estate based upon recent inquiries:

> *There are on the premises an exceeding good House, an excellent barn, together with many useful outbuildings, all of which I am told, want some repairs…there is…a Grist-mill; a good Orchard, some meadow Ground, & plenty of Wood. The distance from N York by land 15 miles, but you may keep a boat & go from your own door to N York by water—Oysters, Fish & wild fowl in abundance—Possession will be given to you in the Spring, when you will take a view of the premises.*

General Dickinson regretted that the legislature had only vested Steuben with life rights and not outright title to the property, saying,

> *This not, my dear Baron, equal either to my wishes & your mind, but 'tis the best I could probably obtain—You'll observe by the Act, that you are to possess it, but not tenant it out, I am ashamed of this clause but it could not be avoided—This may easily be obviated, by keeping a bed & Servants there & visiting the premises now & then—but I flatter myself, from the representation which has been made to me, that it will be your permanent residence; its vicinity to N York, must render it agreeable to you.*

Under these terms, it is likely that the Prussian inspector general contemplated taking up residence at New Bridge. His biographer, Friedrich Kapp, writing in 1859, said only, "Steuben, when informed that Zabriskie, in consequence of that confiscation, was left without means, did not accept the gift, and interposed in behalf of Zabriskie."

Steuben House sign. *Courtesy of Carol Karels.*

New Bridge: History at the Crossroads

Unfortunately, the documented facts do not square with this kindly interpretation. On January 24, 1784, John J. Zabriskie, "now a refugee in the City of New York," filed a claim for compensation from the British government for the loss of his former homestead at New Bridge, which had been "possessed under this Confiscation Law." Zabriskie's 1784 account clearly describes the well-known sandstone mansion that yet stands at this location. Whatever the conflicting sentiments of the Revolutionary War mercenary and dispossessed Loyalist may have been, one fact was equally evident to both: the Zabriskie mansion was not some sleepy country estate that needed only the fires stoked and the slipcovers lifted to make it cozy. It had served repeatedly as a fort, military headquarters, an intelligence gathering post, an encampment ground and the scene of numerous skirmishes. Undoubtedly the abuses of war had rendered the dwelling house uninhabitable, stripped of its furnishings. The old and impecunious Saxon soldier was hardly able to restore its former grandeur. Besides, the legislature had not given the Baron title to the property, but only a right to life tenancy. It would hardly have been worthwhile for him to invest any large sum in the renovation of a property that he did not own.

Before investing in his estate at New Bridge, General Steuben first intended to acquire title to the property in fee simple. On December 24, 1784, the New Jersey Legislature responded to his overtures by passing a supplement to its previous act, which authorized the agent for forfeited estates to sell the property to the highest bidder and to deposit the money in the state treasury. Interest upon the sum was to be paid to the Baron during his lifetime. Accordingly, the Zabriskie estate at New Bridge was sold on April 1, 1785, but its purchaser was none other than the Baron himself, acting through his agent, Captain Benjamin Walker. The purchase price was £1,500. The general's personal interest and familiarity with his Jersey estate was outlined in a letter addressed from New York to Governor Livingston on November 13, 1785, wherein he noted that he had "become the purchaser of that part of the estate of John Zabriskie, lying at the New-Bridge, near Hackensack, and the term of payment being arrived, an order from the commissioners of the continental treasury on the treasury of New Jersey lies ready for the agent whenever he shall please to call for it."

Between 1783 and 1785, General Steuben withdrew $26,000 from the national treasury, including the sum that he used to purchase the former Zabriskie homestead. He apparently spent considerable money to renovate both his leased farmhouse on Manhattan as well as his prized Jersey estate. But his improvident lifestyle and poor management of personal finances outstripped his income and the number of his creditors daily increased. On February 28, 1786, New Jersey Legislature ordered that, if payments on the property were not met by the following March (1787), then the Baron should have the use and benefit of the estate even though he resided in another state. Thus it wasn't until 1786—three years after the initial presentation of the property to Steuben—that the legislature abandoned its stipulation that he should occupy the property in order to receive its profits. With this encouragement, Steuben apparently leased the mansion and mill back to Jan Zabriskie and so enjoyed the rental fees.

By 1787, Steuben's finances were at low ebb. Bankrupt, he placed his affairs under the administration of Ben Walker. In 1788, he moved into rooms in the house of his friends, Benjamin and Polly Walker, on King Street. In May 1788, he set out for his vast estate in the Mohawk country. To pay off his debts and to gain some much needed capital, Baron Von Steuben wrote to Captain Walker on May 23, 1788, giving him full authority to sell his Jersey estate at New Bridge.

Steuben's extensive repairs to the premises are openly stated in his advertisement of sale, published in the *New Jersey Journal* on December 3, 1788, which reads,

> *Long-noted as the best stand for trade in the state of New Jersey. Large well-built stone house, thoroughly rebuilt lately, a gristmill with two run of stone; excellent new kiln for drying grain for export built lately; other outbuildings, and 40 acres of land, one-half of which is excellent meadow. Situated on the bank of the river by which produce can be conveyed to New York in a few hours, and sloops of 40 tons burden may load and discharge along side of the mill.*

On December 4, 1788, Major General Frederick William Baron Von Steuben, of New York City, conveyed his Jersey estate, comprising forty-nine acres at New Bridge, formerly belonging to John Zabriskie, to John Zabriskie Jr. (1767–93) of New Barbados Township, for £1,200. He was the son and namesake of the Loyalist who lost the property. Steuben happily reported in a letter dated December 12, "My Jersey Estate is sold for twelve hundred Pounds N.Y. Money [about $3,000]. Walker and Hamilton are my Administrators."

In 1794, the Baron Von Steuben died in poverty while residing in a crude log house erected in the midst of an untamed wilderness. His loyal aide-de-camp, Ben Walker, buried him without ceremony in a plain pine coffin, wrapped in his military cloak.

WEBSITE OF INTEREST

www.bergencountyhistory.org

Kevin Wright is a regional resource interpretive specialist for the New Jersey Division of Parks and Forestry. He is a past president of the Bergen County Historical Society, a past member of the Bergen County Historic Preservation Advisory Board, a past trustee of both the Bergen and Sussex County Historical Societies and the Borough of River Edge historian. He has served as secretary to the Historic New Bridge Landing Park Commission since 1995. He has written numerous essays on New Jersey and Bergen County history. He has a unique perspective on the Steuben House, for as past curator, he lived there with his family for over ten years. His wife, Deborah Powell, current president of the Bergen County Historical Society, designed and maintains the BCHS website.

Bergen's Loyalists

Todd W. Braisted

In the summer of 1776, an estimated three hundred British ships, under the command of Lord Viscount Richard Howe, arrived in New York Harbor to put down the rebellion. At the time of the Revolution, Bergen County had about three thousand inhabitants, mostly third- and fourth-generation Americans known as the Jersey Dutch. The British aggressively recruited young men in Bergen County, offering generous bounties to those willing to join the King's army. Deals were made in the middle of the night aboard the warships in New York Harbor. Many who signed on were given roles as spies and they wandered freely through Bergen County, observing and reporting back on Patriot activity, including that of their Patriot neighbors. The Loyalists of Bergen County eagerly helped the British, providing supplies and information and recruiting men.

"I hope by the vigorous measures lately adopted, we shall soon reduce that almost totally revolted County of Bergen." Those were not the words of some sinister British general seeking to crush the Patriots of Bergen County. Rather, those words were written in July 1777 by William Livingston, governor of the state of New Jersey.

The American Revolution was as much a civil war as was the later conflict between the states in the 1860s. While differences with the British arose over economic and political issues, many felt an armed revolt leading to an overthrow of the Crown's authority in America was by no means justified. In New Jersey, those who held such views were most numerous in Monmouth and Bergen Counties.

Even before the arrival of British forces in the New York City area, George Washington recognized the conservative tilt of the county, reacting with great consternation upon learning that William Franklin and his guard had stopped at Hackensack en route to Connecticut. One of Bergen's townships was named after the governor, reflecting their sentiments toward him.

During the turbulent campaign of 1776, many Bergen militiamen faithfully did service, both in New York City and helping to build or garrison Fort Lee on the Palisades. But many of those same militia, both officers and men, would join the

> I DO hereby Certify, That *Dirck Brinkerhoof of Bergen County* has, in my Presence, voluntarily taken an OATH, to bear Faith and true Allegiance to His MAJESTY KING GEORGE the Third;—and to defend to the utmost of his Power, His sacred Person, Crown and Government, against all Persons whatsoever.
>
> GIVEN under my Hand at NEW-YORK, this 15. Day of *May* in the Seventeenth Year of His MAJESTY's Reign, Anno. Dom. 1777.
>
> *Mathews*
>
> MAYOR of the City of NEW-YORK.

Oath of allegiance to King George III by Dirck Brinkerhoof, May 15, 1777. *Courtesy of the Clements Library, University of Michigan.*

British when they entered the county in November of 1776. Officers such as Abraham Van Buskirk, John Zabriskie, John Hammell and Peter Rutan would all become officers in the British Provincial forces.

New Jersey raised thousands of troops for King George III, and hundreds of them came from Bergen County. Areas such as Paramus, Hackensack, Closter, English Neighborhood and Ramapough proved fertile recruiting grounds for the British. John Cameron of Ringwood, a discharged soldier from the French and Indian War, joined the regiment of Royal Highland Emigrants, serving in Quebec for much of the war. Mathew Benson joined the King's Orange Rangers, commanded by John Bayard. The Bayard family, while prominent over the border in Orange County, New York, also owned a very large estate on Bergen Neck, in Hoboken. Benson would serve most of the war in garrison in Nova Scotia. John Aldington, whose brewery in English Neighborhood had been converted into a storehouse to serve Fort Lee in 1776, commanded the corps of guides and pioneers, of which John Zabriskie of New Bridge would be captain. Aldington served with his corps from South Carolina to Rhode Island, even helping man the *Tryal* tender in the Hudson River in 1776 to help fend off the attack on the Royal Navy flotilla by fire ships.

THE NEW JERSEY VOLUNTEERS

The vast majority of Loyalist soldiers raised in Bergen County would serve in the Fourth Battalion, New Jersey Volunteers. The New Jersey Volunteers was the largest of all Provincial regiments raised by the British, consisting of six battalions and eventually enlisting over 3,300 officers and men. The corps was commanded by Brigadier General Cortland Skinner, who had served as attorney general in William Franklin's government. It would recruit primarily in areas of strong Loyalist sentiment: the First and Second Battalions from Monmouth, the Third from Essex, the Fourth in Bergen, the Fifth in Sussex and the Sixth Battalion in Hunterdon County. A battalion was later raised in old West Jersey, from Salem, Cumberland and Gloucester Counties.

These battalions were part of the Provincial forces raised by the British throughout the war. Led by their own officers, these regiments were armed, paid, disciplined, uniformed and provisioned the same as the regular British army. They were liable for service anywhere in North America. The regiments were issued new uniforms every year, often changing color and style. Those of the New Jersey Volunteers were green in color during 1777 and 1779 and red in the other years. The troops were paid in hard currency, a private soldier making six pence a day, from which was deducted two and a half pence for his provisions. Those provisions consisted daily of salt beef or pork, bread, biscuit or rice, peas, sauerkraut, cheese, oatmeal, butter, rum and spruce beer.

The commander of the Fourth Battalion, New Jersey Volunteers, was Abraham Van Buskirk, who had served previously as the surgeon to the Bergen County Militia. Van Buskirk described himself as a "Practitioner of Physick," earning £200 per year while he settled on his estate in Teaneck, on the east side of New Bridge. His two immediate field officers were from Hackensack: First Major Daniel Isaac Browne, an attorney, and Second Major Robert Timpany, an Irish-born schoolmaster. Other officers included Captains William Van Allen of New Bridge, Peter Rutan of Franklin and Samuel Ryerson of Saddle River; Captain Lieutenant Hendrick Marsh of New Bridge; and Lieutenant Edward Earle and his brother, Ensign Justus Earle, also of Hackensack. Some other officers did not work out, such as Ensign John Babcock of Ramapough, who was captured in December 1776 and never returned to active duty.

Perhaps the most unfortunate of Bergen's Loyalist troops was Isaac Noble of Ramapough. Slated to be a major in the New Jersey Volunteers, Noble joined the British immediately upon their arrival in Hackensack in November 1776. Along with a number of recruits, he accompanied the army on its march to Acquackanonk, where his widow later picked up the story:

> *He…offered himself a Guide to ford the River at the Head of a Detachment in the Face of the Enemy posted on the opposite Height, which he performed to the Satisfaction of the Commanding general. A Regiment of Loyalists being order'd to be formed in New Jersey, Mr. Noble (in consideration of his Zeal and Services) had the Honor of being named as Major to the…Battalion commanded by Coll: Buskirk, and…was going on Duty as such, when he was attacked by a skulking Party of Rebels near the Camp at Aquakanunk and left by them as dead, having received a violent Contusion on the Head, and the Thrust of a Bayonet in the Eye which was thereby totally lost. On the retreat of the Kings Forces, he was in this lamentable condition conveyed to New York, where for many months he was under the care of Docr: Morris. The wounds having affected the Brain, he was near 18 Months watched and*

The Fourth Battalion New Jersey Volunteers fire a volley while other British and Loyalist troops of the BAR take part in the 225th anniversary of the 1778 British grand forage. Historic New Bridge Landing, 2003. *Courtesy of Susan Braisted.*

treated accordingly, and his Commission of Major was of course never issued. During this Calamity [his wife] *suffered much ill treatment from her neighbours who were disaffected to Government. She was informed of their Resolution to take her into Custody, which to avoid she fled by favor of a dark night, with an Infant of nine months at her Breast, on Foot and unprotected, she suffer'd every thing which can be felt from Terror, inclemency of weather, want of Food and of every Conveniency, by which her Health was much impaired. Finding the impossibility of escaping with more than the Infant at her Breast, was obliged to leave three others to the mercy of the Rebels, who took them the Day after their Mothers Escape, and stript them of every thing necessary to their Infant state even to their Cloaths, at the same time pillaged the House and Farm of every thing portable, and destroyed what they cou'd not carry away. The Children remained Prisoners near 13 months, at the expiration of which time a Flag was obtained from his Excellency Genl: Clinton to bring them to their Parents at New York, which was done at great Expence.*

Isaac Noble could then only find employ as a commissary in the army's civil branches, in which service he was robbed and murdered by some highwaymen on Manhattan Island in 1779.

The rank and file soldiers in the corps reflected a mix of laborers, small property owners and even middle-class farmers such as Abraham Vanderbeck, owner of one hundred acres in Hackensack. Many large families joined en masse, such as the six Ramapough Wanamakers who enlisted under Captain Rutan. Jacob Hemeon of Masonicas joined up with at least four of his sons, all serving as privates. None rivaled the Ackerman family, which provided an impressive sixteen soldiers for the battalion. Not all in the corps were from Bergen County. Arthur Maddox, commissioned a captain in the volunteers on February 14, 1777, had joined the British in South Carolina eight months earlier, while Albert Berdan of Vermont had been confined "in a Dungeon" at Fort Ticonderoga for three months before escaping and joining the volunteers in April 1777.

The battalion served the British faithfully for the remainder of the war, taking part in engagements big and small. Some raids were made in Bergen County, either to gather stores or capture important prisoners, such as future delegate to the Continental Congress John Fell, taken at his home in northern Paramus on the night of April 22, 1777. He was imprisoned in the Cortland Sugar House. Other encounters were true battles, such as on August 22 of the same year when Continental Major General John Sullivan with two thousand troops crossed over to Staten Island, primarily to destroy five of the battalions of New Jersey Volunteers stationed there. He nearly succeeded, totally surprising the First and Fifth Battalions and, if not for the treachery of one of his guides, Van Buskirk's battalion would have shared the same fate. Recovering from the surprise, Brigadier General Skinner "detached Major Tympany with 25 Men to gain Information of the Route which the Enemy had taken. The Major came up with a number of them at the house of Dr. Parker, which they were plundering. He attacked them immediately, killed several, and took the rest Prisoners." After securing the two dozen or so prisoners there, the battalion continued to the kill separating New Jersey and the island,

Bergen's Loyalists

Nineteenth-century wood block print of the Sugar House Prison in New York City.

where they engaged Continentals from the First and Third New Jersey Regiments, who were in the act of crossing back to their native state. Sir Henry Clinton, commanding in New York, sent thanks in orders for the "Resolution & Conduct shown by Col. Buskirk with the Spiritted behaviour of the Officers & Soldiers under his Command." Just a few weeks later, Sir Henry had a chance to personally command the battalion on a large foraging expedition through Bergen County. The one large battle of the expedition took place on September 13 at Acquackanonk, when over a thousand British, German and Provincial troops found themselves confronted by Continental and militia troops, with artillery. Clinton called forth his New Jersey Volunteers to lead the way, writing this in his official report:

> *To try* [the Continentals'] *Countenance, and give an Opportunity to the Provincials, I ordered Buskirk's Battalion to march thro' a Corn Field, with an Intention of taking in Flank a Body of the Rebels posted behind a Stone Wall, and which it would have been difficult to have removed by a Front Attack. The Regiment marched with great Spirit, and their March, with some little Movement to favor it, obliged the Rebels to quit without a Shot.*

The Revolutionary War in Bergen County

Not all would go in their favor during the war. On August 19, 1779, the battalion was nearly surprised at Paulus Hook when the post was attacked by Continentals under Major Henry Lee. While the bulk of the battalion under Van Buskirk was off in English Neighborhood searching for Lee, fifty of the battalion in the post were taken prisoner and two were killed. Sergeant John Taswell was court-martialed and found liable for the loss of the post by abandoning his blockhouse during the attack. The sergeant was sentenced to death, but through the intervention of Van Buskirk the sentence was reduced to being discharged and sent without the British lines. He was immediately picked up by the militia and lodged in Morristown Jail, from which he escaped in 1780 and made his way back to the battalion. Allowed to rejoin the corps, he finished the war as a corporal.

Some of the volunteers would serve in distant theaters during the war. Forty of the corps under Captain Samuel Ryerson volunteered for service in South Carolina in 1780 under the famous Major Patrick Ferguson. Many of these men would never return, becoming casualties during the grueling campaign that year or falling eventually at Kings Mountain. Captain Ryerson, minus his ring finger lost in that battle, and the survivors of the corps would return to New York in April of the following year. The Light Infantry Company of the battalion under Captain Jacob Van Buskirk (the colonel's son) embarked for Virginia in October 1780, where they saw little action before setting sail again for South Carolina a few weeks later. As part of the corps of Provincial Light Infantry, Van Buskirk and his company chased partisans through the High Hills of Santee through the first half of 1781. In one remarkable incident, Ensign Richard Cooper and twenty men of the company found themselves surrounded by ten times their number of partisans under Thomas Sumter. Cooper's commanding officer related the incident:

> *Returning one day from a foraging Party, one of the Waggons, which was bringing a Mill, to grind the Corn, broke down, as it was not above one mile and a half from home, I left an Ensign, whose name was Cooper, with 20 Men, to repair, & bring it on—our Men were but just in and began to dress their dinners; when we heard a centinal firing towards the Line in which he had been left; every Man was instantly in Arms. Suspecting the cause, which was confirmed by the Horses galloping home by themselves. We were soon up to the Spot which was but about a mile for having repaired the Cart, they were proceeding home; when Sumpter wholly surrounded them, & called to him to surrender; but forming his Men in a Circle, round the Trees nearest him, he replied Light Infantry never Surrender, and began firing as hard as they could—seeing us approach, they quitted our Gallant Ensign, & formed to receive us. This business did not last long before they fled, leaving what killed and wounded may be seen by the returns. We took some Prisoners and 30 Horses. Lord Rawdon came the next day, & flattered his young Corps much, by his manner of thanking them, & took that particular notice of Mr. Cooper, he so well deserved.*

Cooper was a rarity in that he came up through the ranks from an enlisted man to become a commissioned officer, ending the war as a lieutenant. The company continued serving in South Carolina through April 1782, when they returned to New

Bergen's Loyalists

York. On September 8, 1781, they fought in the bloody Battle of Eutaw Springs, where Captain Van Buskirk was seriously wounded. Two days earlier the remainder of the battalion had fought their large engagement as part of Brigadier General Benedict Arnold's force attacking Fort Griswold in Groton, Connecticut.

Not all of Bergen's active Loyalists joined the Provincial corps. Those not desirous of the often mundane day-to-day life of a common soldier took up arms in more loosely organized corps, such as the King's Militia Volunteers. The most celebrated of this unit was Lieutenant Weart Banta of Hackensack. This husband and father of three had recruited sixty-one men for both the New Jersey Volunteers and King's Orange Rangers, which was more than enough to entitle him to captain's commission in the Provincial corps. He chose the life of a partisan instead, making a name for himself with his 1778 capture of John Lozier, who had been involved with the murder of a civilian Loyalist, John Richards. Later that year he joined with Thomas Ward and a handful of others in capturing the Continental Muster Master General Joseph Ward at Kakiat. He proved an active guide for British troops, scouting Fort Montgomery up the Hudson River and leading General Grey's column in their attack on Baylor's Dragoons in September 1778. His career as an active partisan effectively ended on March 28, 1779, just fifty-four days after receiving his commission, when a musket ball fired by a Bergen County Militiaman in Closter shattered his knee, leaving him crippled for the remainder of his life.

The nature of a soldier's life being what it is, not all Bergen County Loyalists left home during the war, even some of the men choosing to remain behind. Many of these people took part in what was referred to as "London trading," i.e., bringing their cattle or crops to the British in exchange for gold or imported merchandise not otherwise available in the countryside. Continental commander Major James Moore insisted on moving his command in Paramus each night in April 1780 because of the "great number of disaffected inhabitants about this Place." The militia's orderly sergeants, those tasked with warning inhabitants for their tour of duty, often took their lives into their own hands. Sergeant Benjamin Romaine narrowly avoided being shot while performing this duty near Old Bridge. Sergeant Samuel Banta was not so lucky; he was severely wounded while performing that duty, while others were likewise attacked. Not even the women were to be trusted, as Major Goetschius of the state troops discovered when in September 1780, at Schraalenburgh, they apprehended the wife of a Loyalist guiding six deserters of the Pennsylvania line to the British. Just ten months before, Goetschius had ordered off Gerritie Maybee and her two children to join her husband Abraham within the British lines.

CONFISCATION OF PROPERTY

The state of New Jersey waged its own war of sorts on Bergen's Loyalist civilians, first with imprisonment and later by confiscation of property. In July 1777, Governor William Livingston ordered a detachment of militia drawn from other counties, under the command of Major Samuel Hayes, to proceed from Morristown and arrest

The Steuben House today at historic New Bridge Landing. *Courtesy of Carol Karels.*

forty-nine of the county's residents for remaining subjects of King George III. Hayes and just over one hundred militia (about half the intended force) landed at Secaucus, marched north through English Neighborhood and then west to Hackensack, rounding up just fourteen of the suspects over three days. These prisoners would be lodged in the Morristown Jail, eventually exchanged for a like number of Whig inhabitants imprisoned in New York.

The greater proceedings against Loyalists came from the laws passed allowing for the confiscation and sale of their property. Advertisements announcing "inquisitions" against the Loyalists were published in the papers, listing those who had to appear before the court of common pleas or judgment would be rendered against them. For most, that was impossible. Once judgment had been made in favor of the state, all real and personal property belonging to the Loyalist was seized, advertised for sale and sold at auction. In all, no fewer than 134 properties throughout the county were seized by the state, most famously the home of John Zabriskie at New Bridge, which in turn was given to Washington's drill master, Major General Friedrich Wilhelm Von Steuben. The number of confiscations represented just over 20 percent of all property seized and sold by the state, a greater percentage than any other single county. However, not all the sales were without risk. Captain Jonathan Hopper of the Bergen

County Militia, living in a house at Wagaraw purchased at auction, was killed there by a party of New Jersey Volunteers, which, it was said, drove away the potential buyer of the property of Robert Drummond, major to the Third Battalion of that corps.

WAR'S END AND EXODUS TO CANADA

The end of the war came quietly for the Loyalists, with the acknowledgement of United States independence signed in a peace treaty in 1783. Those who remained loyal to the British were faced with a difficult decision: should they retain their allegiance and leave behind their homeland to settle anew elsewhere under the British Crown, or attempt to make peace with their old neighbors and return home, provided of course that there was still a home to return to. For those serving in the Provincial corps, their regiments would not be disbanded until October 10, 1783. Van Buskirk's battalion had long since lost much of its Bergen County dominance as far as its membership was concerned. Many of the recruits who had entered the unit after its initial raising were actually Continental army (or even a few French) deserters. In July 1781, the corps had been renumbered as the Third Battalion, with three companies of the old Second Battalion being added to it. These men were primarily from Monmouth County, further diluting the Bergen flavor of the unit. On September 3, 1783, those soldiers wishing to remain in the United States, including fifty-five from Van Buskirk's battalion, took their discharge at New York. They included such men as Richard Terhune, John Van Houten, John Van Norden and Casparus Degraw. Many of the remainder, some 356 officers, soldiers, women and children, embarked three days later for the River Saint John in Nova Scotia (now New Brunswick.) Some few others, such as Abraham Van Buskirk and Major Philip Van Cortland, left for England to personally present their losses to a commission set up by Parliament to compensate Loyalists for their losses and services.

These soldiers, joined by tens of thousands of civilian Loyalists from all the colonies, would settle throughout Nova Scotia, Quebec and Upper Canada (Ontario.) Those of the New Jersey Volunteers primarily settled on free grants of land up the River Saint John, near Fredericton. The land was issued out in proportion: one hundred acres to each man, fifty to each woman, child and servant in a family. Those who had served in the military received land in proportion to their rank. The problem however lay in the fact that the land had not been surveyed. Therefore, nothing could be allotted until that was rectified, and that would take almost two years in some places. Mary Fisher, wife of Private Lodewick Fisher of Ramapough, later recalled their first winter in the wilds:

> *Snow fell on the 2nd day of November to the depth of six inches. We pitched our tents in the shelter of the woods and tried to cover them with spruce boughs. We used stones for fireplaces. Our tents had no floor but the ground. The winter was very cold, with deep snow, which we tried to keep from drifting in by putting a large rug at the door. The snow, which lay six feet around us, helped greatly in keeping out the cold. How we lived through that awful winter I*

hardly know. There were mothers that had been reared in a pleasant country enjoying all the comforts of life, with helpless children in their arms. They clasped their infants to their bosoms and tried by the warmth of their own bodies to protect them from the bitter cold. Sometimes a part of the family had to remain up during the night to keep the fires burning, so as to keep the rest from freezing. Some destitute people made use of boards, which the older ones kept heating before the fire and applied by turns to the smaller children to keep them warm.

The land was eventually surveyed, lots were drawn and new settlements finally started. The former residents of the Hackensack Valley finally embarked on the next chapter of their lives. Captain Samuel Ryerson, writing from Burton on May 14, 1784, to his brother George Luke Ryerson in Pequannock, summed everything up: "This cuntery is in a fair way of Being compleatly Settled and I think will Be in a Flurishing Cuntery in a little time. Every thing Now is Peacable the govenor and Council are Verry good Men and have Excerted Them Selves Beyound Every Expectation to get Every Man on his land."

Many of the descendants of these Bergen County families can be found today still in Nova Scotia, New Brunswick or elsewhere in Canada.

WEBSITE OF INTEREST

www.royalprovincial.com

Todd W. Braisted is a lifelong resident of Bergen County. He has served as president of the Bergen County Historical Society and chairman of the West Point Chapter of the Company of Military Historians, and currently serves as president of the Fourth Battalion, New Jersey Volunteers reenactment group. In 2007, he was elected the first American to serve as honorary vice-president of the United Empire Loyalist Association of Canada. He has organized numerous living history commemorations in the county, including those at Historic New Bridge Landing and Fort Lee Historic Park. He is a contributing author of the 1999 Garland Book Moving On: Black Loyalists in the Afro-Atlantic World *and has also had numerous journal articles published. He likewise lectures extensively on Loyalist and local history. Todd has also appeared on the popular PBS show* History Detectives *and CBC's* So Who Do You Think You Are? *His wife, Susan Braisted, is a longtime reenactor and is a cofounder of In Good Company, an eighteenth-century dance group. A number of her photos are included in this book.*

DANIEL'S TALE: THE CAREER OF ONE BERGEN COUNTY MILITIAMAN

ERIC NELSEN

On August 31, 1775, the State Committee of Safety ordered all males age sixteen to fifty to enroll in the militia or leave the state. A few months later, Congress decided to create a Continental army with twenty thousand men. Anticipating a short war, Congress specified that men need only enlist for one year, but had to serve anywhere on the continent. By contrast, militiamen were responsible for protecting local towns and for assisting the main army. When faced with a choice of joining the militia or the Continental army, most Bergen County men chose the militia, which allowed them to stay close to their farms and families. Initially, General Washington expressed frustration that the Jersey Militia came and went as they pleased, and disappeared during planting and harvest seasons. He later praised them, for on numerous occasions the local militia units came out in large numbers to harass the British in their marches across the state and in their multiple foraging attempts. It was the New Jersey Militia that faced raids and skirmishes on a daily basis throughout the war. Eric Nelsen's essay sheds light on the duties of one Bergen County Militiaman—Daniel Vansciver, who lived in the Kearney House at Upper Closter Dock.

June 1832: Daniel Vansciver makes his way on wagon-rutted roads from his home in Closter to the county seat in Hackensack. His purpose is to apply for a federal pension for his Revolutionary War service in the Bergen County Militia—service performed half a century earlier. Such is the length of time it has taken Congress to establish a pension for veterans of the conflict. Many of those veterans by now have died, of course (though their widows might still apply); those still living, like Vansciver, typically are septuagenarians. The application process requires him to provide details of his service and to obtain sworn affidavits from witnesses to it. Applications such as his, though often (and understandably) containing errors as to dates and the like, will become treasure troves for researchers.

> *He entered the services of the United States for one month as a Volunteer under Captain Abraham Haring, and believes it was in the month of August 1776 at the Liberty Pole* [in Englewood]... *and was marched from there to the City of New York, the British then* [having] *possession of Staten Island, this was to Guard and Protect. Served the time and was discharged at Closter.*

The Revolutionary War in Bergen County

Uniforms of some troops that served in Bergen County. From Dumont Heritage. Drawing by Joel Altshuler. *Courtesy of Borough of Dumont.*

Daniel Vansciver (under the irregular spelling conventions of the day, his surname was also recorded as "Van Sciven," "Vanschyven," etc.) casts his recollections back to the summer of the British fleet's arrival in New York Harbor—more than a year after the thunderclap of Lexington and Concord, the summer that saw the largest expeditionary force England had ever mounted, some thirty thousand armed men, encamping on Staten Island. The Americans spent that desperate summer building fortifications in and around New York City. (Affidavits in his application will suggest that Vansciver also worked on the fortifications atop the Palisades, at what would come to be called Fort Lee.)

> *He then entered the Service as a Volunteer for three months under Captain James Christie in the fall of 1776 stationed at the Liberty Pole, Closter, New Bridge and along the North [Hudson] River marching from place to place, their duty on these Stations that of Defending the Inhabitants, the British constantly committing depredations such as plunders, stealing, &c. Served the time [and] was discharged at Closter.*

Daniel Vansciver remembers when he was an eyewitness to the darkest days of the American fight, as first New York City, then Fort Washington and then Fort Lee fell to the British. As the last leaves drifted to the ground that autumn, Washington's army vanished from Bergen County like a retreating tide. He remembers how all, regardless

Daniel's Tale: The Career of One Bergen County Militiaman

of political sympathies, wondered if the end of the year would also see the end of the rebellion. But the new year would instead bring news of Washington's surprising successes in Trenton and Princeton.

In the summer of 1777 he Volunteered for three months under Captain Moris Geotschius…Stationed and Services and duty as before recited. [He served] *the time and was discharged at the Liberty Pole.*

In hindsight, 1777 was the turning point, of course—though none could have known it at the time. As Daniel Vansciver and his fellow militiamen patrolled the shores of the Hudson that summer, more than a hundred miles upstream two armies drew closer together. That autumn the Battle of Saratoga would be fought—and won by the Americans, their first major battlefield victory.

In the Spring of 1778, being drafted for one month under Capt. Abraham Haring, station, duty and services as before recited…In the Summer of 1778 being again drafted for one month under Captain James Christie then stationed at the Liberty Pole and was marched from thence to Aquackonack [Passaic] *when he joined the regiment Commanded by Colonel Tunis Dey. And from thence to Elizabeth town and from thence to New Brunswick…their duty was on this occasion to aid and assist the American Army and that of attacking the British who* [were] *then* [marching] *from Philadelphia to New York and at the same time the Battle of Monmouth took place, when he was marched back with his company through Wood Bridge and from thence to Hackinsack…where he was discharged after having served his month.*

"His month"! A month during which his unit traveled over 150 miles—on foot. A month during which they found themselves at the periphery of the vast and confused Battle of Monmouth, the last major engagement fought in his state.

In the month of September in the same year [1778] *he Volunteered for one month under Captain John Outwater stationed at Hackinsack and Various places in the County of Bergen. Their duty was to guard the inhabitants and that of watching the enemy who had possession of the lower part of the said County* [today's Hudson County]*…Served the time and was discharged at Hackinsack the place of* [enlistment]*…He then Volunteered for two months under Captain Elias Romine. Believes it was in the month of October* [sic] *in the year 1778 stationed at the New Bridge and the Liberty Pole…at which last mentioned place they had an engagement with the British Light horse when a number* [were] *killed and wounded on Both sides* [and] *we* [were] *forced to give way and retreat with the loss of fourteen of our men killed and* [a] *number wounded and taken Prisoner.*

As recounted in Adrian C. Leiby's *The Revolutionary War in the Hackensack Valley*, "On the afternoon of September 22, 1778, British transports and flatboats began unloading thousands of troops at Paulus Hook [Jersey City]. A regiment of dragoons [cavalry] immediately overran the American outpost at Liberty Pole, taking twenty-seven prisoners and killing several of the men." One is reminded of Thackeray's observation in *Barry Lyndon*: "Barry's first taste of battle was only a skirmish…Though this encounter

Statue of Brigadier General Enoch Poor in Hackensack. *Courtesy of Ira Lieblich.*

Liberty Pole Historic Marker in Englewood. *Courtesy of Ira Lieblich.*

is not recorded in any history books, it was memorable enough for those who took part." Even in Leiby's book—at over three hundred pages, still the most comprehensive work on the Revolution in Bergen County—the battle is recounted in precisely *one sentence*. But for Daniel Vansciver and his fellow militiamen stationed at the Liberty Pole, it was a memorable—and terrifying—afternoon indeed. The horses thundered at them, and the dragoons slashed down at them with those swords they kept so razor sharp.

> *He being drafted for one month under Captain Peter Ward in the Spring of 1779 Stationed at Hackinsack, New Bridge and at the Liberty Pole marching from place to place as necessity required, watching the enemy and…Guarding [and] defending the Inhabitants. [S]erved the time and was discharged at Hackinsack the place of enlistment…In the summer of same year does not recollect whether he was drafted or Volunteered for one month stationed at the New Bridge and Closter, Guarding the Inhabitants and…Watching the enemy who were constantly Committing [depredations] on the Inhabitants. [W]as discharged and went home…In the month of September in the same year he Volunteered for one month under Capt. Joseph Board Stationed at Hackensack and various other places in the County of Bergen doing Guard duty defending the Inhabitants and watching the enemy. [S]erved the time and was discharged.*

It had been a dismal time for Bergen's Patriots, especially for those in places such as Vansciver's Closter, where Loyalist raiding parties—composed for the most part of former neighbors and slaves, now refugees in British-occupied New York City—*"the enemy"*—made use of the farm landings along the Palisades to enter the valley beyond and raid their former villages. Barns and houses met the torch; cattle were driven off; men were taken prisoner or left for dead in the wakes of these raids. (Yet somehow life went on. Taxes were collected: in October of 1779, Daniel Vansciver was listed on the tax rolls of Harrington Township as a "single man who works for hire.") The coldest winter of the century would follow.

> *He then Volunteered for [six] months…[with]…Capt. Thomas Blanch. Stationed at Closter, Liberty Pole and Various other places in the County of Bergen. Along the North River their duty on these stations was that of Guarding the shores and Landing places and defending the Inhabitants. In these six months they [were stationed]…with Gen. Washington's Army at Tappan [and] he recollects at one time where they were stationed on the [shore] of the north river Gen. Washington with his life Guards came up to them and [charged] them to be Vigilant and Watchful on this Station…which if could be obtained by the enemy would be a desirable one. Washington further stated that he would send a company of his regular troops to reinforce them which he performed.*

Fifty years later, in the late spring of 1832, Daniel Vansciver remembers the day he met General George Washington.

> *[A]fter the expiration of his six months he again Volunteered under Capt. Thomas Blanch for one month stationed at Closter and along the North River their duty on this station was that of guarding the shores and Landing places and that of defending the Inhabitants. [S]erved the time*

Daniel's Tale: The Career of One Bergen County Militiaman

The Kearney House at Alpine Landing. *Courtesy of Anthony G. Taranto Jr., Palisades Interstate Park.*

and was discharged at Closter the place of enrollment...He then in the spring of 1781 was drafted for one month under Capt. Abraham Haring stationed at Closter and along the North River, their duty was in Guarding and protecting the Inhabitants. [S]erved the time and was discharged...In the summer of the same year he volunteered for one month under Capt. John Huyler stationed on duty as before recited. Served his time, and was discharged.

That fall, word would come of the American and French victory over Cornwallis at a Virginia seaport called Yorktown. For all intents and purposes, the Revolution was ended. Yet it would take months of trans-Atlantic negotiations to get a peace treaty signed. In the meantime, the British continued to hold New York City and its environs.

He then volunteered for one month under Captain Samuel Demarest in the summer of 1782 stationed at Hackensack. Their duty on this station was to Guard and protect the Inhabitants also that of watching the enemy who had possession of the Lower part of County of Bergen...In the fall of the same year Volunteered one month under Capt. Board stationed at Closter and along the north river their duty was to Guard the shores and landing places and that of Protecting [the inhabitants].

A treaty was finally signed in early 1783. The British—and their Loyalist allies, Daniel Vansciver's former neighbors—departed New York City. The war was over. Daniel Vansciver had been about twenty years old when he first volunteered in 1776. He was about twenty-six at the end. He married and had at least two children with Catrina Westervelt. She died, and he remarried to Maria Blackledge, with whom he had at least seven more children. He worked as a laborer and a fisherman. (For a time at least he lived in the house on the Hudson we today call the Kearney House, at the Closter Dock.) He outlived Maria, too. In 1832 he applied for (and was eventually granted) a pension for his Revolutionary service. He died in 1843, at about the age of ninety, and was buried at Demarest. (His tombstone records his having been "in his 95th year," but this seems to be in error. As was the case for many of his generation and station in life, he may not even have known his own true age. And when it came time to sign his pension application, he placed an "X" above his name.)

WEBSITES OF INTEREST

www.njpalisades.org
www.friendsofthepalisades.org
www.outwatersmilitia.com

Eric Nelsen has served as a historical interpreter for the New Jersey section of the Palisades Interstate Park since 1992 and as the director of the park's historic Kearney House at Alpine Landing since 1998. He is the coauthor of Arcadia's Images of America: Palisades Interstate Park, *published in 2007.*

Major General Lafayette: A Passion for Liberty

Arthur Aranda

A number of foreign volunteers arrived to lend their expertise to the Patriot cause, including Thaddeus Kosciusko, a Polish engineer; Casimir Pulaski, a Polish cavalry officer; Baron Von Steuben, a German who trained the army and wrote a military manual; Baron Johann De Kalb, a Bavarian-born military officer; and the nineteen-year-old Marquis de Lafayette, a wealthy French aristocrat. Lafayette, an orphan, became a loyal and trustworthy aide to the childless George Washington, who considered Lafayette a son and a confidante during the roughest times of the war. Lafayette was involved in the court-martial of Charles Lee and the trial of Major André. In the summer of 1825, at the age of sixty-six, Lafayette stopped in Hackensack while touring the country, and was greeted by thousands who had remembered his contributions to the American cause.

> *Humanity has won the battle. Liberty now has a country.*
> *—Marquis de Lafayette*

In the summer of 1780, the Marquis de Lafayette led a troop of elite light troops through the English Neighborhood and camped in present-day Leonia. This I learned from a historic marker on Fort Lee Road, just a block from my Leonia home. Few realize the important role Lafayette played for the Patriot cause. He was responsible, in part, for enlisting the French to aid in the Patriots' effort and helped supply much-needed arms and uniforms to the American army.

Marie Joseph Paul Yves Roch Gilbert du Motier, also known as Marquis de Lafayette, was born in 1757 into wealthy French aristocracy. His father, a colonel of grenadiers, was killed fighting the British in the Seven Years' War, also known as the French and Indian War. A grenadier was a specially trained soldier who lobbed heavy hand grenades at the enemy while closely engaged in face-to-face combat. Lafayette's father's imposing height, physical strength and fearless demeanor were traits he would pass on to his son. Lafayette was only two when his father died and knew of him only from family stories and a portrait that hung in his home, the castle of Chavagnac in Auvergne.

The Revolutionary War in Bergen County

Historic marker in Leonia on Fort Lee Road and Oaktree Place. *Courtesy of Ira Lieblich.*

At the age of twelve, Lafayette's mother also passed away; a few weeks later his grandfather, who had helped raise the young marquis, also died. Lafayette inherited a fortune and became one of the wealthiest orphans in France. At the age of fourteen, following family tradition, Lafayette entered the royal French army. When he was sixteen, he married Marie Adrienne Françoise de Noailles, aligning himself with one of the wealthiest families in France.

Lafayette, like many young aristocrats throughout Europe, had come to embrace Jean Jacques Rousseau's philosophy of "liberty" and the "rights of man." In 1776, he learned of the American struggle for independence during a dinner meeting with the Duke of Gloucester, brother to King George III. The Duke spoke with sympathy of the struggle going on in the colonies and was equally critical of the way his brother was handling the uprising. During dinner, thoughts of adventure and the glory of being engaged in a heroic struggle for these profound ideas fired the young Lafayette's passions. Reportedly he said, "As soon as I heard of American independence, my heart was enlisted."

He made plans to travel to America to lend his services, knowing his plans to assist the colonies against the British would be disapproved of by Louis VI, the king of France. Since the end of the Seven Years' War there had been a fragile peace between the two world powers. Lafayette shared his secret plans with a friend who was also

Major General Lafayette: A Passion for Liberty

seeking to travel to America. After several delays and surreptitious adventures, the two men crossed the Atlantic with written agreements that they would be commissioned major generals when they arrived in Philadelphia.

Silas Dean, a lawyer and Yale graduate, issued the documents and sent a political agent to France to recruit solders and officers and seek financial assistance from the French. After a daunting sea voyage, Lafayette landed near Charleston, South Carolina, on June 13, 1777, and was welcomed with hospitality. He then rode nine hundred miles on horseback to Philadelphia on a journey that took over a month, to present himself to Congress. He offered to serve the military without pay and as a volunteer. Since he represented the highest echelon of French nobility and his motives were so sympathetic to the American cause, Congress commissioned him a major general on July 31. His political connections and his patriotic enthusiasm would prove very useful. Lafayette soon met General Washington and a deep, lifelong friendship developed between the two men. Washington was forty-five and Lafayette was nineteen when they met.

Washington did not have a son and Lafayette had lost his father to war. Together they would lead soldiers in an epic struggle to create a new nation. Washington invited Lafayette into his "family," as he referred to his staff. Lafayette would become part of Washington's inner circle and one of his most loyal and trusted generals. The relationship was described at the time, and since by historians, as one of a father and a son.

During his first military engagement, the Battle of the Brandywine, Lafayette was wounded in the leg by a musket ball. It took two months for him to recover and rejoin the American forces. In December 1777, he was with Washington and the army at their winter quarters at Valley Forge, where the harsh weather was almost unbearable. Several officers tried to have Congress relieve Washington of his command of the Continental army. They unsuccessfully tried to convince Lafayette to cooperate with them, but the plan failed. Lafayette wrote a long letter to Washington, in which he revealed the plans and pledged his loyalty to the commander in chief. Washington wrote back, expressing his sincere appreciation.

Washington learned that he could trust Lafayette with tremendous responsibility and gave him command of a military engagement at Barren Hill on May 20, 1778. Lafayette remained at Valley Forge, improving his knowledge of military tactics until Washington marched out of Valley Forge to meet the enemy in New Jersey.

When Washington learned that the British had evacuated Philadelphia on June 19, 1778, he ordered his troops to pursue the British across New Jersey. As the Americans approached the British, Washington called a council of war at Hopewell, New Jersey, to determine the best course of action. General Charles Lee was opposed to an all-out attack, but Generals Wayne, Greene and Lafayette wrote separate letters to Washington in which each stated that a large detachment of Americans should be sent forward to attack the rear of the British army. If results were favorable, then a general attack should be made.

Washington accepted this plan. He offered the command to General Lee, but Lee was certain the plan would result in disaster. In the meantime, Lafayette requested the command of the advanced position, but Washington told Lafayette it was impossible to turn the command over to him unless Lee would be willing to resign it. When

Lafayette spoke to Lee about giving the command to him, Lee agreed, as he did not desire to command troops when the result of defeat was inevitable. And so, with Washington's approval, Lafayette took command and advanced to meet the enemy.

Lee then reversed his decision, concerned that if Lafayette succeeded in defeating the British, Congress would criticize him for permitting a younger man with less experience to defeat the enemy. He asked Washington to return the command to him, but Washington, since Lafayette held the command, could not displace him. Washington told Lee it was necessary to ask Lafayette and, if he were willing to relinquish the command, then Lee would be restored to the command.

Lee appealed to the generous spirit of Lafayette to return the command to him. Lafayette promised if he did not find the enemy that day he would resign the command in favor of Lee. The day ended without a struggle, and in the evening Lafayette wrote a letter to Lee in which he resigned the command and Lee assumed charge of the division.

The next day, Washington and his army caught up with the British. A favorable moment arrived to make an attack and Washington ordered Lee to attack, planning to advance with the rest of the army in order to defeat the enemy. When Washington arrived with his men, much to his surprise, he found Lee retreating with his division.

Washington stopped the retreat, reorganized the retreating division and ordered an immediate attack. The enemy was driven back, but it was already too late in the day to win a decisive victory, so the soldiers kept their positions and a general attack was planned early the next day. During the night the British retreated and eventually reached New York.

Early in the year 1780, Lafayette's connections with the French monarchy resulted in desperately needed supplies and French troops being sent to aid the Continental army. Until then, the American soldiers had been poorly clad. Even Washington remarked on his troops during the Battle of Trenton, "Many of them were entirely naked and most so thinly clad as to be unfit for service." The French supplied the Continental army with uniforms of coats, breeches and shoes.

So insistent was Lafayette for the French to help the Americans that one day, the Count de Maurepas, chief royal advisor to the King, said to the royal council, "It is fortunate for the King that Lafayette does not take it into his head to strip Versailles of its furniture, to send to his dear Americans, as his Majesty would be unable to refuse it."

He left Paris sailing on the French frigate *Hermione* on March 19. After thirty-eight days, he arrived in Boston. He reported to Washington and then crossed New Jersey again to meet with French representatives of his government in Philadelphia. Lieutenant General Rochambeau was a French officer sent to fight alongside the Americans. His expeditionary army arrived in Newport, Rhode Island, on July 10. The arrival of Rochambeau's army brought new hope to the American cause. In the weeks that followed, Washington and Rochambeau made careful plans so that their campaign would bring definite success. Washington hoped it would be the final victory, resulting in independence.

In the meantime, the British invaded the South with the intent to finish the war once and for all. Washington sent what troops he could spare. The first real movement began

Major General Lafayette: A Passion for Liberty

in the spring of 1781, led by Lafayette, who was sent to Virginia to unite his forces with those of Baron Von Steuben. In the early fall of 1781, Cornwallis and his troops were driven into Yorktown, Virginia. The forces of the Americans and French moved to force him to surrender, as he was also held in from the sea by the French fleet.

As a result of brilliant efforts on the part of the American and the French forces, Cornwallis was compelled to surrender on October 19, 1781. The entire country rejoiced. Consequently, Lafayette went to Washington to request a leave of absence to return home. He went to Philadelphia to secure the permission of Congress, which granted his request and gave him a fine letter of appreciation for his patriotic services.

When Lafayette returned home, he was honored for his service in America. He had done much to strengthen the ties of friendship between France and the United States. Eventually changes came to the French government and Napoleon came to power. Lafayette stood firmly for representative government and never yielded full support for Napoleon. In 1784, Lafayette returned to America on Washington's invitation. During the ensuing years, he befriended and aided Thomas Jefferson, the minister to France, on numerous political and economic matters. He also named his son George Washington Lafayette.

When, in 1800, the French learned of the death of Washington, Napoleon held a memorial service for Washington at Les Invalides. Lafayette was not invited and Napoleon ordered the orator not to refer to Lafayette in his oration.

In 1824, Lafayette accepted an invitation to visit the United States for the fiftieth anniversary of the American Revolution and thus began an extended tour of the country. He was treated like a rock star wherever he went. Being only nineteen when he joined the American forces, he was the last living general of the Revolution.

Lafayette spent a large sum of his own money in support of the Revolution. He eventually was paid back by Congress for "services rendered" during the war. He was also given lands in 1803 in Louisiana. To the end of his life, Lafayette held firm for representative government in his country. Lafayette died in 1834 at the age of seventy-seven. His commitment to American independence will never be forgotten; his name is memorialized on street names, towns, schools and other institutions throughout New Jersey and the rest of the nation he helped to bring into existence. In 2002, he was one of only six others named an honorary US citizen by Congress.

Arthur Aranda is a real estate investment consultant. A native of Wisconsin, he moved to Leonia, New Jersey, in 1986. He has a lifelong interest in American and world history, the history of ideas and Native American culture. He has traveled extensively through Latin America to explore pre-Columbian archaeological sites.

The Significance of the Hopper House

Joan Dater

The Hopper House, formerly located on Ramapo Valley Road or Route 202 in Mahwah, New Jersey, was the home of Patriot and ardent Whig Andrew W. Hopper and his wife, Maria LaRoe Hopper. They lived there during the Revolutionary War and afterward. They operated a prosperous farm and it is believed that the house was used as an inn or tavern during the war. Hopper had several slaves to help with the farm chores.

The Andrew Hopper House/Inn was visited at least five times by General George Washington during the period from 1777 to 1781. It was used as headquarters at least three times. The nearby athletic field at Ramapo College was used as an encampment by the Continental army.

Ramapo Valley Road served as a line of communications during the war. It connected middle New Jersey (Morristown, Pompton) to the vulnerable Highlands to the north (present-day Rockland and Orange Counties). Along it moved supplies and reinforcements, as well as messages delivered on horseback by express riders.

During the course of the war, Andrew Hopper served as a spy for George Washington—according to Benson Lossing, mid-nineteenth-century historian and illustrator—and General George Clinton. Hopper served in the Bergen County Militia as well, under Captains Board and Bartholf. It is likely that he served in the Battle of Millstone, New Jersey, in January 1777.

Most likely at the time of the last visit of August 25–26, 1781, General Washington gave Andrew Hopper either forty-one or forty-two pewter plates. A member of the Mahwah Museum Society has successfully tracked down all of the plates, and six of them were on display for a special exhibit at the Mahwah Museum.

On August 26, 1781, Comte de Rochambeau of France, who had come to our aid, led the French army down Route 202 from Suffern, New York, where they were encamped. They passed the Andrew Hopper House on their way to victory at Yorktown. General Benjamin Lincoln of the Continental army passed through

The Significance of the Hopper House

The Hopper House, from Benson Lossing's *Pictorial Field Book of the Revolution*, 1850–52.

Mahwah on King's Highway (Island Road), south through Ramsey (on Island Avenue) and then linked up with present-day Franklin Turnpike, past the Hermitage, on the way to Paramus to the Old Paramus Reformed Church.

General Washington and the Continental army stayed at Hopper's during the night of August 25 and left sometime before noon on August 26 to pave the way for Rochambeau and the French army. Most likely, they did not meet or confer at Hopper's. Rather, Washington wrote a letter to Rochambeau on August 27 when he had reached Chatham, New Jersey.

Plans are underway to designate the Rochambeau Revolutionary Route from Rhode Island to Yorktown, Virginia, as a national historic trail.

Joan Dater is a writer and editor. She has a Master's degree in teaching and is retired from the teaching staff at William Paterson College. She continues to do research on the Andrew Hopper House and plans to publish her findings. She and her husband, Tom, are members of several local historical societies. She was instrumental in organizing the 225th anniversary celebration of the Washington-Rochambeau March of 1781 in Mahwah during 2006–07. She spearheaded the Mahwah Museum Society's March to Victory exhibit.

A Resourceful Woman in Revolutionary Bergen County: Theodosia Prevost at the Hermitage

Dr. Henry Bischoff

During the Revolutionary War, the Hermitage in Ho-Ho-Kus was the home of Theodosia Prevost. She, the wife of an active ranking British officer, determined to preserve her home, welcomed to the Hermitage General Washington, Alexander Hamilton, James Monroe, William Paterson, Aaron Burr and other Patriot leaders. For more detail on how Theodosia and her family survived guerilla warfare, see Henry Bischoff's book A Revolutionary Relationship: Theodosia Prevost, Aaron Burr and the Hermitage.

In 1775, Theodosia Prevost, a fifth-generation American from an affluent merchant and professional family, resided at the Hermitage, a gentleman's farm near Hopperstown and Paramus, with her husband James Marcus, a Swiss-born English officer on leave from the Royal American Regiment. They had five young children: three daughters and two sons. In the following year, with the outbreak of the Revolution, James Marcus was recalled into British service. He attained the rank of lieutenant colonel and served under his brother, General Augustine Prevost, first in the West Indies and then in Florida. By 1778 and 1779, they served in Georgia and the Carolinas where, with their troops, they captured Savannah and Charleston.

Theodosia, like many others in North America, faced the Revolution as a member of a family with divided loyalties. In addition to her husband and brother-in-law, two of her sons, aged nine and eleven, were enlisted by their father as ensigns in his regiment. In addition, Theodosia had two half-brothers who joined the British service, one in the army and one in the navy. Two of her uncles, as well as her mother's brothers-in-law, also were British officers, one of them a general stationed in Ireland.

However, one of Theodosia's aunts, Lydia Watkins, who favored the Whig cause, moved from New York to Paramus and had a son who became an officer in the Rebel Malcolm's Regiment, which was under the command of Aaron Burr. It would seem that most of Theodosia's Westchester Bartow relatives also were favorable to the Whig cause, but relatives by marriage in that county, the Pells, were mostly Loyalists.

A Resourceful Woman in Revolutionary Bergen County

Reenactors at the Hermitage in Ho-Ho-Kus, 1975. *Courtesy of Claire Tholl.*

The Hermitage, being located in Bergen County, found itself throughout the Revolutionary War in one of the most constantly contested areas in America. There were both Whig and Loyalist neighbors, some of whom were killed, wounded, captured and imprisoned; there was much action by local Rebel and Tory militia companies; and there were many incursions and encampments by foraging and attacking Continental army troops and by British and Hessian regulars. A number of skirmishes took place at nearby Hopperstown and Paramus.

Through the war, the Hermitage property was in the hands of two women and their children. Theodosia Prevost and her three daughters lived in the Little Hermitage near the Ho-Ho-Kus Brook; her mother Ann DeVisme lived with her teenage daughter, Theodosia's half-sister Caty De Visme, in the Hermitage up from the brook. Theodosia, age twenty-nine, took the leadership role. The first major challenge for them in the midst of guerrilla warfare was survival. The women on the Hermitage property were spared attacks from the Rebels because there were no male Loyalists residing there who might fight against the Revolution. In addition, Theodosia saw to it that many Rebel officers were invited as guests to her property. The Hermitage also could count on immunity from attacks by the British, since it was well-known that it was owned by one of their military officers. In fact, the English in 1777 placed a young captured Rebel medical officer, Samuel Bradhurst, a relative by marriage of Theodosia from New York, under house arrest at the Hermitage. He would remain there through the war and would become a good friend of a visitor to the house, Mary Smith, a cousin of Theodosia. They married at the Hermitage in December 1778.

A second major challenge that faced the women at the Hermitage was the threat of confiscation. Since the property was in the name of a man fighting against the Revolution, there were those in New Jersey who wanted to send the women to the British in New York and make the Hermitage a prize to raise money for the Revolutionary cause or to reward one of its major officials. Theodosia exhibited courage and resourcefulness in her extended battle to maintain control of her family property. She sent petitions to the New Jersey State Whig authorities, she requested leading Whig officials whom she knew or would come to know to advocate on her behalf and she made the Hermitage a place that welcomed officers of the Continental army, Rebel militia officers and other Whig persons of rank.

Already in 1777, Theodosia was writing for help to persons she knew in the influential New Jersey Morris family. Later in that year, when her cousin John Watkins was an officer with the Rebel Malcolm's regiment stationed in the Clove above Suffern, she met its commanding officer, the twenty-year-old Lieutenant Colonel Aaron Burr. He stopped at Paramus before and after a daring and successful raid on a British position near Hackensack.

The next July, when the Continental army, after the important Battle of Monmouth, marched north to New Brunswick and the Great Falls of the Passaic toward the Hudson Highlands and was planning an encampment at Paramus, Theodosia sent an invitation to General George Washington to make the Hermitage his headquarters.

She wrote, "Mrs. Prevost Presents her best respects to his Excellency Gen'l Washington. Requests the Honour of his Company as she flatters herself the accommodations will more Commodious than those to be procured in the Neighborhood. Mrs. Prevost will be particularly happy to make her House Agreeable to His Excellency, and family."

Washington accepted Theodosia's invitation and made the Hermitage his headquarters. For four days in July 1778, it was the site for his military planning and correspondence. It also served as a place for rest and recreation for his aides-de-camp and other officers, including Alexander Hamilton, John Lauren, Marquis de Lafayette, General William Alexander (Lord Stirling), James Monroe, Tench Tilghman and James McHenry. The latter later wrote, "At Mrs. Prevost's we found some fair refugees from New York who were on a visit to the lady of the Hermitage. With them we talked and walked and laughed and danced and gallanted away the leisure hours of four days and four nights, and would have gallanted and danced and laughed and talked and walked with them till now had not the general given orders for our departure."

From among those present at the Hermitage on this occasion, Theodosia would later get a letter of protection from Washington, permission to visit relatives in New York from General Alexander of Basking Ridge and letters of advocacy from Monroe, the young aide-de-camp to Alexander. In the fall of 1778, Lieutenant Colonel Burr spent part of a health leave from the army at the Hermitage. He introduced Theodosia to a number of his friends, including William Paterson, who was then the attorney general of New Jersey, and Colonel Robert Troup, who had influential friends in the state, including Governor William Paterson. These advocates would be needed because at that time, the New Jersey Legislature passed a law calling for the confiscation of land owned by Loyalists and others who were acting against the Whig cause.

A Resourceful Woman in Revolutionary Bergen County

In spring 1779, Burr wrote to Paterson asking him to advocate on behalf of Theodosia. Paterson responded in June, stating that he had talked with the commissioners who threatened to confiscate her property. He said he would keep Burr informed about the matter. During the summer, the Bergen County Commissioners for Forfeited Estates threatened to take action. In late September Paterson wrote,

> *I cannot tell you what has become of Mrs. Prevost's affairs. About two months ago I received a very polite letter from her. She was apprehensive that the commissioners would proceed. It seems they threatened to go on. I wrote them on the subject, but I have not heard the event. I am at this place, on my way to a superior court in Bergen. If possible, I shall wait on the good gentlewomen. At Bergen, I shall inquire into the state of the matter. It will, indeed, turn up of course. You shall hear from me again.*

Despite Paterson's efforts, the commissioners served Theodosia with an inquisition, indicating that procedures had begun for the seizure of the holdings that were in her husband's name. Theodosia, for her part, on December 24, 1779, sent a letter to the New Jersey Legislature seeking its support against the commissioners. They then deferred action until their next meeting, March 9, 1780, when it was read and ordered to be filed.

Still, by the summer of 1780 no final action had been taken, but the threat remained. Paterson wrote to Burr in August: "Make my compliments acceptable to the family at the Hermitage. I have a high regard for them, and sincerely wish their happiness. I really pity and admire Mrs. Prevost. Her situation demands a tear; her conduct and demeanour the warmest applause. Tell Mrs. Prevost that she must remember me among her friends; and that I shall be happy to render her all the service in my power."

Despite the advocacy on her behalf of influential friends, the threat to her property continued. In November 1780, she was informed that "there are Inquisitions found and returned in the Court of Common Pleas, held for (Bergen County) on the fourth Tuesday in October last, against the following persons, to wit, James Marcus Prevost." Final judgment was to be rendered in January.

However, as Paterson had indicated, Theodosia still had the support of many friends. An example was a letter written by Troup to an unidentified, influential New Jersey official.

> *I feel irresistibly impelled by a perfect confidence in the intimacy subsisting between us to recommend to your kindest attention one of my female friends in distress. I mean Mrs. Prevost, who has been justly esteemed for her honor, virtue and accomplishments…During the whole course of this war she has conducted herself in such a manner as proves her to possess an excellent understanding as well as a strong attachment to our righteous cause. My character of this lady is drawn partly from the information of the most respectable Whigs in the State. Impressed with those sentiments, I am not ashamed to confess that I feel an anxiety for her welfare…Without the least deviation from truth, I can affirm that Mrs. Prevost is a sincere and cordial well-wisher to the success of our army, which will be an additional reason with you for showing her all the civilities in your power.*

Apparently the prolonged advocacy of Burr, Troup, Paterson and others eventually took effect. The consequences of the fall 1780 inquisition and, in fact, the whole issue of confiscation, disappear from the extant records and letters of all concerned parties. The indictments against the Hermitage properties were not executed. Theodosia's tenacity and the cultivation of influential friends in New Jersey over a considerable period of time seem to have been crucial in her successful retention of the Hermitage.

In the process of the advocacy, Theodosia developed a deepening friendship with Aaron Burr. When, due to battle-related illness, Burr retired from military service in 1779, he undertook the study of law, first with William Paterson and then with Thomas Smith in Haverstraw, New York. By late 1781, while Burr was in Albany preparing for his bar exams, Theodosia received the news that her husband James Marcus had died in military service in Jamaica.

After gaining his law license, Burr began setting up an office in Albany. Then in late June 1782 he traveled to the Hermitage to attend the wedding of Theodosia's half-sister, Caty, and Joseph Browne. With little preparation, Theodosia and Aaron decided that they also would marry and that there would be a double wedding. It took place on June 2, 1782, at the Hermitage. Aaron and his new wife were congratulated by William Livingston, the governor of New Jersey, and George Clinton, the governor of New York.

WEBSITE OF INTEREST

www.thehermitage.org

Dr. Henry Bischoff is director of historical studies at the Hermitage, professor emeritus of history at Ramapo College and has authored seven books, including Mahwah and the Ramapo Valley in the Revolution *and* A Revolutionary Relationship: Theodosia Prevost, Aaron Burr and the Hermitage.

General George Washington and His Command of the Revolution. From Letters Written in July 1778 While Headquartered at the Hermitage

Dr. Henry Bischoff

*D*uring General Lee's court-martial trial in Paramus in July 1778, General Washington and his staff made the Hermitage their headquarters. The letters he wrote while there give us some insight into the quality of his leadership as commander of the Continental army.

At the outset of the American Revolution, with limited military experience and mostly non-professional troops, George Washington faced the forces of what was then the world's leading military power. Two years into the war, in 1778, he had held together and provided training for his troops through some defeats, limited successes and in the face of many difficulties. After leaving a trying winter at Valley Forge, Washington met in battle the main British army marching from Philadelphia toward New York at Monmouth Courthouse in central New Jersey. Despite an unauthorized withdrawal of the troops under General Charles Lee, second in command, Washington rallied his forces, fought the British on a day of intense heat and, despite casualties, held them to a standoff. The British with losses were able to continue to New York City, and the Continentals marched toward a destination north of that city by way of New Brunswick, the Great Falls of the Passaic and a four-day encampment in the Paramus/Hopperstown area of Bergen County.

While headquartered at the Hermitage, July 10–14, Washington wrote sixteen letters and three orders of the day. An examination of these documents—which were sent to the Continental Congress, state governors, fellow generals in the field, the admiral of the newly arrived French fleet off Sandy Hook, intelligence officers and a frontier militia—provide an insight into the way Washington, well into the war, was exercising his leadership.

It was at that time that Washington consolidated his position as the commander of the Continental army. During the past two years he had been subject to doubts, criticism and even a cabal. However, by demonstrating at Monmouth that he could engage the main British force, inflict damage and survive with his army intact; by

The Revolutionary War in Bergen County

Washington at Bourdette's Landing, 1928, by Aileen Ortlip Shea. *Courtesy of the Ortlip family.*

respectful, diplomatic relations with the Continental Congress; and now with his main rival for leadership, Charles Lee, facing a court-martial, Washington's leadership position had become solidified.

Vital to Washington's continued commanding role was the ongoing support of the Continental Congress and its president, Henry Laurens. On the general's arrival at the Hermitage, he received a congratulatory communication from Laurens for his actions at Monmouth. Washington promptly responded on July

General George Washington and His Command of the Revolution

11: "My warmest acknowledgements are due for the indulgent terms in which you express your sense of my conduct, in our late reencounter, with the British army…My dear Sir, there is no man on whose good opinion and friendship I set a higher value than on yours." Then, in a letter written on July 12, we learn that Washington and his troops received praise, additionally, by a unanimous vote of the members of the Congress. This was a positive measure of their approval and support for the continuing leadership of the army by George Washington, for which he wrote that it gave him "the highest satisfaction" and "demands my sincerest acknowledgements."

Additionally, the general received congratulations from William Drayton, a South Carolina delegate to the Continental Congress. Washington, who was not well acquainted with Drayton, took time out of his busy schedule to send him a particularly gracious reply. "It, naturally, is my ardent wish that my well-meant endeavors for the prosperity of my country may meet the approbation of my countrymen…I shall be happy…cultivating a continuance of your friendship."

Washington also kept Congress informed about the movement of his troops and his military plans.

Additionally, the reprimand Washington gave to General Lee, following his failure to follow orders to attack at Monmouth, would enhance the commander's leadership position. Lee challenged the reprimand, held that he saved his troops from destruction by the British and asked to be cleared through a court-martial. Washington granted his request.

The Lee trial was to be a traveling court-martial presided over by General William Alexander. It began in New Brunswick, and there were five sessions at the Reformed Church in Paramus. The trial was cited in the General Orders of July 11. Witnesses included Washington's aides-de-camp, who testified strongly on behalf of their commander, as well as other officers present at the Battle of Monmouth. The trial was concluded in White Plains. Lee was found at fault and suspended from the army for one year. He resigned in bitterness. This action removed an important potential challenge to Washington's leadership position.

A key factor in General Washington's waging of war was his concern for the proper care and the good order of his troops. He saw to it that the time and length of marches and encampments for rest were adjusted to weather conditions. In his letter to Laurens on July 12, Washington stated that he had halted at Paramus "for a day or two or perhaps longer…in order to refresh (the troops) from the great fatigues they have suffered from the intense heat." On the same day in the General Orders, Washington showed concern for the wounded and directed the manner in which they were to be conveyed when the army moved again.

The general also gave attention to provisions for his troops. When deciding where to locate his troops, the availability of food and the opportunities for foraging were a major concern. In a letter to Governor George Clinton of New York on July 11, Washington indicated that he needed to be in a position to obtain the "Flour, which is the Article for which we shall be most likely to be distressed, coming from the Southward."

Old Paramus Reformed Church. *Courtesy of Ira Lieblich.*

General George Washington and His Command of the Revolution

Washington also was aware of the need to bolster the morale of his troops. In the General Orders for July 11, he communicated to them the resolution of the Continental Congress thanking them for their conduct and valor at the Battle of Monmouth. One of the major means of keeping order and discipline in the army was the courts-martial. The General Orders for July 12 listed two courts-martial. A captain from a Virginia regiment was accused of disrespect to a general. It was judged that his actions were improper, but he was acquitted, as it was decided that he had not intended disrespect. The other case involved a lieutenant from a Rhode Island regiment who plundered the property of a woman. He was found guilty and discharged from service.

Washington also was careful to inform the governors of the states into which he planned to move troops. He needed their support for militia and for money and supplies for his army. On July 11, in the letter to New York Governor George Clinton, Washington reported on the movement of the Continental army into his state north of New York City. He also sought the governor's advice on where best to station the troops. On July 14, the commander wrote to Jonathan Trumbull, the governor of Connecticut. He reported that there was the expectation that a British provision fleet was heading for New York and that it may try to reach the city by sailing up the Long Island Sound. Thus, Washington directed Governor Trumbull to gather together frigates and armed vessels from Connecticut and to get like cooperation from neighboring states in order to disrupt this fleet if it did follow this route.

Washington also gave instruction to and sought advice from his generals in the field. On July 13, Washington wrote to General Baron De Kalb: "I am to request that you will cross the North or Hudson's river, as soon as possible, with the Troops now under your command…Some advices I have received this minute require this movement to be made with every degree of dispatch." He had previously written on July 11 to General Horatio Gates, who commanded troops already stationed in the Hudson Highlands, informing him of his plans to move the Continentals northward for a possible attack on the British in New York City. Washington asked advice of Gates, as he had of Clinton, on where best to locate his troops to advantage for foraging and for possible coordinated actions. On July 14, Washington told Gates that he would be in Haverstraw the next day and "I shall be glad to see you there without delay to confer on the several subjects of your letter and on some other matters of importance." Further, Washington had written on July 11 to General Benedict Arnold, whom he had placed in charge of the military in Philadelphia following its evacuation by the British. In addition to updating him on military matters, Washington thanked Arnold for "forwarding a Letter to Mrs. Washington."

An event of the utmost importance in the struggle with England occurred while Washington was at the Hermitage—the arrival of a French fleet off Sandy Hook. This would be the first appearance of direct French military assistance following the treaty of cooperation signed the previous winter. The warships then at the approach to New York Harbor were France's Caribbean fleet headed by Charles Henri

Theodat, Comte d'Estaing, admiral and lieutenant general of the French navy. The letter from Washington to the admiral, sent on July 14, was the first contact between these two leaders, and it was meant to establish friendship and military cooperation. Washington wrote: "I take the earliest opportunity to advise you, that I have been informed of your arrival on this coast, with a fleet of ships under your command. I congratulate you, Sir, most sincerely upon this event and beg leave to assure you of my warmest wishes for your success." The general informed the admiral that he did not have as precise knowledge on the English ships in the harbor as he would like, but that he was seeking more accurate information. Washington told d'Estaing about the location of his troops, and stated, "I shall upon every occasion feel the strongest inclination to facilitate such enterprizes as you may form and are pleased to communicate to me." He told the admiral that he should arrange signals, intelligence and plans through his French-speaking aide-de-camp, Lieutenant Colonel John Laurens, son of the president of the Congress, who was being sent with this letter to d'Estaing. Additionally, Washington informed the Frenchman about the approaching British provision fleet. In a letter to General Gates, Washington described the French fleet as consisting of "a Ship of 90, 2 of 80, 8 of 74, 1 of 64 and 4 of 36 Guns," and that "they fell in with and sunk the (English ship) *Lydia* of 26 Guns on a cruise from New York."

Washington, ever aware of the dangers the Patriots faced in Bergen County, gave extra attention to protection for Laurens, the carrier of his letter to d'Estaing, as he moved from the Hermitage to a sailing point near Sandy Hook. On July 13, he wrote to General David Forman, "As it is of the utmost consequence that Count d'Estaing shd. be immediately acquainted with the strength and posture of the Enemy's fleet and other matters contained in my letter, I entreat you by every means in your power to facilitate and expedite Mr. Laurens getting on board the Admirals Ship."

As Washington had communicated to d'Estaing, intelligence was given major consideration. He told Henry Laurens, "I will try by every practicable means that I can devise to obtain accurate account of the Enemy's fleet in New York." In addition to asking General Gates to gain information on the British ships, Washington wrote to Lieutenant Colonel Francis Barber on July 14: "I have received your favour of yesterday, and am obliged to you for the intelligence it contains. I beg you will continue your endeavours to procure every information you can, concerning the enemy's situation and designs, as well with respect to their naval, as to their land force; which at this time is peculiarly important."

While at the Hermitage, Washington employed a strategy that was flexible, based on opportunities and limitations and that would be adjusted based on the decisions by the French, advice by his generals and the governor of New York, and by the action of the British. He was moving his troops into position for a joint attack on the British in their stronghold of New York City in case the French admiral was willing to enter the harbor and attack the British. If the French admiral decided that he could not carry this off with advantage, then Washington would encourage him to coordinate an attack on the British stationed in Newport, Rhode Island, with the army of General Sullivan. The Continentals would then be in a position north of New York to

General George Washington and His Command of the Revolution

block any attempted British thrust into the Hudson Highlands. The general was still weighing the advantages, for fighting effectiveness and for needed foraging activities, of having both wings of his army on the east side of the Hudson or one wing there and the other on the west side. In his letter of July 11 to Governor Clinton he wrote, "The country on this side (Bergen County) is more plentiful in regard to Forage…We are…in a Country devoted to the Enemy, and gleaning it takes so much from them." However, there would be an advantage to having both wings on the same side if the "enemy mean to operate up the North River."

Additionally, at the Hermitage, Washington kept in touch with the progress of the war on the Pennsylvania frontier. In two letters to John Cleves Symmes, on July 10 and July 14, the commander expressed his sorrow to hear about the attack by the Native Americans, in league with the British, on the Wyoming settlement. He explained that he had sent all the troops that he could dispatch and shared the "intelligence that the Indians are now returning to their homes, which will render assistance from this quarter unnecessary could it be spared at present."

In the days after Washington left the Hermitage and moved north, the French decided that the difficulties in entering New York Harbor, and the strength of the British ships of war there, did not foretell a successful engagement. Instead they sailed to Newport. However, there a failure of General Sullivan to coordinate with the French, followed by a severe and damaging storm, caused d'Estaing, without any helpful engagement with the British, to sail to Boston for repairs and then back to the Caribbean. Nevertheless, the earlier interchange between Washington and d'Estaing did establish a positive connection, and there would be future cooperation when in 1780 the French sent an army of five thousand men under General Comte de Rochambeau to Newport. In the following year the French would march from Rhode Island, join with the Continentals in Westchester County and continue through Bergen County and New Jersey to Virginia for the successful victory over the British at Yorktown.

The July, 10–14, 1778 documents

to John Cleves Symmes, July 10
to Henry Laurens, July 11
to Major General Horatio Gates, July 11
to Major General Benedict Arnold, July 11
to Governor George Clinton, July 11
General Orders, July 11
to William Henry Drayton, July 12
to the president of Congress, July 12
General Orders, July 12
to Baron de Kalb, July 13
to Brigadier General David Forman, July 13
General Orders, July 13
to Lieutenant Colonel Francis Barber, July 14

The Revolutionary War in Bergen County

to Major General Horatio Gates, July 14
to Count d'Estaing, July 14
to John Cleves Symmes, July 14
to Major General Horatio Gates, July 14
to the president of Congress, July 14
to Governor Jonathan Trumbull, July 14

WEBSITES OF INTEREST

www.thehermitage.org
www.loc.gov

These documents can be found in the Papers of George Washington on the Library of Congress website. A lesson plan with material for teachers and questions related to each document for students can be found in Henry Bischoff, *General George Washington at Paramus & Hoppertown: Primary Documents from Washington's Command of the Continental Army While Headquartered at the Hermitage, July 10–14, 1778*, Ho-Ho-Kus, NJ: The Friends of the Hermitage, Inc., 2005.

GENERAL CHARLES LEE:
A DISOBEDIENT SERVANT

BARBARA Z. MARCHANT

Charles Lee was a lieutenant colonel in the British army who had fought in many European wars, where he saw how the common man suffered under tyrants. He fought alongside George Washington in the French and Indian War. He despised King George III for not promoting him in the British army. At the outbreak of the Revolution, he joined the American cause and eventually became the second in command of the Patriot army. He was a brilliant military leader, highly educated and very intellectual, who had the respect of Washington and Congress. But Lee was also extremely egocentric and harbored resentment at not getting the top position when he and others felt he was clearly more qualified. Although he often signed letters to Washington, "Your most humble and obedient servant," he was anything but...

When Carol Karels asked if I'd be interested in writing a profile of Charles Lee for this book of Revolutionary War essays, I agreed, primarily to learn more about this enigmatic and complex man for whom both Fort Lee and Leonia were named. I was not disappointed. What a life he had in his fifty-one years on earth!

A little background on Charles Lee: he was born in Cheshire on February 5, 1732 (which makes him a few weeks older than Washington), and had gone to school in Switzerland. According to the "Anecdotes of the late Charles Lee, Esq. Lieutenant-Colonel of the 47th Regiment, colonel in the Portuguese Service, Major-General and Aid-du-Camp to the King of Poland, and second-in-command in the service of The United States of America during the Revolution to which are added, his political and military essays; also, Letters to and from many distinguished characters, in Europe and America, published in 1797" (in future references, I refer to this work as just "Anecdotes"), he was competent in Greek and Latin, "while his fondness for traveling gave him also an opportunity of attaining the Italian, Spanish, German, and French languages." He was considered a loner but he did enjoy the company of dogs.

Lee first arrived in America in 1752. He met Washington on the Braddock Expedition of 1755 during the French and Indian War. For a time he lived with a

The Revolutionary War in Bergen County

Engraving of Charles Lee from the eighteenth century.

Mohawk woman, who bore him twin sons. As Fischer noted in his work *Washington's Crossing*, Lee was called "Boiling Water" by the Mohawks, probably because of his ill temper. He eventually abandoned his American Indian family and returned to Europe. Even though he was not in America at the time, Lefkowitz noted that Lee, in 1766, wrote to his sister while in Asia Minor, "May God prosper the Americans in their resolutions, that there may be one Asylum at least on the earth for men, who prefer their natural rights to the fantastical prerogative of a foolish, perverted head because it wears a Crown." Through the remainder of the 1760s, he was either a soldier or a soldier of fortune in Portugal, Turkey and Eastern Europe. He returned to England in 1770 and was promoted to lieutenant colonel two years later. Bored by the lack of military action and probably because of his educated background, he became interested in politics. Lee became an anti-monarchist, partially because George III had not followed through on promised promotions. Lee had been paying attention to the activities in the colonies. Hearing about the not-so-peaceful state of affairs in the Americas whetted his appetite for more adventure. This man of action returned to America in 1773. In May 1775, Lee was offered and accepted a commission in the U.S. military. Since he still was a member of the British army, he sent a letter resigning

General Charles Lee: A Disobedient Servant

his commission in His Majesty's service. Not considered to be the handsomest of men, in today's terms he would be thought of as ugly and, in fact, one of his headquarters during the Revolution became known as "Hobgoblin Hall," according to Lancaster in *The American Revolution*. He was also very unkempt, even when dressed in his uniform, and it is alleged that his dogs smelled better than he did.

Lee resented the fact that Washington had been appointed commander in chief in 1775 by the Continental Congress. Among the generals, Lee was the only professional soldier in the U.S. Army. He had fought in the French and Indian War and other conflicts overseas and had felt that with his experience, he should have been put in charge of the American forces. Lee believed that he should not have been appointed as a major general or third in command to Washington. (Major General Artemus Ward had been appointed second in command, but since Ward was in poor health, Lee was considered by most to be second. It was not until Ward retired after the evacuation of Boston that Lee was officially the second in command.)

However, Congress would not have made a soldier who had been born in England head of the American army. Since Lee lost his property in England because of his having joined the American force, he wished to be compensated. George Washington was willing to work for expenses only. Since Washington was from the South and most of the troops were from the Northeast, Congress felt that it was a good political move to have Washington in charge. Lee did have his supporters in Congress, but Washington prevailed.

Lee had been in charge of the Continental army in New York, but had been ordered to the South in early 1776, where he did an admirable job of defeating the British in Charleston. Lee returned to the Northeast on October 14 and was given a new command north of King's Bridge in New York. Because of his victory over the British forces in the Battle of Charleston, Fort Constitution was renamed Fort Lee on October 19, 1776.

Less than one month later, on November 16, Fort Washington fell into enemy hands. It had been defended courageously by troops led by Colonel Robert Magaw. Both Magaw and General Nathanael Greene, commandant of Fort Lee, had advised Washington that Fort Washington could be defended even though Washington felt that the troops should be moved west to New Jersey and, according to Hibbert in *Redcoats and Rebels*, abandon Fort Lee. As Schecter noted in *The Battle for New York*, when Lee heard that with the surrender of Fort Washington, the British had taken capture of 230 officers and 2,600 soldiers, he was enraged. He felt that if Fort Washington had been called Fort Lee, it would have been evacuated. This belief was realized when Fort Lee was abandoned on November 20.

In the 1936 Bergen County book *Boys and Girls of New Jersey Now and Long Ago*, in writing to Lee, Washington stated,

> *Yesterday morning the Enemy landed a large Body of troops below Dobb's Ferry, advanced very rapidly to the Fort called by Your Name. I immediately went over, and as the Fort was not tenable on this side and we were in a narrow neck of land, the passes out of which the enemy was attempting to seize, I directed the troops to move over to the west side of the Hackensack River.*

Washington had been upset over the loss of both Forts Lee and Washington and his state of mind did not improve over his discovery that his trusted aide-de-camp, Joseph Reed, had been corresponding with Lee. On November 21, Reed wrote to Lee advising that Washington had wanted to abandon Fort Washington but listened to Greene instead. In *Memoirs of Charles Lee*, Reed wrote to Lee, "Oh, General! An indecisive mind is one of the greatest misfortunes that can befal [sic] an army: how often have I lamented it this campaign."

General Lee himself never was part of the retreat from Fort Lee, even though Washington's instructions to Lee had left little doubt about what should have happened. Lee's approximately four thousand troops did not merge with General Washington's forces until mid-December. Lefkowitz in *The Long Retreat* noted that Washington's instructions to Lee were issued on November 10, even before the struggle for either Fort Lee or Fort Washington had begun, "If the Enemy should remove the whole, or the greatest part of their force, to the West side of Hudson's River, I have no doubt of your following, with all possible dispatch."

Lee had been at Peekskill on November 20 when Fort Lee fell. Washington wrote to Lee while on retreat through northern New Jersey, as noted in Michael R. Yesenko's *General George Washington's Campaigns of 1775, 1776 and 1777*: "I would have you move over by the easiest and best passage [to New Jersey]." Lee felt that Washington's letter was more in the form of a suggestion than a command and did not move his troops immediately across the Hudson. He also felt that it was a disgrace that both Fort Washington and Lee had been taken by the British. According to Hibbert in *Redcoats and Rebels*, by not moving his soldiers immediately to join the retreating troops in New Jersey, Lee hoped that there would be a way to show Congress that he was by far the better general, since with Washington in charge there had been defeat after defeat during the autumn of 1776. Lee gave myriad excuses as to why he did not join the main force under Washington. However, in early December, Lee slowly moved four thousand of his troops into New Jersey.

Washington probably admired and was more than a little in awe of Lee. This was most likely the reason that he hesitated to give a direct order to his second in command. Lee was just about everything that Washington wanted to be (except for smelly and ugly). Lee was well traveled; Washington had never left the United States except for a two-month trip to Barbados in 1751. Lee was well educated; Washington had a minimal education. Lee was conversant in several languages; Washington only knew English. Lee had extensive military experience in several different countries; Washington had some, but only in North America.

Lee still had not joined Washington's main body of troops on December 8, and according to Yesenko, Lee wrote to Washington on that date that "it will be difficult, I am afraid, to join you; but cannot I do you more service by attacking their [the British] rear? I shall look about me tomorrow, and inform you further." In his book *George Washington in the American Revolution*, James Thomas Flexner mentions that, unfortunately, "Lee had a propensity for sleeping in strange places (and with strange women)." Sometime between December 12 and 14, by lingering too long at the Widow White's Tavern in Basking Ridge, Lee was captured by six British troops. The troops

General Charles Lee: A Disobedient Servant

Drawing depicting the capture of Major General Charles Lee. Source unknown.

had been led by a young second lieutenant with the unforgettable name of Banastre Tarleton under the supervision of Colonel Harcourt of the British Light Horse. Lee sent word to General Howe that he was willing to show how the Americans could be defeated, but Howe did not want to speak with Lee. It had been thought that he was turning on the Americans, but he could have been trying to help them. According to Schecter, Lee gave the British no information about the American army. In fact, the information that he tried to give the enemy would have made them spread their forces thinly over the United States, which would have reduced their strength.

At one point during his captivity, Lee had requested that "my dogs should be brought as I never stood in greater need of their company than at present." The British thought that the capture of Major General Lee was the best news possible and that the Rebels would soon be squashed. However, as Fischer pointed out in *Washington's Crossing*, "It delivered Washington from a very difficult problem of leadership…Washington at last succeeded in drawing together the fragments of his army."

Fortunately, Lee's troops had been a distance away from him at the time of his capture in Basking Ridge and were able to join up with the main body of Washington's forces. On April 6, 1778, Lee was returned to the Americans in exchange for Major General Prescott.

On June 28, 1778, Lee had been given the command of the army's vanguard at the Battle of Monmouth. Initially, Lee had been given the command but did not want it. Lafayette took command, and then Lee changed his mind and wanted it back again. Rather than have Washington take the command from him, Lafayette handed it over to Lee. Without notifying Washington, Lee gave the order for his troops to retreat after only one volley was fired. Washington was on his way to reinforce Lee's troops with more men. Washington was aghast that Lee had been disobedient. Since Lee had no faith in Baron Von Steuben's training of the troops, he felt that the Americans would be defeated. Of course, Lee had not been involved in day-to-day operations of the army between mid-December 1776 and early April 1778. He might not have realized how well the Americans had been training, but the commander in chief knew and was excited at the thought of seeing his confident army attack the British. When confronted by Washington about his retreat during this battle, Lee sputtered that he disapproved of the attack by what he considered American amateurs against British professionals. Washington advised that no matter what Lee's opinion of him was, Washington still expected his commands to be carried out as ordered. Whether Washington swore at Lee has been the subject of many discussions, and in "Anecdotes" Lee writes to Washington, "From the knowledge I have of your Excellency's character, I must conclude, that nothing but the misinformation of some very stupid, or misrepresentation of some very wicked person, could have occasioned your making use of such very singular expressions as you did, on my coming up to the ground where you had taken post: they implied that I was guilty either of disobedience of orders, of want of conduct, or want of courage." Washington's reply to Lee was, "I am not conscious of having made use of any singular expressions at the time of my meeting you. What I recollect to have said, was dictated by duty, and warranted by the occasion."

Because of Lee's actions on the battlefield in Monmouth in June 1778, he was court-martialed and charged. From "Anecdotes," the three charges were as follows: "First, for disobedience of orders, in not attacking the enemy on the 28th of June, agreeable to repeated instructions. Secondly, for misbehaviour before the enemy on the same day, by making an unnecessary, disorderly, and shameful retreat. Thirdly, for disrespect to the commander in chief, in two letters, dated the 1st July, and the 28th June." The trial then followed along with the army's movements. One trial location was at the Old Paramus Reformed Church in Ridgewood. According to "Proceedings of a General Court Martial, Held at Brunswick, in the State of New Jersey, by order of His Excellency General Washington, Commander in Chief of the Army of the United States of America, for the Trial of Major General Lee, July 4th 1778," the court met in Paramus five times between Saturday, July 11 and July 15, 1778. Lee handled his own questioning and gave a spirited defense. However, on August 12, the court handed down his sentence: Lee was to be suspended from military service for

General Charles Lee: A Disobedient Servant

one year. He tried to have the sentence commuted, but to no avail. He then went to his estate in western Virginia, where he lived with his horses and, of course, his dogs. On October 2, 1782, he died alone in a tavern in Philadelphia. According to Hibbert in *Redcoats and Rebels*, Charles Lee stated in his will, "I desire most earnestly that I may not be buried in any church, or church-yard, or within a mile of any Presbyterian or Anabaptist meeting-house; for since I have resided in this country, I have had so much bad company while living, that I do not chuse [*sic*] to continue it when dead." Lee was a true original, even unto death.

Barbara Z. Marchant dedicates her essay on Charles Lee to another Englishman, her late husband Peter, who made twenty-one years of her life jolly good fun.

"The Enemy...will have no Mercey upon our Loaded Barns": British Foraging at Hackensack, September and October 1778

JOHN U. REES

Crown forces occupied New York and areas adjacent from September 1776 to December 1783, hosting a large garrison and serving as the command center and central staging area for British, German and Loyalist units intended for service farther afield. As such, huge quantities of food and forage were needed to sustain soldiers, civilians and animals alike. Closely situated as it was to New York, Bergen County suffered the attentions of both Continental and Crown troops; this study examines one of the largest and longest British foraging incursions in that locale during the war.

From 1776 to 1781, territory in proximity to British-held New York was always in danger of sporadic Crown force's sorties, often with the sole purpose of gathering foodstuff for their troops and livestock on Manhattan, Long and Staten Islands. In mid-September 1777, while two large armies of American regulars were confronting invasions in southeastern Pennsylvania and northern New York, approximately four thousand British troops crossed the Hudson (North) River to forage the area around Hackensack, opposed only by New Jersey Militia with "a foundation of C[ontinental] troops." This 1777 forage operation was both short-lived and seemingly successful.

A second, larger incursion commenced on September 22, 1778, when British forces under Lieutenant General Earl Cornwallis landed in New Jersey and proceeded to occupy a position from English Neighborhood on the Hudson River to New Bridge on the Hackensack. Seen from the contemporary American point of view, the fog of war is quite evident, with Continental commanders initially unsure of the British objective. New Jersey Governor William Livingston wrote General George Washington that "the Enemy is very hungry as well as their horses and your stores at Morris Town are rather too well furnished to satisfy the stomachs of the former, & the latter will have no Mercey upon our loaded barns," while Brigadier General William Maxwell noted on September 22 that he had received intelligence "that they are either going on some Expedition or they are going to leave New York. Some says there is two expeditions on foot one up the sound the other up the North River and through this way but they say this may

"The Enemy...will have no Mercey upon our Loaded Barns"

Militia and Continental troops from the Brigade of the American Revolution taking part in the 225th anniversary of the 1778 British grand forage. Historic New Bridge Landing, 2003. *Courtesy of Susan Braisted.*

be with a design to get fresh Provisions and cover their embarkation." After capturing an American picquet at Liberty Pole and occupying the adjacent villages, the enemy proceeded to build a fortification on the west side of the Hackensack River at New Bridge to cover parties gathering food and forage for the New York garrison during the upcoming winter.

General Maxwell's brigade of New Jersey Continentals remained in the vicinity of Elizabethtown monitoring enemy activity on Staten Island that seemed to indicate a landing nearby. In a September 26 letter, Maxwell told militia Brigadier General William Winds, "There has been the greatest preperating...yesterday to come here... The Enemys Boats now heaves in sight, we expect they will attempt to land in half an Hour at least." Governor Livingston related

> *that a large Body of the Enemy were lying on their arms on Staten Island and that a number of armed vessels and flat-bottomed boats were collected...it was expected they would land at Elizabeth Town point with eleven or twelve sail of Briggs Sloops & Gallies, & their flat boats in the rear. The weather being hazey, &...General* [Maxwell] *not being able to see their rear, supposed them to be coming in force, and therefore ordered the alarm gave & signals to be fired. The Militia turned out...*[the] *General with his Brigade marched down with great spirit to give them a continental Reception. But they turned about and stood up Newark Bay and thence up Hackensack river.*

The uncertainty kept the four New Jersey regiments in a continual state of alarm for the first few days of the enemy's raid. Second New Jersey Regiment Colonel Israel Shreve, writing on September 29, said, "I have not had one night sleep since Last Friday."

At the same time as the ongoing foraging operations, Colonel George Baylor's Third Light Dragoon Regiment suffered a severe defeat at the hands of the British. Deputy Quartermaster Joseph Clark noted,

> *When the enemy came to Hackensack, Col. Baylard's regiment of dragoons and a detachment of* [light] *infantry, who were posted there, retreated to Paramus. Sunday, the 27th* [September], *Col. Baylard's regiment removed to the neighborhood between Tappan and Clarkstown, where before day next morning they were surprised in their quarters by a party of the British horse and infantry, who had come up the river and landed below Tappan… Upwards of a dozen men were killed on the spot, and most of the wounded were mortally so.*

The same day General Washington informed General Maxwell that with "the Enemy now on a forage …You will…immediately march to the high grounds west of acquncanuck with your Brigade in order the better to cover the Country [and] the public stores at Morristown—give confidence to the militia—and promote the driving off [of] the Cattle &ca." Washington's orders were not put into effect until October 2, Maxwell having written him on September 29 that "General Winds [and his militia]…occupies partley the same ground that You have aloted for me; that the Enemy makes no Moves over the Hackensack &ca…We think that had Your Excellency been informed [of that, and]…the likelyhood of the Enemy crossing here and pillageing this part of the country…You would not have ordered me up to Acquackinac or in that neighbourhood, I have therefore concluded to stand fast with my Brigade" at Elizabeth Town until the commander in chief directed otherwise, or the enemy "make some advances to the Westward, in [which] case I shall move Immediately and endeavour to fall on their flank or Rear." A September 28 deserter's account provided details of British activities:

> *Michael Mullen a Deserter from Lord Rodon's* [Rawdon's] *Corps—says he left his Corps yesterday Morning between Hackinsack and the Liberty Pole…he amagins there is about 6,000 Troops on that side the River…Lord Cornwallis Commands…* [and] *they are repairing the Old Bridge, at Hackinsack, to get their Cannon over…there is no Troops on the West side of the River, but British & Hessians…* [and they] *take from the inhabitants all their Cattle, Hogs, Fowles & Forage of every kind.*

According to British Major John André, no German units were involved, only the British Grenadier and Light Infantry Battalions, Guards Battalions, Third and Fourth Brigades, Rawdon's Loyalist Volunteers of Ireland and a dragoon detachment.

On October 2, Maxwell finally moved some of his troops from Elizabethtown at the behest of New Jersey Major General William Alexander, Lord Stirling, who wanted "two Reg[iment]s. at least at Aquaquanunk Bridge to encourage and support

"The Enemy...will have no Mercey upon our Loaded Barns"

the Militia." At 11:00 a.m. that day, Colonel Shreve noted, "In one hour the first and Second Regiments are to march...to watch the motions of the Enemy that Lay three miles North of Hackensack, we are to join Lord Sterling at Paramus, with Gen Woodfords [Virginia] Brigade and Some other Regt., I Expect to hear the Enemy are on the Move out of Jersey Every hour, as their Vessels Are Going down the River from Hackensack Loaded with hay Grain." From Paramus, on the morning of October 4, Lord Stirling informed Washington that having "had [the British] lines reconitred yesterday from Hackinsack Bridge to Tapan," it was found that "they are fully employd in foraging." That afternoon, from Acquackanonk, he added, "I find here General Winds with about 600 Militia General [Nathaniel] Heard with about 1,000 & General Maxwell with the first & Second Rejiments of his Brigade. Colonel [Elias] Dayton with the other two [New Jersey regiments] & Col. [John] Neilson with...[a force of] Militia are at Elizabeth Town." At this juncture the situation was not promising, Major General Stirling related,

The Militia are all home Sick and are every hour apply[ing] *for leave to return to their families. I have used every argument to induce them to Stay at this Critical Juncture and Get the Officers to exert themselves to perswade them what I believe is really the truth, that the Enemy have nearly Compleated their forage on the East side of Hackensack River and if they have anything further in View it must take place in the Course of two or three days. Intelligence of what the Enemy are particularly at is difficult to Obtain but I have put every Engine to work to get at it.*

Belatedly, the remainder of the New Jersey Brigade moved to oppose the enemy force in and around New Bridge. Lord Stirling told Washington that

About Eight oClock this Morning [5 October] *we were Alarmed with Accounts of the Enemy's Advances through Hackensack, soon after that about 300 of them were on the heights behind Arent Schuylers house...near the head of the polyfly* [River] *about one Mile SW from Hackensack...These movements may be to Cover their forage. Boats going down the River, as they have been grossly Insulted within these two or three days. I have sent for Colonel Dayton to come up to the heights near Second River with the 3d & 4th* [New Jersey] *Regts. & what Militia is at Elizabeth Town, which I have reason to belive are very few...I have but little hopes of any reinforcement till it will* [be] *too late to prevent them at least forageing this Side of Hackensack River and perhaps of pushing further into the Country.*

Operating in close proximity to enemy lines increased the danger and added to the discomfort of the troops involved. Virginia Brigadier General William Woodford wrote from Paramus on October 4 that he had his troops "shift our Camp every night to guard against a surprise—the last night gave us a thorough soaking."

Only ten days remained until the last of the British foraging force returned to New York and adjacent posts. During this time, Continental forces were able to ensure their enemy remained between the Hackensack and Hudson Rivers, though this was likely due more to the designs of the British than American strength and

The Revolutionary War in Bergen County

Troops from Lamb's Artillery wheel a three-pound field piece into position during the 225th anniversary of the 1778 British grand forage at Historic New Bridge Landing. Reenactors from the Brigade of the American Revolution. *Courtesy of Susan Braisted.*

effectiveness. Major André succinctly related the undertaking's salient points from the British point of view. For September 30 and October 2 and 5: "Foraging party in front"; on October 8, he wrote, "Foraging. The hay collected during our stay in Jersey was put on board Sloops, and conveyed from the Forks of Hackensack and Overpeck to New York." Finally, on October 13, André recorded, "The foraging having been completed and cattle collected, the Troops hutted their position between Hudson's and Hackensack Rivers, and marched on the 14th to Bergen, and on the 15th crossed from Forbes' Hook [Paulus Hook] to their former positions on York Island, Long Island and Staten Island."

Writing on October 13, Lord Stirling recounted the British incursion, which lasted from September 22 to October 15, and his efforts to counter it:

On the Enemy's Invadeing this part of New Jersey, His Excellency General Washington thought proper to Order General Woodfords Brigade and Colonel [Stephen] Moylens [4th] Regiment of Horse to March into this State in addition to General Maxwells Brigade which was already here, and was pleased to honor me with the Command of the whole. We have for above a fortnight been within five or six miles of the Enemy and although their Army Consisted of seven thousand foot and a Considerable body of Horse and Mine of less then two thousand, they have gained not the least advantage of us; On the Contrary they have been

"The Enemy...will have no Mercey upon our Loaded Barns"

Confined to a Narrow district of Country... They have taken off every kind of forage in their power, and have burnt the houses of such of the Inhabitants as were known to be friends to the Cause of Liberty. They have this Morning thought proper to retire and are now on their way to New York... I shall tomorrow move the troops to New Ark & Elizabeth Town in order to Watch the Motions of the Enemy on that side.

The British operation was ruinous to many local inhabitants, Loyalist and Whig alike. Quartermaster General Timothy Pickering took into account family needs when confiscating food for the American army in 1781, estimating "that they be allowed to retain":

For 4 persons in family   35 bushels of wheat- | for bread
20 bushels of corn - | for seed
2 horses—3 tons of hay & 10 bushels of corn, oats, or buckwheat
3 cows—2 tons of hay
4 hogs—20 bushels of corn or buckwheat
And so in proportion for a smaller or larger family.

Given the circumstances, it is unlikely the British would have held to such niceties.

John U. Rees's work, focusing primarily on the common soldiers' experience during the War for Independence and North American soldiers' food, 1755 to the present, has appeared in the ALHFAM Bulletin *(Association of Living History, Farm and Agricultural Museums),* The Brigade Dispatch *(Journal of the Brigade of the American Revolution),* The Continental Soldier *(Journal of the Continental Line),* Journal of the Johannes Schwalm Historical Association, Military Collector & Historian, Minerva: Quarterly Report on Women and the Military, Muzzleloader Magazine *and* Percussive Notes *(Journal of the Percussive Arts Society). He is a regular columnist for* Food History News, *and has contributed entries to the* Oxford Encyclopedia of American Food and Drink, *as well as the revised Thomson Gale edition of* Boatner's Encyclopedia of the American Revolution. *A partial article list plus many complete works are available online at www.revwar75.com/library/rees. Additional articles, including a monograph on the March 23, 1780 Paramus action, may be found at http://www.continentalline.org/en/newsletter.html*

The Baylor Massacre

Edmund A. Moderacki

On September 21, 2003, the Bergen County Board of Chosen Freeholders commemorated the 225th anniversary of the events of the Baylor Massacre at the Baylor Massacre Burial Site, a Bergen County historic park in River Vale. It was there that American soldiers were the victims of a surprise attack by British soldiers on the night of September 28, 1778, a night referred to as one of "savage cruelty." The site was threatened in 1967 but is now protected and is the official burial site of six Patriots who were hastily buried in tanning vats. Ed Moderacki's essay on the massacre was written for the 2003 commemorative program, and is reprinted here.

In September 1778, British General Cornwallis occupied southern Bergen County with a force of about five thousand soldiers. Their purpose was to gather forage, or food, to feed the army that would be garrisoned in New York City during the coming winter. Bergen County, with its fertile land and industrious Jersey Dutch farmers, was a major source of food for both armies during the Revolution.

The Continental army had units stationed around the Old Paramus Reformed Church, in today's Ridgewood. Additionally, the American militia occupied the village of Tappan, New York, with a force of four hundred militiamen and was in a position to launch harassing attacks against British foraging parties.

The Third Continental Light Dragoons were one of four regiments of dragoons authorized by the Continental Congress. At that time in the Revolution, dragoons were cavalry used as scouts and messengers. The Third CLD was commanded by Colonel George Baylor.

Baylor was born in 1752 in Virginia, his family being part of the local aristocracy. When the Revolution began, Baylor was recommended to George Washington and made his aide-de-camp. Baylor distinguished himself at the Battle of Trenton in December 1776, and was given the privilege of bringing the news of the American victory and a captured Hessian flag to the Continental Congress in Baltimore. Baylor was rewarded with the command of one of the

The Baylor Massacre

A Baylor dragoon, by George Woodbridge. *Courtesy of County of Bergen.*

newly authorized dragoon regiments, which had about 120 officers and men when it was in the field.

After an absence of several months spent enlisting soldiers and equipping his regiment, Baylor rejoined his command on September 22. During his absence, the regiment was commanded by Major Alexander Clough. Under Major Clough, Washington had used the regiment to gather intelligence in Bergen and in the Hudson Valley. On September 27, the regiment was ordered to take a position between the American forces and the foraging British. River Vale was known by several names in the eighteenth century, one being the "Overkill Neighborhood," as it was over the kill (river) from Tappan. Like much of Bergen County, the inhabitants were divided in allegiance. Some, known as Patriots, supported the Continental Congress, and others, known as Loyalists, remained loyal to the Crown. Baylor was alerted that the area had its share of Loyalists.

At this time, the British General Clinton said that his mission "was to take a forward position, procure supplies of provisions, observe the motions of the Rebel army and favour an expedition to Egg Harbor." Accordingly, on the September 22, he requested Lord Cornwallis to take a post between New Bridge on the Hackensack River in Jersey and Hudson River and Lieutenant General Knyphausen between Wepperham on the "last of these rivers and the Bronx." One column, under the command of General Charles Grey, was to cross the Hackensack River at New Bridge and then move to the Hudson from the west.

The previous year, Grey's men had inflicted casualties on Pennsylvania troops under the command of General Wayne at Paoli. In order to ensure the surprise of a nighttime attack, Grey had ordered his men to remove the flints from their muskets to prevent an accidental gunshot and to rely only on their bayonets. He was given the name of "no Flint Grey" because of his tactics. These tactics were used again in River Vale, with the same brutality.

It was late in the afternoon when Baylor and his men arrived in the neighborhood and met the militia driving the cattle away from the British. The weather was unseasonably cold, and Baylor allowed his soldiers to sleep in six barns located between the Hackensack River and Prospect Avenue. Four houses along Rivervale Road housed the officers. A sergeant's guard was dispatched to watch over the bridge over the Hackensack at the intersection of modern Rivervale and Old Tappan Roads and to watch the roads to the south and east.

It is not known who alerted the British to Baylor's disposition, but it is likely that one or more Loyalist farmers carried the information south on Kinderkamack Road and met Grey's advancing column. Grey immediately saw the opportunity to conduct another night attack. One column was dispatched across the farm fields that are today Edgewood Country Club in order to surround the houses and barns. The second column traveled east on Piermont Avenue before turning onto Rivervale Road and attacking the guard detachment at the bridge. The attack commenced about 1:00 a.m. on September 28.

Baylor and Clough were alerted by the noise of the attack and tried to hide from the British by climbing up into the chimney of the large Dutch fireplace

The Baylor Massacre

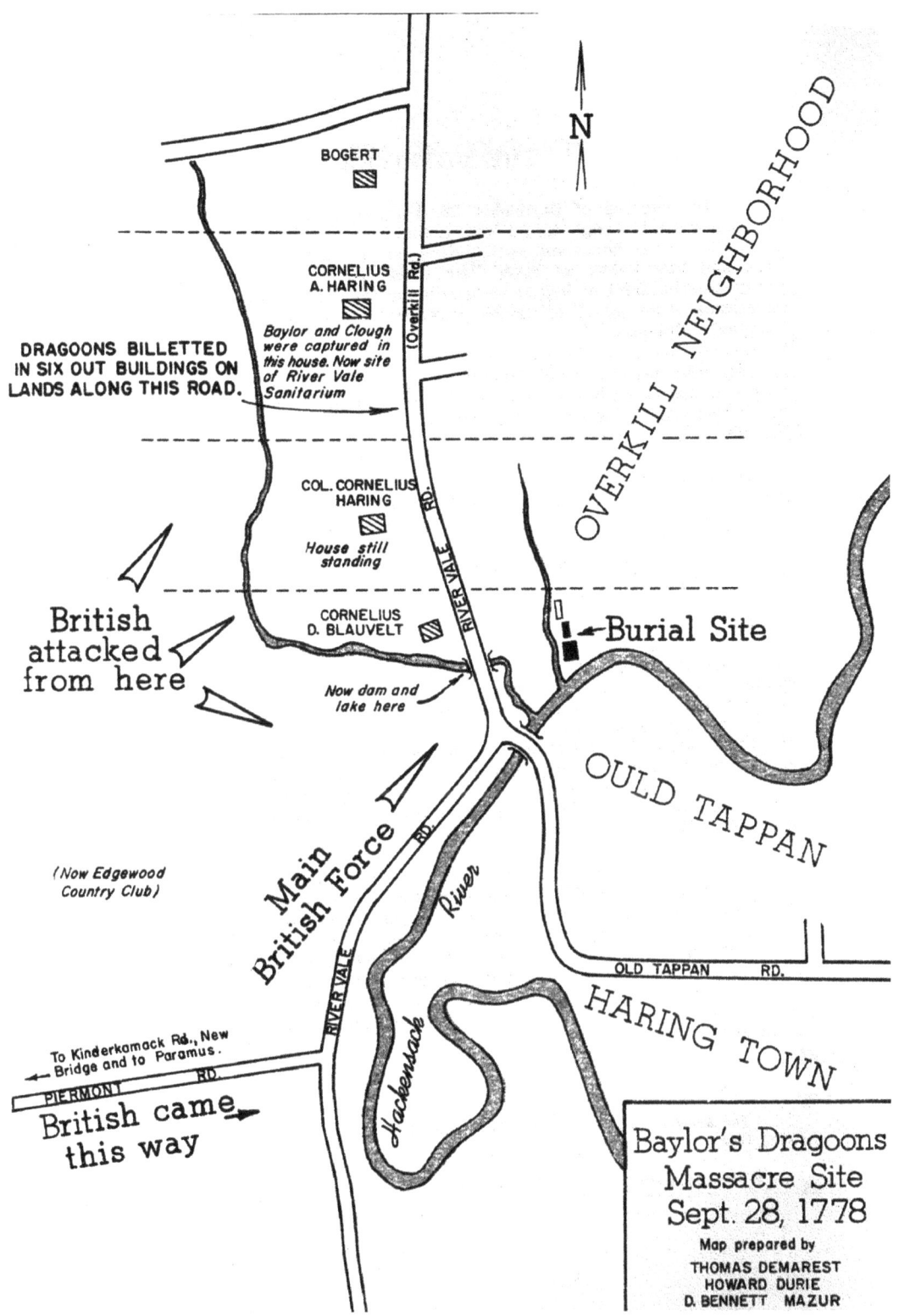

Map of Baylor massacre site in River Vale. *Courtesy of County of Bergen.*

Baylor Massacre Historic Marker in River Vale. *Courtesy of Carol Karels.*

The Baylor Massacre

of the house in which they were quartered. The British brought them down by bayoneting them.

The British used their bayonets to stab, and their muskets to club, the sleeping dragoons. Baylor had 116 officers and men when he arrived on September 27; 11 of his dragoons were killed immediately, and 2 more enlisted men and Clough died of their wounds in Tappan the following day. Records indicate that as many as 22 men died, some several weeks later, of their wounds. Although most of them were wounded, 2 officers and 37 men escaped into the night. One British soldier was killed when shot by a dragoon.

Grey's men did not stay long in River Vale, but gathered their prisoners and captured American equipment, and continued north to Tappan. Fortunately, the militia had been alerted of the movement of the British and had evacuated Tappan.

The next day, a detachment of the Bergen County Militia was dispatched to River Vale to locate any survivors. Finding six of the dead Patriots at the bridge, they were faced with the problem of burying the men. Fearing the possible return of British troops, they hurriedly buried them in three abandoned leather tanning vats located by the Hackensack River.

The location of this burial was passed on by word of mouth for many generations. The only physical marker was the abandoned millstone from the tannery. Abram C. Holdrum removed the millstone from the site around 1900, to demonstrate the strength of his new team of oxen. His son later donated the stone to the River Vale Schools, where it was displayed in front of the Holdrum School for many years.

In 1967, Thomas Demarest, then a resident of Old Tappan, became alarmed that a housing development, already under construction, would destroy this historic Revolutionary War burial site. Through careful research, the approximate location of the burials was identified. Mr. Demarest contacted County Freeholder D. Bennett Mazur for help. As a result, the county sponsored an archaeological dig that was able to locate six sets of remains and many artifacts. Through the actions of the Board of Chosen Freeholders, the county acquired the site and dedicated it as a county park, preserving it for future generations. In 1974, the six sets of remains were reinterred in the park, next to the Hackensack River. The original millstone was donated by the River Vale Board of Education to serve as the gravestone for the buried Patriots.

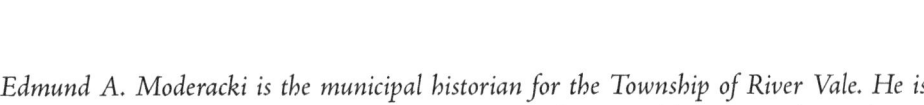

Edmund A. Moderacki is the municipal historian for the Township of River Vale. He is the former adjutant general of the Brigade of the American Revolution and lectures on the Baylor Massacre and art and music in colonial America throughout the metropolitan region. His Images of America: River Vale *has been published by Arcadia Press. He is a music teacher in the River Vale schools and conducts the popular Waldwick Band.*

The Hard Winter of 1779–80

Robert Griffin

In his essay, Robert Griffin writes of how extreme weather both helped and hampered the efforts of the American army. From nor'easters to record-breaking hot and cold spells as well as unprecedented snowfall accompanied by subzero temperatures, he shows that weather truly was the third combatant in the war. Worst of all was the winter of 1779–80, known as "the Hard Winter."

Even casual students of the Revolutionary War have a sense of the role that weather played throughout the conflict. Well-known paintings of General Washington crossing the ice-laden Delaware River on Christmas night in 1776 and kneeling in prayer at snow-covered Valley Forge in 1778 provide powerful images that help us envision the difficult conditions of war during the winter. The extreme heat of ninety-six to one hundred degrees at the Battle of Monmouth reportedly killed at least sixty-two British and Hessians and thirty-seven Americans on the battlefield. British soldiers were required to wear fully buttoned wool coats regardless of the weather. Weather, it seemed, acted as a third combatant in the war, capriciously favoring the Patriots at one point and the British at another, often hindering both. But it was especially the harsh winter weather that took its toll on men and horses.

During the first winter of the war, Colonel Benedict Arnold lost 450 of his 1,050 volunteers during their trek through Maine to Quebec in early November 1775. The remaining 600 gaunt, ragged men, their clothing "torn in pieces…hung in strips, many without hats, beards long and visages thin and meager" attempted a disastrous attack on the fort in a snowstorm that began at dawn on the day of the attack, December 30, 1775. The Americans' combined forces totaled 900. There were 60 casualties and 426 captured. Arnold refused to give up—despite being outnumbered by 3 to 1—and insisted on keeping the remnants of his force around the city for the sub-freezing winter, with the expected devastating results.

An unseasonably cold nor'easter on August 28, 1776, initially hampered American forces attempting to defend Brooklyn Heights from British attack. "We had no tents to

The Hard Winter of 1779–80

screen us from its pitiless pelting," wrote one officer. However, the same harsh weather also served to keep the British fleet out of the East River, leaving the Americans a precious avenue of escape. During the night of August 30, the nine thousand Americans evacuated Long Island. A heavy fog the following morning provided perfect cover for the Americans to complete their escape from the greatly superior enemy forces.

As the war finally advanced to Bergen County and New Jersey, weather continued to dog both the Americans and the British. During the winter retreat from Fort Lee in late November of 1776, eyewitnesses told of barefoot soldiers marching in an icy rain into Hackensack. However, a month later, it was the Americans who benefited from a terrific snowstorm on Christmas night, providing cover for their surprise attack on Trenton. After a second success at Princeton several days later, Washington wisely decided to send his army into winter quarters near Morristown. The British outpost withdrew to New Brunswick and Amboy, with the main forces quartered in New York City. There was no more military activity during the winter of 1776–77. There was much snow, but few severely cold periods.

But even under the best of conditions, winter weather proved to be deadly to the poorly equipped Americans. During the encampment at Valley Forge near Philadelphia, during the winter of 1777–78, 2,500 soldiers died. Far worse, however, was the winter of 1779–80. Called "the Hard Winter," it is the only time in recorded history when the Hudson River froze completely between Manhattan, New Jersey and Staten Island. Two previous landmark winters were somewhat comparable, but all agreed that the winter of 1779–80 topped them all. Thomas Jefferson in Virginia reported there had been nothing similar in the American experience.

General Washington had again decided upon Morristown for his winter encampment, and the various units marched to Jockey Hollow, arriving between the first week of December and the end of the month. Among the most detailed firsthand accounts of the war is that of Dr. James Thatcher, surgeon of the American army. He described the arrival of the American forces from Connecticut:

> *We marched to Pompton on the 9th, and on the 14th reached this wilderness, about three miles from Morristown, where we are to build log-huts for winter-quarters. Our baggage is left in the rear, for want of wagons to transport it. The snow on the ground is about two feet deep, and the weather extremely cold; the soldiers are destitute of both tents and blankets, and some of them are actually barefooted and almost naked. Our only defence [sic] against the inclemency of the weather, consists of brush-wood thrown together. Our lodging the last night was on the frozen ground…We could procure neither shelter nor forage for our horses, and the poor animals were tied to trees, in the woods for twenty-four hours without food, except the bark which they peeled from the trees…Our baggage has at length arrived, the men find it very difficult to pitch their tents on the frozen ground and notwithstanding large fires, we can scarcely keep from freezing. In addition to other sufferings, the whole army has been for seven or eight days entirely destitute of the staff of life; our only food is miserable fresh beef, without bread, salt, or vegetables.*

The snow season had actually begun a month prior to the Americans' arrival, with a light fall on November 2 and another on November 7. Just prior to the November 2 storm, General Anthony Wayne had moved his Pennsylvania light infantry from Haverstraw to join with General Lord Stirling's New Jersey Line at Paramus. A false alarm of a British invasion at Fort Lee had caused the Americans to consolidate their forces in Bergen County. In the process, they collected from sixty to a hundred wagons from the farmers in the vicinity. On November 2, the day of the first storm, Wayne moved his troops on a huge forage as far south as the "Overpeck Creek between Fort Lee and Paulus Hook," where he collected "upward of one hundred head of fat cattle and a considerable quantity of grain."

Wayne's timing couldn't have been better. Heavy snowstorms hit on November 26 and December 5, dumping nearly nine inches each time. Severe cold set in, and another heavy snow on December 18 deposited seventeen inches of new snow. But the worst was still to come. An outstanding series of three major blizzards ravaged the entire East Coast from Virginia northward. They came in quick succession during a ten-day period.

The first storm was a combination of rain and snow accompanied by violent wind, and continued at least six hours. The depth of new snow measured at New Haven was eighteen inches. The second storm began during the early afternoon of January 2. Reverend Henry Muhlenberg, reporting from Trappe, just west of Philadelphia, wrote in his diary on January 2, "After service it began to snow heavily again, accompanied by a stormy northeast wind." His entry on January 3 continued: "Since yesterday afternoon and throughout the night there was such a snowstorm that the house and yard are so circumvallated that one can scarcely get out or in, and the snow is still falling. Had some time for reading and writing. The cold wind still continues. It kept up its frightful howling the whole night."

Dr. Thatcher's diary entry described the second of the three storms:

> *On the 3d instant, we experienced one of the most tremendous snowstorms ever remembered; no man could endure its violence many minutes without danger of his life. Several marquees were torn asunder and blown down over the officers' heads in the night, and some of the soldiers were actually covered while in their tents, and buried like sheep under the snow...But the sufferings of the poor soldiers can scarcely be described; they are badly clad, and some are destitute of shoes. The snow is now from four to six feet deep, which so obstructs the roads as to prevent our receiving a supply of provisions. The consequence is the soldiers are so enfeebled from hunger and cold, as to be almost unable to perform their military duty, or labor in constructing their huts.*

The third storm was a nor'wester with gale force winds that caused great drifting, with only intermittent snowfall. At the conclusion of the ten-day period, Dr. Thatcher reported snow cover had reached the depth of four feet on the level with drifts as high as ten to twelve feet.

January 1780 is rated as the most persistently cold calendar month in the history of the Eastern United States. At Philadelphia, the thermometer rose above freezing only once, and that for a short time. A temperature of negative sixteen degrees for New York City was mentioned in diaries of the period. Hessian General Wilhelm

The Hard Winter of 1779–80

Knyphausen had been left in charge of the British and Hessian forces in New York City when Sir Henry Clinton sailed on December 26 to invade Charles Town, South Carolina. Washington knew Knyphausen to be more aggressive than Sir Henry, and he feared the enemy would move by sleigh up the Hudson River and attack West Point. To ensure that Knyphausen would remain on the defensive, Washington ordered General William Alexander, Lord Stirling, to mount a substantial raid on Staten Island. In spite of the difficult conditions—or perhaps trying to take advantage of them—Lord Stirling with 2,700 men and 500 sleighs on January 25 launched his attack across the ice on the Tory Abraham Van Buskirk's Fourth New Jersey Volunteers, who were quartered on Staten Island. But the weather conditions were too severe to take full advantage of their victory, and the nearly frozen men hurried back into Bergen County with only a few prisoners and booty. According to Dr. Thatcher, 500 men were "slightly frozen" and 6 were killed in the skirmish.

The frigid weather eventually shut down every seaport along the Atlantic Coast. By mid-January, the entire Upper Hudson Bay froze over so that ox-sleighs could go back and forth from Staten Island to Manhattan and Brooklyn—a condition never known to have occurred before or since.

In retaliation for Stirling's attack, Van Buskirk attacked Elizabethtown in the dead of night on one of the coldest days of the winter, January 25, 1780. They captured about fifty American officers and men without the loss of a single man and with only a few scattered shot. On January 29, it was reported that heavy loads and even large cannon were dragged across the ice to fortify the British position on Staten Island. But the harsh weather conditions by this time caused all major military action to cease.

On February 10, three hundred British light horse descended upon the town of Hackensack to attack the Continental post at Paramus Church. Finding the snow very deep and the roads impassable, they returned to New York having inflicted little or no damage.

A warm early March brought hope that the winter was finally abating, but it was not over yet. Another storm on March 16 and again March 31 brought more snow. Dr. Thatcher noted, "An immense body of snow on the ground…there had been four snowfalls in February and March brought six more." Another entry in his journal read, "For the last ten days we have received but two pounds of meat a man, and we are frequently for six or eight days entirely without bread."

Before this winter was over, plans for a major attack on the town of Hackensack came to light on March 22, 1780. An appeal was sent to General Washington for help from the Continental forces stationed at Paramus. But his approval arrived too late. That evening, three hundred British Regulars under the command of Lieutenant Colonel Duncan MacPherson, of the Forty-second Regiment—the celebrated Black Watch—launched their attack from Manhattan. Crossing the Hackensack River at Little Ferry at midnight, they arrived in Hackensack around 3:00 a.m. An aborted attempt was also made to attack the Continental forces stationed at the Old Paramus Reformed Church; it was the village of Hackensack, however, that suffered the worst of the affair.

Led by Tory sympathizers, the British and Hessian troops set the Hackensack Courthouse afire and systematically tried to burn every Patriot's home in the village.

Conrad Bender portraying an officer of the Forty-second, or Royal Highland, Regiment of Foot. *Courtesy of Ira Lieblich.*

The Hard Winter of 1779–80

Only luck and a favorable wind prevented their total success. Nonetheless, the doors and windows of every Whig's house were broken down and everything of value taken. Not only that, but the raiders also took virtually every grown man in town, fifty or sixty in all. Thirteen weeks would pass before all of the prisoners were finally exchanged and returned home.

The "Hard Winter" was still not finished! Another storm brought four to five inches of snow on April 5. Eleven days later, on Sunday April 16, the British mounted another attack on Paramus Church. This time they were not interested in wasting time on inflicting vengeance on civilians at Hackensack. At 1:00 a.m., about one hundred cavalry from Staten Island joined forces at English Neighborhood with three hundred Hessian cavalry, who had been ferried across the Hudson at Fort Lee earlier in the night. An hour later, they attacked the Continental guard at New Bridge, consisting of one officer and thirty men. After a brief skirmish, the British pushed on, leaving fifty men to protect the bridge. The main force arrived at Paramus at sunrise.

The Continental forces consisted of 250 troops of the Third Pennsylvania Regiment under Major Thomas Langhorne Byles. They were stationed along the road west of the Paramus Church. In addition to the picket at New Bridge, Major Byles posted a second picket a mile and a half east of the American headquarters. Cornet George Spencer, of the Queen's Rangers, was ordered to push rapidly forward past the picket and on to the American headquarters, which he did. The surprised Americans sought shelter in the stone house belonging to Mr. John Hopper. Cornet Spencer set fire to the corner of the shingled roof and demanded the surrender of the Americans. After determining that their cause was lost, Major Byles reluctantly surrendered, but not before he was mortally wounded in the chest.

As soon as they received the alarm, large numbers of Bergen County Militiamen turned out to harass the retreating enemy. Firing from behind stone fences and trees, they continued their attack from Paramus to Fort Lee, inflicting heavy casualties and forcing the retreating troops to slow their march and throw out flanking parties to protect their main force. The result was that a great many prisoners escaped and much of the booty had to be abandoned, including four wagons and sixteen horses retaken at the very water's edge.

As if to punctuate the disastrous winter, one final storm swept across the Northeast on May 1, 1780. In all, twenty-eight individual storms occurred during "the Hard Winter." The economic consequences of the snow and ice conditions were devastating to a country already strained to the breaking point by the hardships of five years of warfare.

Robert Griffin is chairman of the Historic New Bridge Landing Park Commission in River Edge (Bergen County), a Revolutionary War site. He is also past president of the Bergen County Historical Society, a past chairman of the Bergen County Historic Sites Advisory Board (a County Freeholder Board) and served as Teaneck Township historian and on Teaneck's Historic Preservation Commission as vice-chair. He is president of Bergen Historic Books, Inc., a book sales and publishing company that specializes in local histories and genealogies about northern New Jersey.

Thomas Ward and the Woodcutters of Bergen

Todd W. Braisted

Bergen County served as the breadbasket, armory and a source of wood for both armies for the duration of the war. Todd Braisted's epic tale of Thomas Ward and his woodcutters portrays the lawlessness, treachery, plundering and pillaging, and the daily terror of guerilla warfare that was carried on in Bergen County, the neutral ground, during the war.

While battles are often won by superior tactics, the side with superior logistical support often wins the war. Fuel, provisions, ordnance, ammunition, transport and clothing are essential supplies for any army. Today petroleum, oil and lubricants may be necessary fuel products, but in eighteenth-century America *it was wood*.

The British army in America had been fighting to suppress the rebellion there for nearly five years by the winter of 1779–80. Human terms aside, it had cost the British Treasury a small fortune to keep its troops properly supplied. Part of their logistic train was the Barrack Master General's Department, one of the civil branches of the army. A major task of this organization was to see that the army, its posts, garrisons and barracks were properly supplied with wood, both for cooking and heating. That winter would strain the department's resources to and beyond its limits, as it was to be no normal season. Temperatures plummeted to lows not ever recalled by the local inhabitants. The Hudson River froze to such a degree that cavalry and heavy artillery safely crossed on the ice between New York City and Paulus Hook (now Jersey City). Staten Island, joined by the ice with both New Jersey and Manhattan, was supplied with provisions from the latter by sleighs. The Reverend Charles Inglis of New York noted in his diary "this has been the severest Winter Known in the Memory of Man—the Sexton of St. Pauls [Church] measured the Depth to which the Frost had penetrated, & he found it to be 4 feet 1 inches thick."

The British faced a daunting challenge. Not only was there an acute shortage of firewood in British-held New York City, but there was also a shortage of manpower in the form of woodcutters. A stopgap solution was found by employing Loyalist

Thomas Ward and the Woodcutters of Bergen

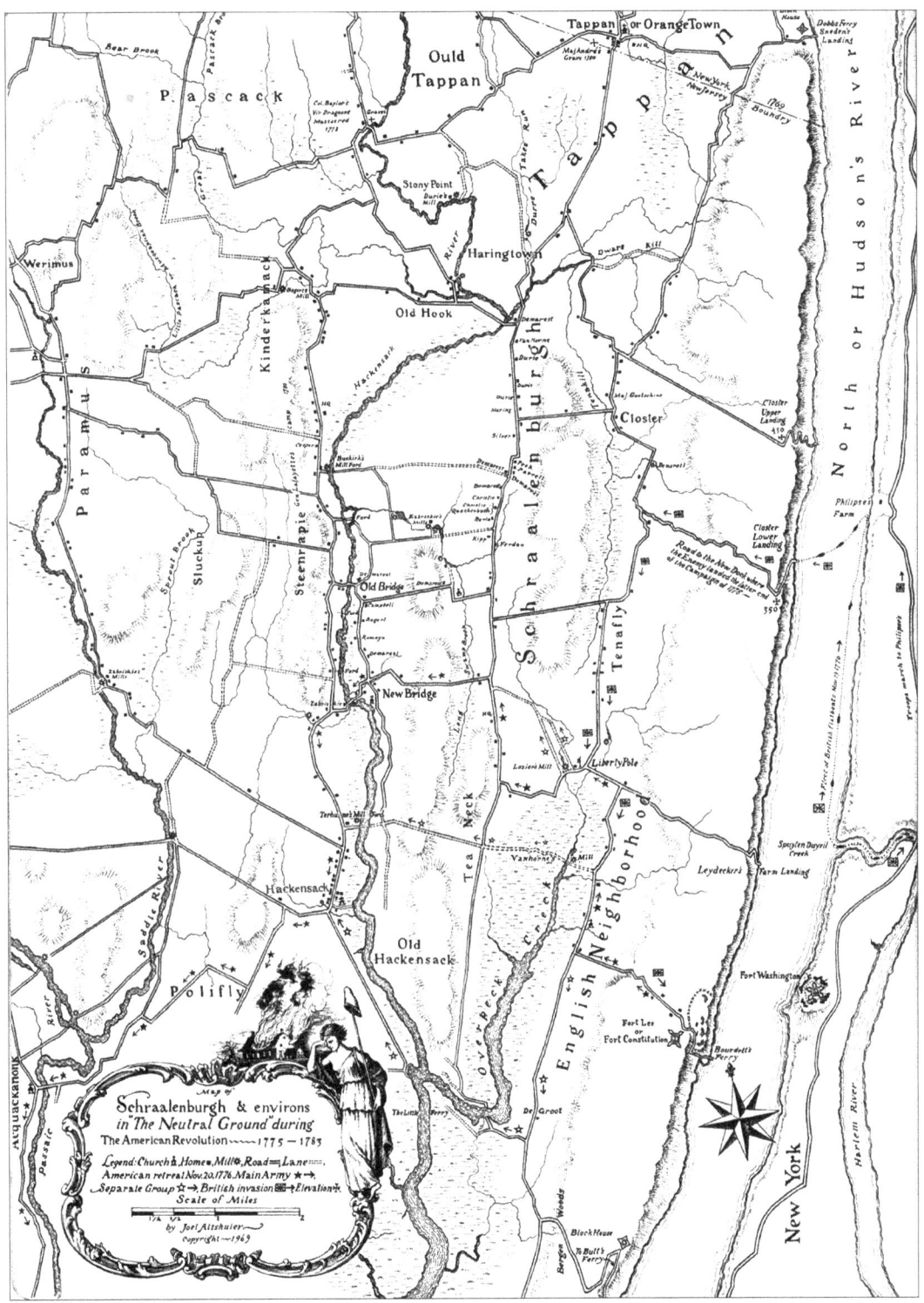

A map of the neutral ground from Dumont Heritage Book, drawn by Joel Altshuler. *Courtesy of Borough of Dumont.*

refugees residing in New York City to work as woodcutters across the Hudson, in such places as Bergen Point, Communipaw, Hoboken and Weehawken. Some of these refugees, such as Lucas Buskirk and Aaron Banta, were from Bergen County. While these measures (and such things as dismantling old ships for their wood) got the city and troops through the long, hard winter, a more reliable source of supply would be needed. Enter Abraham C. Cuyler.

Cuyler was the former Loyalist mayor of Albany, New York, and father of Lieutenant Colonel Cornelius Cuyler of the British Fifty-fifth Regiment of Foot. Imprisoned early in the conflict, he sought to serve the British by raising a corps of woodcutters. The corps proposed by Cuyler was a hybrid of a military unit and commercial enterprise. While the group would be armed, it would not be a part of the British army, but rather serve under contract directly for Cuyler, and by extension have an exclusive financial deal with the Barrack Department. The men were to be paid for the amount of wood they cut and delivered to the fuel yard in New York City, from which proceeds they would supply their own needs with regard to arms, ammunition, provisions, etc.

During that fierce winter of 1779–80, Cuyler met with little success in raising his corps, so much so that recruiting was put on hold in January. He used the hiatus to solicit the support of the men who would become his principal officers, to wit: Thomas Ward, David Babcock, Philip Luke and John Everet. When recruiting resumed in April 1780, these were men responsible for organizing the military end of the operation, leaving the financial haggling of wood prices and deliveries to Cuyler. Of the four men previously mentioned, Thomas Ward would rise to the top as the chief officer. Ward was not a typical Loyalist officer, who generally came from the gentleman class of society, espousing the British cause from the start of the conflict. Ward was a resident of Newark, New Jersey, and also owned seven hundred acres of land just over the border at the Clove, Orange County, New York. Rather than joining the British on their entry into New Jersey in 1776 though, as many Loyalists did, Ward threw in his lot with Washington's army and enlisted as a sergeant on April 3, 1777, in Malcolm's Additional Continental Regiment. A change of heart occurred, and Ward soon deserted to the British, providing them with someone who would serve as an outstanding partisan leader until the end of the war. Even before his association with Cuyler, Ward made a name for himself by leading a small expedition of volunteers to Kakiat, where they took the Continental army's muster master general and his deputy prisoner, safely transporting them to New York City, although vigorously pursued the entire route. At the time of his appointment to the Refugees, Ward had been busily employed gathering intelligence in Bergen and Orange Counties, enhancing his reputation as a bold partisan.

On May 1, 1780, Cuyler gathered up his corps in New York City, crossed the Hudson to Paulus Hook and marched eight miles north to Bull's Ferry. This site was picked for several reasons: the large amount of available wood for cutting, ease of ferrying the wood to New York City, defensibility in case of attack and relatively easy access to the interior of Bergen County. That last item was of importance for an unstated role of the corps: that of raiding the countryside. While the wood contract

Thomas Ward and the Woodcutters of Bergen

1904 drawing of the Bull's Ferry blockhouse. *Courtesy of Bergen County Historical Society.*

with the British would be lucrative, the additional need of food to eat and cash to purchase such things as medical supplies, weapons, tools, wagons, etc. would far exceed their initial revenue. The men put this to the test on their first foray into the countryside, raiding Closter on June 7, 1780. The thirty men involved were ordered "not on any Pretence whatever [to] Hurt or injure any of the well disposed loyal inhabitants" and "endeavor to Sieze Kill or Apprehend the Rebel Guards in that or any other part of the Country you may March through also every other disaffected person that is known to be Aiding or Assisting the Rebellion." Thus was started a cycle of raids and attacks that would rage throughout Bergen County and the adjacent countryside for the next two years.

One of the first orders of business at Bull's Ferry was to establish a post, in the form of a blockhouse. This small fortification was common in the eighteenth century as a place of defense against surprise or limited attack. Their work was inspected on July 11, 1780, by Lieutenant William Fyers of the British Corps of Engineers, who found a substantial two-story blockhouse mounting two four-pound cannons on the upper floor. A stockade (wall) surrounded the blockhouse to the edge of the Palisades, sixty feet in front of which was an abatis (sharpened stakes nine feet in length pointing outward).

The new post and its occupants did not go unnoticed by the rest of Bergen County. Major Lemuel Trescott, commander of the Continental army outpost at Paramus, reported on May 8, 1780, to George Washington on the arrival of the Refugees and sent a patrol to ascertain their strength and purpose for being there. For two weeks Trescott's command observed the Refugees, who during that time did nothing more odious than round up horses in English Neighborhood to equip a troop of light horse, then being raised under Captain Joshua Miller. Trescott requested permission from Washington to take his command and attack the post. Washington said it should not be attempted without an almost certain chance of success. Under that admonition, Trescott and his men stayed put at Paramus. The county's Whig inhabitants were likewise curious about the new threat on the west shore of the Hudson. On May 26, 1780, a party of Bergen County Militia, commanded by Captain Thomas Blanch, advanced clandestinely to the blockhouse with plans to, if possible, attack it. Realizing, as Major Trescott had before them, that the post was too strong for their numbers, they retired. Coming near the Three Pigeons tavern, they encountered between six and nine Loyalists. They killed John Berry of Hackensack (aka John or Jack "The Regular") along with another, and took prisoner a lieutenant and private. The prisoners captured were described as members of the New York City Militia. Berry was the stuff of folk legends in the county, whose veterans later recounted the Loyalist as having killed anywhere from thirteen to forty-eight Whigs!

The business at hand for the Refugees, however, was the cutting of wood and fulfilling contracts with the British in New York City. Already by June 24, Cuyler began to complain to Ward that the wood work was going too slow. Disagreements also started with the inhabitants on whose property the wood was being cut. The "Bergeneers," as the residents near the town of Bergen were known, were often paid less than the stipulated price. Other inhabitants of Bergen County, desirous of British gold, had for years brought their produce clandestinely to New York City to sell at market. With the blockhouse at Bull's Ferry, however, the Refugees there insisted on buying the goods at a reduced price, or trading for merchandise they had stockpiled in their post.

THE ATTACK ON BULL'S FERRY BLOCKHOUSE

All this was irrelevant to the Continental army and the Pennsylvania troops serving under Brigadier General Anthony Wayne. Encamped at Totowa in July 1780, Wayne devised a plan to collect cattle for Washington's army and to destroy the blockhouse at Bull's Ferry. On July 21, Wayne led a force of 2,000 infantry, cavalry and artillery, including about 90 state troops commanded by Major John Mauritius Goetschius of Schraalenburgh, over New Bridge with a grand plan to attack the Refugees. Stationing half his force to guard the approaches at Fort Lee, the roads leading up from Paulus Hook and covering New Bridge, Wayne took his remaining three regiments and the artillery and started a furious bombardment on the blockhouse. Just the day before, Cuyler had warned Ward to abandon the post if a force with artillery was sent against him. Seeing it was too late for that, Ward positioned the 115 officers and men under his command throughout the attack and prepared to repulse an attack by seasoned troops outnumbering his by 10 to 1.

The attack was started by a ferocious artillery barrage that lasted ninety minutes or more. Four six-pound field pieces were advanced to within seventy yards of the blockhouse, with each gun hurling 110 shots into it, dismantling the Refugee's artillery pieces and killing four or six men in the upper story. Moses N. Combs of Newark, one of the artillerists, later described the desperate battle: "I was with the last gun that retreated when but three men beside myself were left to manage the gun, the rest having all been killed or wounded—or employed in carrying off the wounded and dead. Of our 4 horses, one was killed & two wounded. Two men who served the cartridges were shot. I served the remainder until the last was expended."

The effect of the artillery was disputed afterward. Wayne said the six-pound iron cannon balls bounced off the wooden blockhouse. British Commander in Chief Sir Henry Clinton, who visited the post the next day, counted fifty-two holes in just one wall. Even the British adjutant general, the famous John André, commented on the discrepancy in his commemorative poem of the event, called "The Cow Chase": "No shot could pass, if you will take The Gen'ral's Word for true; But 'tis a d----ble Mistake, For ev'ry Shot went thro'."

Not seeing any advantage in continuing the attack, as well as receiving word that reinforcements may be coming from Kingsbridge to aid the Refugees, Wayne ordered his troops to be drawn off. However, through either confusion or a disregard for the orders, Lieutenant Colonel Thomas Robinson of the First Pennsylvania Regiment, with an "extreme excess of bravery," led on his corps and the Second Pennsylvanians in a futile charge against the abatis, stockade and blockhouse. The Pennsylvanians would find no easy way into the blockhouse. From within, Ward had his men keep up an incessant fire until nearly all their ammunition was gone. After fifteen terrifying minutes, Robinson ordered a retreat; his horse was shot in two places and "his Coat riddled by Musket ball & buck shott."

For Anthony Wayne, it was a humiliating and costly defeat. Indeed, July 21 was the bloodiest day of the war in Bergen County. "This act of intemperate valour," as George Washington termed it, cost the Continental army at least sixty-four dead and wounded, including eighteen-year-old Lieutenant Jacob M. DeHart of the Second Pennsylvania Regiment.

The British were rather astonished that Ward and his woodcutters had actually survived, let alone beat Wayne and his force. Ward's total loss was perhaps six killed, and anywhere from six to fifteen wounded. André continued his taunt of the U.S. accounts and their contention that the work had been proof against artillery: "Five Refugees ('tis true) were found Stiff on the block house floor, But then 'tis thought the shot went round, And in at the back door." Staff Captain F.A.J. von Wagenheim of the Hessian Jäger Corps wrote home to Germany: "These men [the Refugees] defended and deported themselves better than the sharpest, best-trained officers with the best troops. In Europe they would have made the name of their commander eternally famous, and this was done by farmers. I am concerned that this event will receive no recognition in Europe, but it happened just the way I described." Sir Henry Clinton took the extraordinary step of not just publicly and personally thanking Ward and the Refugees, but also sending home an account of the action to Lord George Germain, the secretary of state for American affairs. Germain called the action a "very extraordinary instance of courage" and reported the action to King George III himself, who "approved" of their "intrepid behaviour."

The Revolutionary War in Bergen County

THE KING'S MILITIA VOLUNTEERS

Although the woodcutters were the toast of the town, the fame indeed proved fleeting. The business relationship between Cuyler and Ward quickly deteriorated after the attack at Bull's Ferry, with charges that much of the wood at the post was being secretly shipped to private hands in the city and sold on the black market. By August 6, Cuyler told Ward and the others to "Stop all unfair Practices" or he would govern himself accordingly. It was irrelevant anyway, as a few days later the British ordered the post abandoned, leaving six hundred cords of firewood on the ground. Cuyler, having no interest in continuing his dealings with Ward and some of the other officers, used this circumstance to terminate the contract. Thomas Ward and the remainder of his now nearly defunct corps would need a new benefactor. They did not search long before finding one.

William Franklin, the last royal governor of New Jersey and president of the newly created Board of Associated Loyalists, was a man in search of a military. The Associated Loyalists was intended to be a political body coordinating all aspects of Loyalist politics and activity that did not fall under the control of the British commander in chief. Franklin had spent over two years as a prisoner in Connecticut, during which time his wife passed away, leaving him bitter toward those who had imprisoned him. Upon his exchange in November 1778, Franklin immediately sought to organize companies of Refugees for military service outside the formal control of the British military. Thousands of Loyalists were already serving in Provincial regiments, corps modeled, uniformed, armed, paid, disciplined and provisioned the same as British soldiers, and most importantly, subject to the commands and orders of the military. This led to extended periods of mundane garrison duty and only limited opportunities of combat against their Rebel countrymen. Hoping to employ those Loyalists who either wished a more active form of service or who, from their station in life, were unsuited to serve as private regular soldiers earning six pence a day, Franklin drew together an interesting collection of officers and men, including a number from Bergen County.

While the focus of the corps under Franklin's patronage would still be the cutting of wood for profit, the military aspects would become better organized and more aggressive in their forays. For six months, the period between September 1780 and March 1781, the Board of Associated Loyalists sponsored Ward and his corps, providing them with arms, artillery, entrenching tools, armed and transport shipping and, most importantly, a powerful lobbyist with the British.

The new base of operations would be Bergen Point, modern Bayonne, on the southern tip of Bergen Neck, opposite Decker's Ferry, Staten Island. It offered some protection from the northern approaches by the post at Paulus Hook, with the rest protected by water. These barriers to attack would be needed, as their new fortification was a sad replacement for the formidable work at Bull's Ferry that had served them so well.

By the spring of 1781, the situation at Bergen Point was becoming untenable, for local inhabitants were growing increasingly hostile. Constant complaints were being made to the British in New York, causing work slowdowns and disruptions for depositions and investigations. By early March, the inhabitants refused to let any more wood be cut on their property unless the price was raised from one dollar per cord to three. Without work, Ward once again needed to find other means of support and accordingly, on the evening of March 11, marched 160 men of the corps with a field piece north to attack the blockhouse defending the ferry crossing at Sneden's Landing on the New Jersey–New York border. Intercepted en route by Captain Thomas Blanch and a party of Bergen County Militia, Ward's force never advanced beyond Closter, three miles shy of their destination, where they contented themselves with gathering cattle and plundering some property from the Whig inhabitants.

This expedition was the last function of the corps as a part of Franklin's Associated Loyalists. The separation was precipitated by the wording of the commissions as proposed by both the board and Sir Henry Clinton, which was rejected by Ward and the officers under his command. Franklin asked for and eventually received the arms and accoutrements he had procured on their behalf.

Now free from higher authority and seeking a short-term solution to their financial woes, Ward proposed returning to Bull's Ferry where they would remove (and sell) the wood left behind the previous August. That may have been the purpose for a foray into the county on May 5 that seemed to accomplish little more than gathering provisions and inflicting a few casualties on the militia. A complete change of venue, one closer to the heart of the county, was in order.

THE REFUGEES AT FORT LEE

On the morning of May 14, 1781, a fleet of small vessels carrying over two hundred Refugees arrived off Fort Lee. After landing with their artillery and horses, the troops marched into English Neighborhood and dispersed a militia picket posted there. A party of militia returned later that day to find the Refugees had started work on a new blockhouse, built upon the remains of old Fort Lee. They commenced firing from a "stone house" a hundred yards away, but the Refugees stormed the house and drove them out.

Colonel Theunis Dey, from his home in Preakness, put out the call for the militia. In a gathering not seen since the beginning of the war, hundreds of militia flocked from across the county, joined by state troops stationed at Hackensack. They knew a post at Fort Lee would give Ward's men a perfect vantage point to range far into the countryside, bringing the war into every corner of the county. The fort was, as Private Harman Blauvelt of Harrington recalled it, "a nest of Tories, Refugees and British."

After rendezvousing at Liberty Pole, Colonel Dey led as many as four hundred men to attack the Refugees at Fort Lee. They engaged in a spirited contest, but the militia was again driven off, once more retiring to Liberty Pole to lick their wounds and count their losses. (Among them was Private John Devoe of Hackensack, who was taken prisoner *after* being shot, bayoneted, clubbed *and* cut down by a cavalryman's sword. He not only survived his ordeal but was exchanged and serving again in about seven weeks.)

The Revolutionary War in Bergen County

Edmund Moderacki surveys construction of the blockhouse while refugees continue working during the 225th anniversary of the Fort Lee blockhouse battle, 2006. *Courtesy of Susan Braisted.*

For the next couple of days there was a lull in the fighting—giving Ward and his Refugees a chance to fortify their position. For security, they retired to their ships each night, rather than stay on shore and be open to a surprise attack. Each morning the troops would land from their shipping and march up to the works, probably from the area that is now Edgewater. The militia, taking note of this routine, laid an ambush for them in the defiles leading up to the works. After initially capturing a lieutenant and a private of the Refugees, the militia pursued the fleeing Loyalist advance guard. Ward countered by bringing his artillery to bear on them; this, coupled with a flanking maneuver and bayonet charge, forced the militia to retire from the field. After five days, each side was stalemated: the militia could not force the Refugees away, and the latter could not spend enough time building their blockhouse.

George Washington, from his headquarters at New Windsor, New York, was apprised of the situation by May 17, when he ordered Colonel Alexander Scammell to proceed to Fort Lee and drive off the Refugees. Colonel Scammell was at the time in Westchester County, putting in order a new corps of Continentals formed to handle events such as this. This force proceeded across the river to Nyack where, to their

Thomas Ward and the Woodcutters of Bergen

surprise, no food was waiting for them. With no food of their own, Scammell and his men were delayed some time before provisions arrived from West Point.

The British high command in New York City was well aware of the fighting at Fort Lee, as well as Colonel Scammell's moves and his intention of attacking the Refugees. Sir Henry Clinton, the British commander, ordered almost two thousand crack troops in motion, including cavalry, Hessian riflemen and the Loyalist New Jersey Volunteers, many of whom were also from Bergen County. Sir Henry at the same time dispatched his adjutant general, Lieutenant Colonel Oliver DeLancey Jr. to Fort Lee to assess the situation for himself. DeLancey reported that the Refugees had made little progress in fortifying their position, and that he doubted their ability to do so in the future. Clinton ordered Ward to cease his efforts and return to their shipping. Grudgingly, the Refugees left Fort Lee for good. The other troops were ordered to return to their quarters, thus ending the chance for a major clash of armies.

Scammell and his men, finally fed, remained unaware that the Refugees were on the point of withdrawing. From Nyack, his corps proceeded south as far as Closter, where an immense rainstorm not only soaked the men, but also wetted their ammunition. There Scammell would have to stay, spending the night in wet clothes, sharing barns with the farmers' livestock. On the morning of May 22, examining the state of his men and their arms, he determined they were in no shape for any action and reluctantly ordered them north to Tappan. He was heartened, however, to hear from an officer he had sent to scout Fort Lee that the Refugees had abandoned their position and were on board their shipping. So ended the Fort Lee experiment.

Despite all the setbacks and missteps, Ward's men were still the primary source of wood coming into the British lines. The safety and security of the corps and their important work was in the British army's interest. With that in mind, the British on May 23 dispatched Major Archibald Robertson, an accomplished engineer, along with Major Oliver DeLancey Jr., the adjutant general, over to Bergen Neck to meet with Ward to fix on a new post there, about three or four miles above their old post at the point. Their fourth establishment would be dubbed Fort DeLancey in honor of their visitor, and would prove the last outpost the corps would occupy.

Over the ensuing summer the Refugees grew in strength to 344 officers and men, organized in eight companies. The woodcutting proceeded at an accelerated pace. Between July 3 and 16, 1781, a total of 220¾ cords of wood were delivered to the Barrack Master General's Department from the post at Bergen Neck, earning the Refugees £884, 5 shillings.

In addition to procuring vital supplies, the Refugees undertook more important military operations, requested specifically by the British command in New York City. Throughout the end of July and all of August 1781, Ward and his men conducted patrols large and small in efforts to find out whether or not the massing Continental-French army under Washington was positioning itself to attack New York. Ward, now going by the rank of major, received his first orders on July 29, requesting patrols be sent as far north on the road to Snedens Ferry as was safe.

September started no differently than August had left off, with more raids. Captain William Harding quietly led eleven Refugees up to Closter, where

Sergeant Benjamin Romaine of the militia lay with some others. Romaine later recalled the terror of that night:

On the 6th day of September 1781, myself with five others, while in arms at Closter, was taken by surprize of the enemy, who was led to the place of our nightly seclusion, to which we were accustomed to retire, when off of duty, not daring to Sleep in our houses. This place of seclusion was in the thick woods, and near it were driven our horses and cattle for safety. They were led to it by one Samuel Cole, who perpetrated this act of treachery: he was of Closter, a Tory resident of our neighborhood. He led on the enemy in his own person, we were made prisoners, though not then in actual enlistment, and with our horses and cattle were hastened down to this City, where we were put in prison and held for seven weeks. Our exchange was effected nearly the exact time Cornwallis was taken, we returned to our homes, and I entered on military duty in my company beat as theretofore and continued therein till the end of the war. At our capture, one Elias Day was pierced through the thigh with a bayonet, and myself was slightly wounded in the arm with a like weapon, by Captain William Arden [sic: Harding] the Chief of the Gang; who saith, it was only his intention to make me feel a little for abusing Sam Cole, their Guide.

The approaching end of the war presented familiar challenges and difficulties to the Refugees. While their particular form of *petit guerre* took its toll on the inhabitants of Bergen County, it did little to affect the larger course of the war being played out at Yorktown, Virginia. The only appreciable part Ward played in the abortive British attempt to rescue Cornwallis and his army in Virginia was possibly filling a request for wood for the fleet taking Sir Henry Clinton's army southward. But the greatest battle Ward would fight was not with militia or Continental soldiers, but rather with the inhabitants on Bergen Neck whose wood his men had cut.

For the last half of 1781, just about every British or Loyalist figure of authority in New York City received complaints from about fifteen to twenty households on Bergen Neck where Ward's men were cutting wood. After enough complaints came in, Abraham Cuyler was appointed to enquire into the matter. After two days of meeting with the aggrieved inhabitants as well as Ward and his principal officers, plus a tour of the lands, it appeared to them that nearly £9,000 was due for the wood cut by the Refugees. That money was owed directly by Ward and his agents, as they had been paid by the Barrack Master's office for all the wood delivered. Ward in turn used a variety of tactics to delay or avoid paying the inhabitants. A court of enquiry, composed of two Loyalist field officers and two prominent civilians, was convened and found that the sum of £3,577 and change was still due from Ward to the inhabitants, an amount far less than that claimed but still far more than Ward could afford to pay. Van Schaack would still be pleading his clients' case in 1784 in England, long after the end of the war.

While the surrender of Cornwallis's army at Yorktown brought an end to the major campaigns of the Revolution, the end of the war was still two years away. An April 30, 1782 order from Sir Henry Clinton put an end to offensive hostilities in the New York City area. For the Refugees, it meant no more excursions for the purpose of rounding

Thomas Ward and the Woodcutters of Bergen

up cattle (or plunder). Ward found himself at the end of a lawsuit instigated on behalf of the inhabitants whose wood the Refugees had cut. The cloud of debts and lawsuits hanging over him was almost certainly a factor in a decision to once again change location. This time, however, the Refugees would not be switching locales in New Jersey, but rather have the dubious honor of becoming the first Refugees from the New York area to seek asylum in Nova Scotia. The *New Jersey Journal* happily reported in its October 9 edition, "Last Saturday the groveling Major Ward, with his nefarious motley crew of refugees, fell down from New York, bound to Nova Scotia. They carry with them a year's provision, and implements of husbandry." The departure of Loyalists for Nova Scotia would become commonplace the following year. What made Ward's departure unique was that it came well before any preliminary treaty of peace had been signed recognizing the independence of the United States.

Thomas Ward settled with his family in Digby, Nova Scotia, along with some members of his former corps. The only woodcutting the Refugees would be doing there was clearing their new land and building homes for their families. What was the legacy of the woodcutters' thirty-month career? While their excesses were of no small distress to the militia and Whig inhabitants of Bergen County (and more than a few Loyalists), they were an absolute necessity for the British. As William Crosbie, the British barrack master general, noted in August 1781, "Were it not for the exertions of the Refugees under Major Ward and Captain Harding at Bergen Point, who have received from the Commander in Chief every encouragement to persevere in this business, and to whom I pay ten Dollars a Cord, I could not, from any other resource, that I have knowledge of, carry the Army thro' half the approaching Winter Weeks."

The Hanging of Major André

Steve Kelman

And now I've closed my epic strain,
I tremble as I show it,
Lest this same warrio-drover, Wayne,
Should ever catch the poet.
—"The Cow Chase," by Major John André

The third canto of the "Cow Chase," a satirical poem written by British Major John André about the Bull's Ferry Raid, was published in Rivington's Gazette the same day André himself was captured carrying incriminating documents given to him by the traitorous Benedict Arnold. After a trial, André was sentenced to death by hanging, as the Patriot spy Nathan Hale had been a few years earlier. Unlike most British military men, André was well educated, spoke four languages fluently (including Dutch), wrote poetry, painted and studied music and dance. He reportedly "went a-courting" throughout Bergen County during the Revolutionary War. He joined the British army when he was twenty, and by thirty he was General Howe's chief of intelligence. Among other Bergen County events, he was involved in the Baylor Raid.

By the morning of his execution, October 2, 1780, Major John André, the British spymaster, had resigned himself to his fate as a convicted spy. André had, of course, been part of the most treacherous betrayal in American history—he had plotted with the American traitor General Benedict Arnold to turn over the West Point garrison to the British. If this plot had succeeded, the American Revolution would most surely have been dealt a fatal blow.

Waking early in his room at Mabie's Tavern, the current location of the '76 House Restaurant in Tappan, New York, André busied himself by "making a self portrait without a mirror, the figure full face sitting at a table." He presented the sketch to one of his guards, Jabez Tomlinson of Connecticut, who later presented the drawing to Yale University.

The Hanging of Major André

André had requested that he have an honorable soldier's execution—death by firing squad—but was essentially kept in the dark as to his fate until moments before. General George Washington, who was in his headquarters at the nearby DeWint House, was first inclined to grant him his request.

Four days earlier, on September 29, André had been sentenced to death after what was a speedy but thorough trial. The trial took place inside the Old Dutch Church, a stone's throw from Mabie's Tavern, where André would live out his last days under constant guard. The church had previously served as a military hospital for Washington's forces after the Battle of Harlem Heights in 1776.

For the trial, Washington had appointed one of his most trusted generals, Nathanael Greene, to serve as president of the board, one that also included Generals Marquis de LaFayette, Frederick Von Steuben and Henry Knox. Colonel Alexander Hamilton was the secretary during the proceedings.

The main charge against André centered on the fact that he had entered American lines "in a private and secretive manner." It was Greene who had argued against putting André to death by firing squad, while the rest of the generals on the board were inclined to grant it.

According to local author Jules Loh in his booklet *Treason—The Arnold–André Plot*, Greene spelled out his reasoning: "André is either a spy or an innocent man. If the latter, to execute him in any way would be murder. If the former, the mode of death is prescribed by law." Greene went on to state that because of the "alarming crisis of our affairs," the public safety called for a "solemn and impressive example. Nothing can satisfy it short of execution of the prisoner as a common spy," he proclaimed. That meant hanging.

André's date with the executioner came ten days after his capture on September 23 by a local militia group. He had been traveling under an alias, John Anderson, and had been en route to White Plains, the location of the closest British lines. By a quirk of fate he was stopped near Tarrytown while wearing civilian clothes, questioned and searched. Guards found in his boots detailed drawings containing sensitive information about the troops, armaments and defense at West Point. There were twelve in all—six in each stocking.

Major André had received the incriminating documents from Benedict Arnold, the commander at West Point, the night before his capture. The British had offered Arnold a fee of £10,000 British for them. Arnold's betrayal was an extremely serious matter, for Washington regarded West Point as "the linchpin of the Hudson corridor and therefore the most strategic location in the entire northern theater."

When he received word of André's capture, Arnold fled to British lines; André was turned over to Major Benjamin Tallmadge, an American intelligence officer, and kept under heavy guard. The two spymasters would spend the next few days together. They had much in common and reportedly got on well together.

André was first taken to Fort Putnam, one of the West Point strongholds, and then later to Stony Point. From there he marched with Tallmadge and a squad of one hundred dragoons to Washington's headquarters in Tappan.

Years later, Tallmadge recalled his time with André in a letter. "He was very inquisitive to know my opinion as to the result of his capture…I endeavored to evade

The Mabie Tavern (Old '76 House) in Tappan today. *Courtesy of Ira Lieblich.*

the question." In this same letter, Tallmadge described his friendship with Nathan Hale, the Patriot spy hanged by the British. "I said to him that I had a much loved classmate at Yale College who entered the army with me in the year 1776 by the name of Nathan Hale." Then Tallmadge recalled that he asked André if he remembered Hale's fate, to which André replied that he had been hanged as a spy. "But surely you do not consider his case and mine alike," André said. Tallmadge responded by saying that the two cases were "precisely similar and similar will be your fate." Tallmadge then observed that André became "more troubled than I had ever seen him before." The two cases were quite similar indeed. Like Hale, André had "been caught red handed in the act of espionage and could not escape his fate."

Barnet Schecter, in his 2003 book *The Battle for New York*, noted that "André not only fit the same profile as Hale (who was also captured wearing civilian clothes) but was captured and executed under strikingly similar circumstances." Unlike André, Hale, who was caught scouting out enemy positions in Brooklyn, was not even brought before a tribunal of officers, as André had been.

André spent the last hours of his life passing time with his guards inside of Mabie's Tavern. His last breakfast arrived from the DeWint House at eight and was prepared by Washington's steward, Samuel Fraunces, who had prepared all of André's meals throughout his confinement at Mabie's to ensure their valuable charge wasn't poisoned.

The Hanging of Major André

André Hill Marker, site of execution. *Courtesy of Ira Lieblich.*

After his final meal, André packed all of his belongings into two trunks, gave the keys to his servant Peter Laune and told him where he wanted them delivered. The servant handed André his familiar red British regimental uniform that he would wear as he marched to the gallows.

In all, about fifteen hundred soldiers and onlookers witnessed the hanging, which took place at high noon on October 2, 1780, on a hill behind the tavern. When the time came, André told his guards, "Gentlemen, I am now ready to obey your call."

With that, each officer took an arm and the three men stepped outside the door and began the walk to the hanging trees. According to reports, when André caught sight of the gallows he became startled and hesitated in his step. His guard gripped his arm and asked, "Why the emotion, Sir?" to which he responded, "I am reconciled to my death but I detest the mode."

Tallmadge, who had been André's constant companion in the days leading up to his execution, was among the many officers who attended the execution. Washington, however, would have no part of it, choosing instead to draw the blinds so he would not have to witness the event. Washington, who had great admiration for André as both a person and an officer, wrote French General Rochambeau, in a letter dated October 10, 1780, that André was "more unfortunate than criminal. While we yielded to the necessity of rigor, we could not but lament it."

Today the hill where André was hanged is a residential street called André Hill, located off Old Tappan Road. At the top of the hill is a commemorative marker that reads, "His death, according to the stern code of war, moved even his enemies to pity and both armies mourned the fate of one so young and brave." His remains were moved to Westminster Abbey in 1821.

Mabie's Tavern, where André lived out the last hours of his life, is still in operation today as the '76 House Restaurant and is one of the oldest continuously operating taverns in the United States. The restaurant, the church where the trial took place, the monument and the DeWint House (Washington's headquarters) are all located within the Tappan Historical District.

WEBSITE OF INTEREST

http://www.76house.com/history_tavern.html

Steve Kelman is a reporter for a weekly newspaper in Bergen County covering the towns of Bergenfield, Dumont and New Milford. He often covers stories of historic interest in the county. He also writes a feature column for a monthly journal called Prime Times. *A lifelong history buff, he grew up in Northvale, two blocks from the Tappan, New York border.*

W3R: The March to Win a War

Carol W. Greene

At the 2007 Bergen County Historic Preservation Award Ceremony, Carol Greene was directly involved with five of the awards given out for her efforts on behalf of the 225th anniversary celebration of the Washington-Rochambeau Revolutionary Route (W3R) of 1781, when seven thousand American and French troops marched four months to Yorktown. She writes of this march, and the reenactment in 2006, here.

In 2006, New Jersey and eight other states observed the 225th anniversary of the Washington-Rochambeau march of 1781. Their celebrations took place under the banner of "W3R," which stands for the Washington-Rochambeau Revolutionary Route of 1781—the road taken by allied American and French soldiers on their "March to Victory" at Yorktown, Virginia. The battle fought there turned the tide of the Revolution, ultimately leading to America's independence from England.

We know why Britain's King George III was involved in this fight: the intractable American colonies were, after all, part of his empire. But a question everyone asks is, "Why did the French get involved in the American War for Independence?"

Let us begin our story with Benjamin Franklin, celebrated American scientist, inventor, philosopher and printer—as well as a shrewd, artful player in the game of foreign diplomacy. He had traveled to France on behalf of the colonies in December 1776 to seek French aid against the British. To a degree, he succeeded. King Louis XVI was willing to covertly provide arms and money to the Continentals, even though he was cautious about openly entering the war.

At the time Franklin arrived in France, there was little sympathy in that country toward the rebellious American colonies. France had already been at war with Britain for almost a century, and it had suffered a humiliating defeat at British hands in the French and Indian War (1754–63). Thus, at the outset the American War for Independence was not a tempting enterprise for the French.

Franklin, however—in spite of his democratic beliefs and humble attire—was embraced by the French aristocracy for his amazing intellect, joie de vivre and a charming irreverence—not to mention the fact that he, like they, was an enemy of Britain. Settling into his home in the Paris suburb of Passy, Franklin bided his time, awaiting the right moment to persuade the King to make a more serious commitment to the American Revolution.

On December 4, 1777, momentous news reached the French court: American forces had achieved a stunning defeat of Burgoyne's British and Hessian army at Saratoga, New York. Now Franklin could urge the French to join the winning campaign in America. Would King Louis XVI be persuaded? After all, if France regained a foothold in America, the country would benefit from America's vastly rich resources—while Britain would be commensurately deprived.

The answer was not long in coming. France officially recognized American independence on February 6, 1778, when the two sovereign states signed the Treaty of Amity and Commerce, as well as the secret Treaty of Alliance, at Versailles. France promised to fight on the Americans' side, and to make no separate peace agreement until Britain formally recognized American independence.

While Franklin pursued diplomacy in France, General George Washington continued his valiant struggle on American soil. Since he was short on troops, funds and supplies, his strategy was to inflict damage upon the British whenever possible, but only if it could be done at minimal loss to the Americans. With the British under General Henry Clinton occupying New York City, Washington positioned troops in the Hudson Highlands and the hills of New Jersey. But he was restricted to fighting a war of attrition that the Continentals had little hope of winning.

The effectiveness of inserting French troops was uncertain—were there still hard feelings because of past hostilities? Yet help was sorely needed. Finally, on February 2, 1780, King Louis XVI approved a plan to send both ships and troops to America.

The plan was soon implemented. On May 2, 1780, 5,800 French troops under the command of Jean Baptiste Donatien de Vimeur, Comte de Rochambeau, set sail for America from Brest, on the western tip of Brittany. There were thirty-two transport vessels, and warships including seven ships of the line, two frigates and two smaller warships, with crews totaling about 7,000 sailors.

The convoy reached Narragansett Bay, Rhode Island, on July 11, 1780, but to the disappointment of the Continentals, the French troops were not ready to spring into action immediately. Many French sailors and soldiers were ill, mostly from scurvy, after more than two months at sea; they needed time to recover. Beyond that, a monumental task awaited the French quartermaster general: to assemble supplies, provisions, draft animals and horses for a probable land march of thousands of soldiers, and to set his French engineers and cartographers to work planning and preparing the march routes for French and Colonial troops.

Rochambeau, the French commander, was a distinguished veteran of many campaigns. He was fifty-five years old and known to be level-headed, able to compromise for the sake of the mission and willing to work with fellow officers—all characteristics crucial to cooperation with the Americans.

W3R: The March to Win a War

Comte de Rochambeau. *Courtesy of W3R-USA.*

When Rochambeau met with Washington on September 21, 1780, in Hartford, Connecticut, an immediate mutual respect developed between the two men. Some officers at this meeting, including the Marquis de Lafayette—and Washington himself, still stung by the memory of being routed from New York City by the British—favored a campaign to retake that important prize. But the planners had to concede that even with the additional French troops, such an operation could not succeed without French naval support.

On April 9, 1781, with winter having come and gone and no progress made, Washington wrote despairingly, "We are at the end of our tether, and…now or never our deliverance must come."

Rochambeau importuned the King for more money and a second division of infantry. The King did provide the funds, but he declined to send more troops, advising

The Revolutionary War in Bergen County

Admiral de Grasse's flagship, the *Ville de Paris*. *Courtesy of W3R-USA.*

Rochambeau instead to continue his efforts with Washington and to cooperate with Admiral de Grasse, whose fleet had left Brest for the West Indies on April 5, 1781.

On May 21–23, 1781, Washington and Rochambeau met at Wethersfield, Connecticut, to discuss joint strategy. Rochambeau favored a campaign in the Chesapeake, arguing that if British General Charles Cornwallis, who was occupying the Carolinas, could be lured into an engagement, the allies might inflict a decisive blow. An attack on New York City, on the other hand, was risky. Even if more French warships were available, they had a deeper draft (twenty-seven feet) than comparable British ships (twenty-two feet): the sand banks in New York Harbor, a significant obstacle, would restrict their movements to times of high tide.

Washington, however, still favored an operation to retake New York City. Since Clinton had dispatched troops to the Chesapeake in support of Cornwallis, it may have weakened New York defenses. Despite misgivings, Rochambeau agreed to Washington's plan. On May 28, 1781, he sent a message to Admiral de Grasse in Saint-Domingue (today's Haiti), urging him to sail north with all the troops he could transport, and to bring additional funds. Two weeks later, French land forces who were encamped at Newport set out for New York.

The French and Continental armies met in White Plains, and on July 22–23 they jointly conducted a "grand reconnaissance" of New York City to locate suitable avenues of approach and to identify the weak points in British defenses. But much to Washington's chagrin, the reconnaissance showed that recapture of the city was out of reach. On August 1, 1781, he wrote in his diary, "Therefore, I turned my views more seriously to an operation to the southward."

Meanwhile, Cornwallis had settled upon a base in the Chesapeake Tidewater—the small port of Yorktown, Virginia. It was a strategic site that could be easily supported by the Royal Navy, the source of supplies, reinforcements—and, if needed, a means of evacuation for British troops. If Cornwallis was to be trapped here, the French naval force would have to position itself between Cornwallis and the Royal Navy. Now, everything depended upon de Grasse.

In a letter dated July 28, de Grasse wrote to Rochambeau that he was en route to the Chesapeake, but that he could remain there only until October 15. De Grasse's letter reached the French headquarters at Philipsburg, New York, on August 14. Immediately, Rochambeau and Washington set a new plan into motion.

With barely any notice, thousands of soldiers, plus hundreds of vehicles, several thousand animals and miles of wagon trains carrying supplies, began the 450-mile march to Yorktown, Virginia.

On August 17, the first American forces crossed the Hudson River at Dobbs Ferry, followed the next day by more American infantry and the French artillery. The French infantry followed on August 19 via Peekskill and Stony Point, New York. Thus commenced the largest allied troop movement of the Revolutionary War: it was exquisitely timed, brilliantly orchestrated, amazing in its practical planning—and destined to succeed.

MARCHING THROUGH NEW JERSEY

As the allied American and French forces prepared to enter New Jersey, it was crucial to have the British think that New York City was targeted for attack. To accomplish this purpose, American scouts and patrols ranged back and forth in New York State just north of the city and on the west side of the Hudson River, in eastern Bergen County. Thus, while making a show of interest in New York, the Continental troops prevented enemy reconnaissance and kept allied commanders informed of British activities as the allied forces marched for Philadelphia

Washington cloaked the operation in deception by various means: inserting false information into communications likely to be intercepted by the British; building

March of Rochambeau's Troops through New Jersey*
August 26, 1781 – September 2, 1781

Date	Route	Miles
26 August	Suffern to Pompton Meeting House	15.0 miles
27 August	Pompton Meeting House to Whippany	14.5 miles
28 August	stay in Whippany encampment	-
29 August	Whippany to Bullion's Tavern (Liberty Corner)	16.0 miles
30 August	Bullion's Tavern (Liberty Corner) to Somerset Courthouse (Millstone)	13.0 miles
31 August	Somerset Courthouse (Millstone) to Princeton	15.0 miles
1 September	Princeton to Trenton	12.0 miles
2 September	Trenton to Red Lion Tavern, Pennsylvania	17.5 miles
	Total mileage	103.0 miles

Total of 103 miles on 7 marches, Suffern (8/26/1781) to Red Lion Tavern, PA (9/2/1781) this averages 14.71 miles per day's march (not counting 1 day of rest)

Total mileage in New Jersey only: appr. 86.5 miles

*Source: Howard C. Rice, Jr., and Anne S. K. Brown, *The American Campaigns of Rochambeau's Army 1780, 1781, 1782, 1783. Vol II: The Itineraries, Maps and Views.* (Princeton, NJ and Providence, RI: Princeton University Press and Brown University Press, 1972), itineraries pp. 52-74, maps 50-56 and maps 64-71.

Rochambeau march schedule through New Jersey. *Courtesy of Carol Greene.*

boats, supposedly to ferry the army to Staten Island; having foodstuffs delivered to Continental magazines (supply depots) in the area; spreading rumors that would be overheard by spies; and entrusting only a chosen few officers with the real plans.

The feint worked! Clinton remained convinced that New York City was the object of attack, and the massive troop movements of seven thousand soldiers along five routes into and through New Jersey took place unimpeded. Had the march been thwarted, the war could have been lost right here in Bergen County. On August 24, Major Sebastian Baumann's detachment marched into New Jersey through present-day Ringwood in Passaic County, en route to Pompton. The other four routes crossed into New Jersey via Bergen County. On August 25, 1781, General Moses Hazen and his New Jersey regiment marched from Sneden's Landing on the Hudson en route to Paramus, while on the same day General Benjamin Lincoln entered New Jersey at Suffern, briefly marched on the Ramapough valley road, turned down the King's Highway of 1703 (now Island Road—Franklin Turnpike) and proceeded south to join Hazen's forces in Paramus.

Also on August 25, Generals Washington and Lamb marched down the Ramapough valley road, from Suffern to Pompton. They were followed on August 26 by the First Brigade of Rochambeau's French forces from Suffern en route to Pompton. These troops had encamped in the area of Suffern's Tavern on the night of August 25.

The allied troops averaged fifteen miles a day, traveling at two and a half miles per hour. To avoid the summer heat, they sounded reveille about 2:00 a.m. and

W3R: The March to Win a War

commenced the day's march by 4:00 a.m. Only occasionally did they rest a day or two at the same place. The campsites were located twelve to fifteen miles apart, which meant that the columns would arrive at their new location about noon. This allowed local inhabitants to get a firsthand look at the dashing French soldiers, and to sell provisions to them. People were glad to deal with the French, because they traveled with wagonloads of silver and paid handsomely for needed supplies.

The Americans, on the other hand, were severely underfunded and had only scrip money, which people were reluctant to trust. Unfortunately, many damage claims were later brought by citizens against the Continental army for lost livestock and property. Sometimes people locked their doors when they saw the army coming, and hid their horses so they wouldn't be confiscated.

There were poignant disparities between the Continental and French armies. Sometimes the Continentals could not afford uniforms and dressed poorly—often, indeed, they lacked shoes. Their rations were scant, and some have maintained that the American army was left to starve. During encampments, the Americans had to ask local inhabitants for the use of their ovens to bake bread, while the French simply paid to have the bread baked for them.

The French troops were not only well fed, but they also had unusually beautiful uniforms and regimental flags in glorious colors. There were a number of regiments, each led by noblemen: les Régiment de Saintonge, de Royal Deux-Ponts, de Bourbonnais et de Soissonnais; les Régiments d'artillerie d'Auxonne et de Metz; les Volontaires-étrangers de Lauzun ("Lauzun's Legion"); et les Régiments de Gâtinais, d'Agenais, de Touraine et de Dillon.

Wisely, Washington and Rochambeau had agreed at the outset of the alliance to keep the armies separate. The march routes through New Jersey and logistics of the troop movements reflect this policy. But whichever of the groups was passing through, they had a significant impact on the landscape.

Imagine the people in sparsely settled neighborhoods—maybe a dozen houses, if that—reacting to thousands of soldiers coming through on narrow dirt roads. It took hours for some of the columns to pass by; what an astonishing sight that must have been!

It took all divisions only nine days–from August 25 to September 2—to march the 86½ miles from the New York–New Jersey boundary line at Suffern/Mahwah to Trenton; from there they crossed the Delaware River into Pennsylvania.

WITNESS SITES

Historic sites that existed at the time of the march are called witness sites—and many still stand today as National Landmarks.

Prominent among them in Passaic County are Long Pond Ironworks and Ringwood Manor on Sloatsburg Road in Ringwood. Robert Erskine, Washington's surveyor-general, lived in an earlier house at the site and managed the Ringwood Company and the Ringwood Iron Mines until his premature death in 1780.

The Revolutionary War in Bergen County

Filling Canteens in the Ramapo Valley, Mahwah, by David R. Wagner. The setting for this painting is an original, eighteenth-century section of Ramapo Valley Road at Sun Valley Farm, near an old spring. The Ramapo River and Mountains are in the background. *Courtesy of David R. Wagner.*

In Bergen County, witness sites along Ramapo Valley Road—the primary W3R route—include:

THE HOPPER GRISTMILL SITE, Route 202, Mahwah. The mill served as a supply depot for Washington's clothier general, and provided troops with grain.
THE LAROE–HOPPER–VAN HORN HOUSE, Route 202, Mahwah, which dates to the mid-1700s.
THE HAVEMEYER MANSION, Route 202, Mahwah, across from Ramapo College. The site of Patriot Andrew Hopper's house. Washington was at the Hopper House on August 26, 1781. He left early in the day to pave the way for Rochambeau and the French army to march down Route 202 from Suffern, New York, where they were encamped.

W3R: The March to Win a War

EXTANT HOUSES OF JOHN MAY, GARRET GARRISON (now called "Waternook") AND JOHN BERTHOLF (now called "Amberfields"), Route 202, Mahwah.

EXTANT DEMAREST FAMILY DWELLING HOUSES, Route 202, Oakland.

THE VAN ALLEN HOUSE AND MILL, Route 202, Oakland, where Washington had headquartered July 14–15, 1777.

Among witness sites on the King's Highway of 1703 (Island Road–Franklin Turnpike, a secondary W3R route) are the following:

A SECTION OF THE ORIGINAL ROUTE OF THE KING'S HIGHWAY OF 1703, which lies in the cemetery behind the Education Building of the 1798 Ramapo Reformed Church, Mahwah—another eighteenth-century road section not covered over by pavement or destroyed by development.

SITE OF ROBERT ERSKINE'S BELLGROVE STORE, west of Island Road, Mahwah.

SITE OF LUTHERAN CHURCH BUILT PRIOR TO 1739, Island Road, Mahwah.

OLD STONE HOUSE, Island Road, Ramsey. This was a tavern where—according to local lore—Aaron Burr would stop on his way to the Hermitage.

"PETERSFIELD," Franklin Turnpike, Allendale. Residence of Continental Congress member John Fell.

Moving across New Jersey, by David R. Wagner. This painting shows troops at the Van Allen House in Oakland. Note the straw bundle on the pole at right. *Courtesy of David R. Wagner.*

The Revolutionary War in Bergen County

The Hermitage, Franklin Turnpike, Ho-Ho-Kus. It is here that Aaron Burr courted Theodosia Prevost.

Old Paramus Reformed Church, East Glen Avenue, Ridgewood. The predecessor to the current church structure served as a barracks and hospital during the Revolutionary War, and many soldiers who did not survive their wounds are buried in its cemetery.

"America's March to Yorktown"

Despite its importance to the ultimate success of America's quest for independence, the Washington-Rochambeau March of 1781 was relatively unknown—until 2006. Every child had heard of the Battle of Bunker Hill and the Boston Tea Party, but few Americans realized that the War for Independence lasted seven long years, and fewer still appreciated the enormity of effort and the complex logistics that marked the last major campaign of that war. Likewise, many know the names of Lafayette and Von Steuben as Europeans who came to our aid, but the names of Rochambeau and de Grasse, whose contributions were huge, are rarely mentioned.

All that changed in 2006, thanks in part to the efforts of a small group of history enthusiasts who call themselves the "America's March to Yorktown" (AMtY) reenactors. Not content to simply talk about their passion for Revolutionary War history, these reenactors put that passion into action: they undertook the monumental task of retracing the steps of the French and American forces all the way from Providence to Yorktown.

As much as possible, the group duplicated the marching and encampment schedule of the French and American forces 225 years earlier, which meant hikes averaging fifteen miles daily—rain or shine, with no recourse to vehicles. The marchers also strove for historical accuracy in other ways—sleeping in tents on the ground, eating the kind of rations that sustained the eighteenth-century troops and wearing the clothing those soldiers wore. To complement their Continental army and French regiment uniforms, they carried a thirteen-star American flag, a French Tricolor and a banner of the Bourbonnais Regiment.

Their quest for historical accuracy was greatly aided by the practical professionalism of Rochambeau's army, which included not only soldiers, but also scribes and mapmakers. These latter produced itineraries of the entire march, as well as beautiful maps depicting each day's march route and campsite in meticulous detail.

The itinerary is remarkably accurate, describing landscapes on Ramapo Valley Road that still exist today:

> *Passing several houses on the right, you ford this little river. The bridge is in bad condition. You then go uphill, the road turns right…The left-hand road goes to Paramus, Hackensack, etc.*

W3R: The March to Win a War

The AMtY marchers arrive at the New York–New Jersey border. *Courtesy of Tom Dater.*

The Revolutionary War in Bergen County

Here, after crossing the Mahwah River bridge, the reenactors with police and military escort march up the same hill mentioned in the Rochambeau itinerary. *Courtesy of Alex Rainer.*

The soldiers had to ford the Mahwah River near today's Brake Shoe Place. Now, the river flows under a modern bridge; but the road still goes uphill, and bears right; the left-hand turn is Island Road (the Kings Highway).

The itinerary continues:

> *Reaching a fork, take the right; the left-hand road leads into the New York road.*

The "New York road" is today's West Ramapo Avenue; it led to the Kings Highway, the traveled way to New York City.

Farther down Ramapo Valley Road, in Oakland,

> *The road runs mostly through the woods, along the side of the hill, up and down, and sometimes very bad. You reach Fallanel's [Van Allen's] Mill, where there is a pond on the left and a mill on the right.*

The terrain here is very irregular; surely, the soldiers stopped to rest at Van Allen's mill—as did the re-enactors on their modern-day march.

The AMtY reenactors' trek of six hundred plus miles was meant to raise public awareness of the historic march, and to encourage establishment of a nationally recognized Historic Trail along the primary march route (in Bergen County, Ramapo Valley Road) covering the nine states traversed by the allied American and French troops.

That process is still underway. "A bill to amend the National Trails System Act to designate the Washington-Rochambeau Route National Historic Trail" was introduced in both houses of Congress on July 26, 2006. Its supporters hoped to have it passed by October 2006, in time to commemorate the 225th anniversary of the Yorktown victory. Regrettably, Congress did not achieve that goal, but the legislation has been reintroduced in both houses, and the Senate held hearings on the issue in late April 2007. If the bill succeeds, the result will be an official National Historic Trail that includes a self-guided auto route, hiking trails, visitors' centers, signage and related literature, all of which will allow history-minded families to discover the W3R Route for themselves—though probably not entirely on foot, as the AMtY marchers did!

On August 25, 2006—225 years to the day after Generals Washington, Lincoln and Lamb did so—the reenactors crossed the New York–New Jersey state line at Suffern. And Mahwah, and Bergen County, were ready for them.

Despite torrential rain, the marchers were welcomed with a border crossing ceremony attended by many area residents, along with Bergen County Executive McNerney, Mahwah Mayor Martel and many other dignitaries. Also on hand were New York and New Jersey Girl and Boy Scouts who participated in a ceremonial flag hand-off across the state line, and VFW representatives from Suffern and Mahwah who passed the Light of Freedom—an actual copper lantern—from one state to the other.

As the reenactors and their "camp followers" headed south toward Pompton with the American red, white and blue, the French Tricolor and the blue, purple and white French Bourbonnais Regimental flag fluttering in the breeze, they were protected from vehicular traffic by police and military escorts fore and aft. There were colorful "W3R" highway signs and festive banners along Ramapo Valley Road.

In 1781, French engineers had marked the routes with straw bundles on top of poles as an "all clear" signal. For the occasion of the march 225 years later, bundles were tied to the W3R sign posts. The signs and banners are still in place as an ongoing reminder to area residents of Bergen County's significant role in the Revolution, and the epic march that echoed through the Ramapough Valley so long ago.

W3R REPORT BY DR. ROBERT SELIG

Much of the new information about the Rochambeau march through New Jersey was developed by Dr. Robert Selig, the nation's foremost authority on French involvement in the American War for Independence. In connection with the proposal to designate the Washington-Rochambeau Route a National Historic Trail, he was engaged by the National Park Service as its W3R consultant, and performed studies of all nine states along the route, including New Jersey.

The Revolutionary War in Bergen County

The W3R banners and signs—complete with straw bundles—still remain as a reminder of the Rochambeau march of 1781 and its reenactment in 2006. *Courtesy of Alex Rainer.*

Dr. Selig visited Mahwah and Bergen County numerous times to develop information on the march routes in this area, consulting with local historians Dick and Carol Greene, Tom and Joan Dater and others.

Dr. Selig's three-volume, nine-hundred-plus-page report, a treasure trove of original research, is available free of charge from the New Jersey Historic Trust, which funded the New Jersey study.

Special thanks to:
The AMtY marchers, for sharing their adventure with Bergen County.
Dr. Henry Bischoff, for his support of W3R events in Bergen County. Dr. Bischoff is an authority on the Revolutionary War in northern New Jersey, particularly the Ramapough Valley.

Dr. Robert Selig, for generously sharing his knowledge at lectures and during visits to New Jersey and Bergen County.

David R. Wagner, for permission to illustrate this text with his paintings. A Connecticut artist and historian, he has painted over fifty scenes interpreting the Washington-Rochambeau march, with focus on the French. Combining meticulous research, artistic talent and imagination, David Wagner brings alive the landscape of the Revolution.

WEBSITES OF INTEREST

www.W3R-NJ.com
www.W3R-US.org
www.MarchtoYorktown.org
www.americanrevolution.org
www.davidrwagner.com—"Revolutionary Route Series"

Carol W. Greene, a lifelong Mahwah resident, has served the cause of history education and historic preservation for more than twenty-five years. She was a longtime board member, and ultimately chair, of the New Jersey Historic Trust, and served for eighteen years on the Bergen County Historic Preservation Advisory Board. In Mahwah, she has been a member of the Historic Preservation Commission since 1980, and is a cofounder and past president of the Mahwah Museum Society. In 2007, the Bergen County Division of Cultural and Historic Affairs, Historic Preservation Advisory Board, awarded her the Claire Tholl Award for lifetime achievement in historic preservation. The Ramapough Chronicles, her history of northern Bergen County, is scheduled for publication in 2007. She is vice-chair of W3R-New Jersey. Her husband, Dick Greene, brought the eighteenth-century road at Sun Valley Farm to prominence, and with daughter Lindsey Greene coordinated W3R–AMtY march events there on August 25, 2006.

BLACK LOYALISTS IN BERGEN COUNTY AND "THE BOOK OF NEGROES"

Arnold E. Brown

Slavery was widespread in Bergen County before, during and long after the Revolutionary War. Most Jersey Dutch managed their large and prosperous farms with the assistance of slaves imported from Africa and the West Indies. Initially, slaves weren't allowed to join the American army, but after the British offered them freedom in 1775, Washington changed his tune and welcomed them. Those who sided with the British, the black Loyalists, were evacuated to Nova Scotia at the end of the war; those who fought for America were granted their freedom in some states, but not in New Jersey. In 1800, New Jersey had more slaves than ever, with most of them in northern New Jersey. It wasn't until 1804 that New Jersey passed its first abolition law, an Act for the Gradual Abolition of Slavery. New Jersey was the last Northern state to pass such a bill.

Enslaved Africans sought their lost freedom as they struggled against their captors in Africa, while in slaveholding pens awaiting sea-bound slave ships, while they crossed the cruel middle passage and until the moment they landed in the North American colonies. They took the opportunity brought on by the Revolutionary War to again seek their freedom. Some slaves sought freedom through service to the American armies; far more joined the British forces of King George III of England. In the early 1770s, when talk of freedom from the British ran high, there was much slave restlessness in New Jersey, and they too became outspoken about their own freedom. Race relations were strained, and many farmers feared slave uprisings. On July 10, 1775, the Continental Congress decreed that no "stroller, Negro or vagabond" might enlist in the military. On November 7, 1775, the royal governor of Virginia, John Murray, Earl of Dunmore, was forced to declare martial law and flee due to the American Rebels. While he was aboard the ship *William* off Norfolk, Virginia, directing his loyal forces, he issued a proclamation, declaring in part: "All indentured servants, negroes, or others (appertaining to Rebels) free, that are able and willing to bear arms, they joining His Majesty's troops, as soon as may be, for the more speedily reducing this colony to a proper sense of their duty, to His Majesty's Crown and dignity."

Black Loyalists in Bergen County and "The Book of Negroes"

Historic marker regarding slave cemetery in Leonia, Broad and Vreeland Avenues. *Courtesy of Carol Karels.*

This call to arms brought an immediate three hundred free and enslaved Africans to Murray's side. His Ethiopian Regiment was formed and their crest of arms was "Liberty to Slaves," which became a British slogan. Word that enslaved Africans would be freed upon a British victory quickly spread throughout the African American community in both Northern and Southern states. Those who aided the British, either out of loyalty to the Crown or for the hope and promise of liberty, were called "black Loyalists."

The Americans feared that hordes of enslaved Africans would desert their masters and join the British forces, thereby obtaining their freedom. The Americans countered by opening the way for free blacks to serve in the Continental army. This led the way for various states to make provisions for the use of blacks, free and slave, in the military. Black men and women who joined served as cooks, nurses, scouts, Indian interpreters, wagon drivers, trench diggers, foragers, pilots and guards. Later, men often fought alongside whites in battle.

The British did much to encourage black slaves to flee from their owners. Daniel Jones, chief of the New York Police Department, issued an order on June 7, 1779, as follows: "All Negroes that fly from the enemy's Country are free. No person whatever can claim a right to them. Whoever sells them shall be prosecuted with the utmost severity."

On June 30, 1779, British Commander in Chief Sir Henry Clinton issued a proclamation from headquarters at Phillipsburg: "I do most strictly forbid any Person to sell or claim Right over any NEGROE, the property of a Rebel, who may take refuge with any part of this Army; and I do promise to every Negro who shall desert the Rebel Standard, full security to follow within these Lines, any Occupation which he shall think proper."

The wave of runaways became so great that Major General James Pattison had his aide write a letter dated May 25, 1780, indicating that "not only the Male but Female Negroes with Children take advantage of your Post in New Jersey, to run away from Masters and come into this City…they must become a burden to the Town…The General therefore requests you will be so good as to prevent their passing the North River."

At the close of the Revolutionary War, peace negotiations were conducted in Paris. In some colonies, African slaves who served for three years in the military were given their freedom, and their masters were paid full compensation for the loss of their slave. Other enslaved Africans who served in the state militia as substitutes for their masters were returned to slavery after the war. One such person was Samuel Charlton, who was born into slavery in English Neighborhood, Bergen County, circa 1760. Samuel served as a substitute for his owner in the New Jersey Militia. He served in the baggage train and after the war he returned home to enslavement. When his owner died he was freed and given a pension.

On November 30, 1782, a Provisional Peace Agreement was signed between His Majesty's government and the United States of America. The Americans were pressured by the slave holding gentry to protect their property rights in their enslaved Africans. This resulted in the creation of Article VII, which stipulated:

> *All Hostilities both by Sea and Land shall from henceforth cease all prisoners on both sides shall be set at Liberty and His Britannic Majesty shall with all convenient Speed and without Causing any destruction or carrying away any Negroes or other property of the American Inhabitants withdraw all his Armies, Garrisons, and Fleets, from the said United States.*

New York City was the last place that the British occupied. Sir Guy Carleton, commander in chief of His Majesty's forces, was responsible for the evacuation of New York City by the British forces. He interpreted the Provisional Peace Agreement to mean that blacks who were already with the British before November 30, 1782, and who claimed freedom by the proclamation were free, and therefore could not be considered as American property on that date. Only confiscated slaves and those who came after the Peace Agreement were covered by Article VII.

General George Washington interpreted Article VII as meaning that any slave who had at any time been owned by an American was American property, and therefore was required to be left behind as the British evacuated the United States. There was great clamor among the slave owners, for they feared that the British would take all runaway slaves with them. General George Washington insisted that Sir Guy Carleton meet with him at Orangetown, Rockland County, New York. On May 6, 1783, they

Black Loyalists in Bergen County and "The Book of Negroes"

met at the home of John DeWint. Sir Guy Carleton took the position that he would evacuate any slave pleading the Proclamation. He stated that he would keep a written record of all blacks being removed from New York City so that compensation could be paid to legitimate American claimants.

General Washington acceded to Sir Guy Carleton's position and they created a Board of Inquiry with representatives from both sides. The Black Loyalists were brought before the Board of Inquiry, which assembled at Fraunces Tavern in downtown New York City every Wednesday between 10:00 a.m. and 2:00 p.m. Brigadier General Samuel Birch went around town and issued certificates to every black who could prove the minimum residence required. His certificates were based upon the proclamation issued in 1779 by the British commanders in chief, Sir Henry Clinton and Sir William Howe, who promised "every Negro who shall desert the Rebel Standard, full security to follow within these lines, any occupation which he shall think proper."

"THE BOOK OF NEGROES"

The ships were inspected by the British and Americans for the names of all black persons departing from New York City for Nova Scotia. This record is known as "The Book of Negroes, Book 1 and 2." It is also known as the *Inspection Roll of Negroes*. It covers the time period from April 26, 1783, to November 30, 1783. There are listed 1,336 black men, 914 black women and 750 black children, for a total of 3,000 black persons. The list contains the name of the ship, its commander, the destination of the ship, name of the black person, age, description, age and place of residence of the claimant, name of person in possession of and remarks.

Among some of the last of the African Americans to be evacuated were members of the Black Brigade, also known as the Black Pioneers. These African Americans served in the British army, and as "pioneers" their duties were to provide support by being teamsters, performing camp cleanup and maintenance work brigades, preparing sites for camp, fortifying camps and general engineering duties. The "pioneers" did not bear arms. There were African Americans who did bear arms and fight for the British as well as the Americans.

The Black Pioneers were first formed into a company by General Henry Clinton in April of 1776, when he led an expedition to North Carolina and seventy-one enslaved African American runaways joined his forces. When General Clinton came north to New York City, he continued to attract runaways, including some from Bergen County and other parts of New Jersey. The Black Pioneers never exceeded seventy to eighty in number. These men served General Clinton, Captain Allan Stewart and Captain George Martins. They were used in Newport, Rhode Island, in December of 1776, Philadelphia in 1777, New York City in 1778, Charleston, South Carolina, in December 1779 and finally they returned to New York City, where they remained until the end of the war, when they were evacuated to Nova Scotia. Some Black Pioneers were sent to Nova Scotia prior to 1783 to prepare for the flood of Loyalists that were to come in 1783. A town in Nova Scotia where a great many African Americans were relocated was named Birchtown in honor of the efforts of Brigadier General Samuel Birch, who issued passes to Nova Scotia to the fleeing blacks in New York City.

The following is a partial listing of an annotated transcript of those records for black persons, 128 free and 18 enslaved, who resided in Bergen County, New Jersey, and the vicinity. The abbreviations: [BB] is Black Brigade, [F] is free, [S] is enslaved:

ALBERT, SAMUEL. *20 years of age, stout lad, M[ulatto], formerly slave to Samuel Tin at Hackensack, New Jersey, says he was made free by the death of his master 7 years ago. Possession of Samuel Mann. Sailed April 23, 1783 aboard ship Grace bound for Port Roseway. Ship Master William Oxley.* [F]

ALMIN, *32 years of age, stout healthy man, formerly the property of Williams at Tappan in New Jersey, came in on Sir William Howe's Proclamation. Sailed April 23, 1783 aboard ship Camel bound for St. John's. Ship Master was Tinker.* [F]

BANTER, THOMAS. *24 years of age, stout black, formerly a slave to Albert Banter, Paramus, New Jersey, left him about six years ago. Possession of Colonel Tyngl. Sailed April 23, 1783 aboard Grand Dutchess of Russia bound for St. John's. Ship Master Stephen Holman.* [Note: The name "Banter" may be Banta.] [F]

BANTER, JOHN. *2 years of age, mulatto boy, free man. Possession of Colonel Tyngl. Sailed April 23, 1783 aboard Grand Dutchess of Russia bound for St John's. Ship Master Stephen Holman.* [Note 1: The name "Banter" may be Banta. Note 2: Effie Douglas, who was listed next to John, may be his mother.] [F]

BAYARD, SAM. *45 years of age, stout tall man. Possession of Matthew Tankard. Formerly slave to Peter Bayard, New Jersey, came off about 5 years. Sailed April 23, 1783 aboard ship Polly bound for Port Roseway. Ship Master John Browne.* [Note 1: Samuel Bayard is listed as head of family in the "Muster Book of Free Blacks, Settlement of Birchtown, 1784." Note 2: Peter Bayard is probably related to William Bayard of Hoboken, then in Bergen County.] [F]

BERRYAN, SARAH. [BUNYAN] *27 years of age, stout wench, formerly slave to Gerrit Smith, Cacyte, New Jersey, left him 4½ years past by Proclamation. Possession of Charles O. Bruff. Sailed April 23, 1783 aboard London frigate bound for Port Roseway. Ship Master Hugh Watts.* [Note: Gerrit Smith was a Tory and a Loyalist.] [F]

BLAVELT, DINAH. *20 years of age, large wench, 1 child named JACK, 1 year old, formerly slave to Blauvelt, Tappan, New Jersey. Possession of Charles O. Bruff. Sailed April 23, 1783 aboard London frigate bound for Port Roseway. Ship Master Hugh Watts.* [F]

Black Loyalists in Bergen County and "The Book of Negroes"

BOGERT, WILLIAM. *20 years of age, stout male, formerly slave to John Bogert, Tappan, New Jersey, left him about five years ago in consequence of Proclamation. Possession of Charles Oliver Bruff. Sailed April 23, 1783 aboard London frigate bound for Port Roseway. Ship Master Hugh Watts.* [Note: William Bagart is probably William Bogert, and he is listed in the "Muster Book of Free Blacks, settlement of Birchtown, 1784" as head of family.] *[F]*

BOURDET, HARRY. *18 years old, stout fellow. Oliver Bourdett of St. John's, claimant. Possession of Oliver Bourdett. Property of Oliver Bourdett, born in his father's house* [English Neighborhood]. *Sailed June 13, 1783 aboard Brig Tartar bound for St. John's River. Ship Master Andrew Yates.* [Note: Oliver Bourdett's father, either Peter or Stephen, operated the Burdett's Ferry about one mile south of Fort Lee.] *[S]*

BRINKERHOOF, THOMAS. *34 years of age, very short ordinary man, formerly slave to Cornelius Boggard near Hackensack, New Jersey, left him 5 years past. Sailed April 23, 1783 aboard ship Sovereign bound for St. John's River. Ship Master William Stewart.* [Note: Cornelius Boggard is probably Cornelius Bogert, who was found guilty of treasonable activities by the Committee of Safety of New Jersey and held in Morristown by the Americans, to be used for exchange for American prisoners held by the British.] *[F]*

BROWN, MARMORY. *58 years old, stout fellow, formerly the property of Derrick Van Ryper, Bergen, New Jersey, left him 7 years ago. Sailed July 31, 1783 aboard L'Abondance bound for Port Roseway. Lt. Phillips, Commander.* [Note: Marmory Brown is listed in the "Muster Book of Free Blacks, Settlement of Birchtown, 1784" as head of family.] *[F]*

BROWN, MARY. *69 years old, worn out, formerly the property of Cornelius Van Ryper, Bergen, New Jersey, left him 7 years ago. Sailed July 31, 1783 aboard L'Abondance bound for Port Roseway. Lt. Phillips, Commander. [F]*

ELLIS, DINAH. *25 years of age, very little wench, formerly slave to Ellis Remain, Hackensack, New Jersey, left him 3 years past. Possession of Stephen Shakespeare. Sailed April 23, 1783 aboard ship Providence bound for Port Roseway. Ship Master John Richee. [F]*

ELLIS, LUCY. *3 years of age, fine girl. Possession of Stephen Shakespeare. (Daughter of* THOMAS *and* DINAH ELLIS). *Sailed April 23, 1783 aboard ship Providence bound for Port Roseway. [F]*

ELLIS, SAMUEL. *5 years of age, fine boy, formerly slave to Ellis Remain, Hackensack, New Jersey, left him 3 years past. [F]*

ELLIS, THOMAS. *25 years of age, stout little fellow, formerly slave to Ellis Remain, Hackensack, New Jersey, left him 3 years past. [F]*

KIPP, HENRY. 23 years of age, stout fellow, formerly slave to Abraham Kipp, Hackensack, New Jersey, left him 6 years past. Possession of Timothy Maham. Sailed April 23, 1783 aboard Baker & Atlee bound for Port Roseway. Ship Master Eramus Roberts. [Note 1: Henry Kipp is listed in the "Muster Book of Free Blacks, Settlement of Birchtown, 1784" as head of family. Note 2: Henry Kipp petitioned in 1791 to go to Sierra Leone.] *[F]*

LIVSA, SALLY. 20 years old, stout wench, formerly the property of John Lashley of Acquackanung, New Jersey, left him 6 years ago. Sailed July 31, 1783 aboard Clinton bound for Annapolis & St. John's. Ship Master Lt. Trounce. [F]

LYDACRE, FANNY. 3 years of ago, traveling with her mother LUCY LYDACRE. Possession of John Kingston. Sailed April 23, 1783 aboard Elizabeth bound for Port Roseway. [F]

LYDACRE, LUCY. 24 years of age, snug little wench, ¼ M[ulatto]*, formerly slave to William Lydacre,* [New] *Jersey, left him in the year 1776 by Proclamation. Possession of John Kingston. Sailed April 23, 1783 aboard Elizabeth bound for Port Roseway. [F]*

LYDECKER, THOMAS. 32 years old, stout fellow, formerly property of Garret Lydecker of Hackensack, New Jersey, left him 6 years ago. Possession of John Mercereau. Sailed July 10, 1783 aboard Townshend bound for River St. John's. Ship Master J. Hog. [Note: Reverend Garret Lydecker resided in English Neighborhood, now known as Englewood.] *[F]*

Arnold E. Brown, JD, is the president of Brown & Associates, a business consultant firm, and a real estate sales associate with Coldwell Banker of Fort Lee. He is the founder and president of Du Bois Book Center, a retail e-commerce bookstore specializing in used, rare, out-of-print and new books about and by African Americans. He is a member of the Afro-American Historical Society Museum, Jersey City, New Jersey; member of the Bergen County Historic Preservation Advisory Board; and a member of the New Jersey Chapter of Afro-American Historical and Genealogical Society. He is the coauthor of Arcadia Publishing's Images of America: Englewood and Englewood Cliffs, *published in 1998.*

GEORGE WASHINGTON:
FIRST OF THE BIG-TIME SPENDERS

MARVIN KITMAN

While doing research on his book The Making of the Prefident 1789 *at the New York Public Library, media critic Marvin Kitman came across ledger books containing George Washington's handwritten expense accounts from the Revolutionary War. History books are filled with Washington's great feats during the Revolutionary War, but few are aware of what a great job he did keeping track of his expenses during those years. Kitman continued his research on this subject at the Library of Congress. This essay is adapted from his book* George Washington's Expense Account, *which was published by Simon & Schuster in 1970.*

Like most American schoolboys, I had heard the story of how George Washington offered to serve his country during the Revolutionary War without salary. In one of the most stirring speeches in the annals of patriotism, after his election as commander in chief in June 1775, he explained that all he asked of his new country was that it pay his expenses in the war against British tyranny. He promised to keep a careful record. The speech brought tears to John Adams's eyes.

Nothing much is heard in the classroom, however, about the equally stirring expense account General Washington handed in after the war. I stumbled across a copy of it in the stacks of the New York Public Library while researching my book, *The Making of the Prefident 1789*, the story of how the "Mount Vernon machine" engineered the first election, in which General Washington ran unopposed and won unanimously.

Washington's expense account was first published by the chief clerk in the registrar's office of the Treasury Department in June 1843, under the title *Accounts, G. Washington with the United States, June 1775 and Ending June 1783, Comprehending a Space of 8 years.* I was a freelance magazine writer at the time I discovered this document. And if there's anything freelance writers are authorities on, it's expense accounts.

There are forty-three basic principles of expense account writing. Washington used forty-two of them. The rules include: *be specific about smaller expenses and vague on the larger ones.* (Describe in some depth the purchase of a ball of twine, for example, brown, 2¾-inch circumference, purchased at, say, Moore's Hardware in Leonia…$1.98, and casually throw in dinner for one army…$1,100.)

DAR retreat sign at Liberty Pole in Englewood. *Courtesy of Ira Lieblich.*

George Washington: First of the Big-time Spenders

Another rule is: *Use descriptive adjectives,* as in one of the general's better-written entries:

July, 1775 ☆ **127**

George Washington's handwritten expense account. *Courtesy of the Library of Congress.*

Sometimes, instead of "household expenses," he used the more gripping "Hd." In both forms, they covered a multitude of sins, such as eating. I found by checking accompanying receipts, located in the Library of Congress, that among things the steward paid for were "geese, mutton, fowls, turkey, veal, butter, turnips, potatoes, carrots, and cabbage." The troops not on the expense account were eating less well later at Valley Forge and Morristown.

When the general was being more expansive, he used the synonym "miscellaneous." Or as he put it, "misc."

The Revolutionary War in Bergen County

The general, to his credit, followed basic rule #12 (*omit nothing*) for eight long years.

There is a tendency in the postmodern world to belittle George Washington's achievements in war and peace. But in expense account writing, my study concluded, he is second to none. If the general had gone on the payroll, as Congress proposed after his election as commander in chief, he would have been paid $500 a month, or $6,000 per year. His take-home pay for the eight years of the war would have been $48,000.

The expense account he submitted in lieu of salary was for $449,261.51. It included an interest charge for money laid out of his own pocket on behalf of his new potential country and a surcharge for depreciation, caused to some degree by a loss of confidence in his military leadership. Anyway, it was what he charged for, as well as how much, that made the eight years of Washington's Revolutionary War the golden age of expense account writing.

As I sat in my old Leonia home reading the general's original accounts, I found myself whistling in admiration at the man's writing. Some might be impressed by the bar bills. The amount of alcohol consumption that went on during the Revolutionary War period was staggering. But Washington never drank more than a bottle of Madeira a night, as all historians concur, besides rum, punch and beer. He also often drank cider, champagne and brandy.

And he wasn't the only one drinking on the job. The troops left Fort Lee in such haste on November 20, 1776, when they learned of the British invasion that they left the cook fires burning. When British troops entered the abandoned fort, they found a large number too drunk to participate in the retreat but invited the Redcoats to party with them.

Still others may be more impressed with Washington's shopping expeditions. The first day on the expense account he bought everything new: from a new horse and a new carriage to a new gun to a book on the art of war at J. Sparhawks, the Barney's of its day. The shopkeepers of Philadelphia were sad to see him go to the front in Boston. But he was soon to be a boon to Bergen County's economy and everywhere else he traveled on the tab.

The general has not received credit either for being a leader in the mail-order catalogue shopping field. His shopping lists and letters to London merchants before the war should make every Yuppie's heart beat faster. And like the rest of us, he was continually in debt. Fortunately, he had married the richest widow in Virginia. To Washington's credit, no matter how bad his financial plight at Mount Vernon, he didn't stop spending extravagantly during the war for "necessaries," as the *Account* called anything he craved because of his consuming passion. Teddy Roosevelt gets credit for the phrase "Charge" at San Juan Hill. But it was the battle cry that rung through Saville Row and Regent Street, when the ships arrived carrying the general's orders.

But what really impressed me most was the way he charged for scouting and night patrols. Entry Number 149 on July 23, 1776, was for $489 for "Reconnoitering the Country as far as Perth Amboy."

Entry No. 147, for July 15, 1776, also caught my eye: "To my own & Parties expenses laying out Fort Lee—on the Jersey side of the No. River…$217.50."

When I was a soldier at Fort Dix, scouting and night patrols and digging foxholes were considered a routine part of the job. It never occurred to us to put in a chit to

George Washington: First of the Big-time Spenders

The Retreat, by Mahonri Young, 1916, on Fort Lee Road in Leonia. *Courtesy of Carol Karels.*

the paymaster when we got back in the morning from chores necessary to defend ourselves or that we would be able to charge the country extra. It was part of the job.

Even more impressive was his entry on January 1, 1777: "No.2. To Sundry Exps. paid by Myself—at different time & places in passing from the White plains by the way of King's ferry to Fort lee—and afterwards on the retreat of the Army thro' the Jerseys into Pennsylvania—& while there…$3,281.53."

Some authorities might argue that since an army is paid to go forward, not backward, soldiers might take themselves off the payroll totally when retreating, on the grounds they were not doing their job. Washington wasn't one of them.

I thought about all of this as I sat in my Leonia home, a few hundred feet away from the retreat route down Fort Lee Road, imagining the troops marching past the Leonia Presbyterian Church and the Mahonri Young plaque commemorating the march, the rear guards struggling with the general's boxes of receipts, which he handed in at the end of the war.

Others would have made it up, as we expense account writers sometimes do today in times of emergency, but not Washington. He had the foresight to keep the bills for the eight years of the war, much of which was spent retreating on the tab. That's why he was first in expense account writing!

The retreat went up Grand Avenue, past the old English Neighborhood Dutch Reformed Church, Pastor's Drug Store and Sonny's Pizzeria in Englewood, under

Route 95, then left at Palisade Avenue, past Baumgart's Restaurant, across the Erie railroad tracks, before turning right at the Liberty Pole and up to New Bridge. All went on the expense account without his usual detail.

As already noted, the basic principle was being vague on major expenses, a principle the general strictly adhered to. For example, there were his charges "for secret service." Amazingly, he included the founding of the nation's first intelligence arm on his personal expense account. Of course, he couldn't name names of who was informing on their neighbors.

Nobody likes to argue with officers of higher rank. But to this day I think the commander in charge made a wrong turn on this expense account trip. Instead of heading toward Valley Forge as the terminus of this retreat "thro' the Jerseys," he could have easily turned right and gone up to the Ramapough Mountains. Fidel Castro and other rebel groups learned from Washington's mistakes and always took to the hills. In the Ramapoughs, our Rebel army wouldn't have had to deal with the patriotic Quaker farmers who wouldn't sell food to troops lacking gold.

Not that this was an impediment to George Washington and the expense account crowd. General Knox, for example, started the war at 230 pounds and ended at 285.

By no means am I suggesting that George Washington invented expense accounts. Paul Revere, for example, handed in an expense account for his famous ride (it's in the Massachusetts State House in Boston). I'm only implying that a careful reading of this least widely read of the thirty-two volumes of Washington Papers in the Library of Congress shows he may have been the founding father of the American way of life known as expense account living.

What might have seemed like a petty cash item to John Adams when he hailed Washington's no-salary offer as "a monument to patriotism" turned out to be the forerunner of cost over-runs in Congressional dealings with the military.

Congress, by the way, paid the expense account to the penny without a question. Coincidentally, when General Washington offered the same deal after his election as president in 1789—no salary, just expenses—Congress made him take a salary of $25,000 per annum (at a time when Thomas Jefferson as the secretary of state was being paid $3,500). It was the country's first economy wave.

Marvin Kitman is the author of The Making of the Prefident 1789. *Currently, he is also the only living coauthor of General Washington. The book* George Washington's Expense Account, *as it says on the cover, was written by "Gen. George Washington & Marvin Kitman PFC (Ret.)" Marvin was the TV/media critic at Newsday for thirty-five years. His most recent book is* The Man Who Would Not Shut Up: The Rise of Bill O'Reilly. *He ran for president as a Lincoln Republican in 1964, and lost. Among his other achievements was serving in the U.S. Army at Fort Dix, where in only two years he rose to the rank of private first class. He asked for no fee for this monograph, only that the publisher pick up his expenses while writing the essay.*

Military Actions in Bergen County and Vicinity, 1776–1781: A Timetable

Dr. Henry Bischoff

1776

General George Washington and the Continental army marched from Boston through Connecticut to New York City and western Long Island during the spring with eighteen thousand troops.

A British fleet arrived in New York Harbor in late June with thirty thousand troops under General William Howe. They landed on Staten Island.

The British troops at the end of August moved to western Long Island (now Brooklyn), where they surrounded the Continentals and defeated them in battle.

The Continental troops escaped at night across to Manhattan.

The British pushed the Continentals out of most of Manhattan into Westchester County. New York City was burned and Fort Lee engaged the British warships several times through September and October.

Washington decided to move the main body of his troops across the Hudson at Kings Ferry (Verplanck) on November 12 and on to Hackensack.

Washington left a force of seven thousand troops in Westchester under General Charles Lee and three thousand at Peekskill under Major General William Heath. The latter was to protect a major fortification at Fort Montgomery (Bear Mountain).

On November 13, General Heath sent four hundred soldiers to establish Camp Ramapough at Sidman's Bridge in the Clove north of Suffern.

A major body of British troops (five thousand) crossed the Hudson at New Dock (Huyler's Landing at Cresskill) on November 19–20.

General Nathanael Greene evacuated Rebel troops from Fort Lee. They moved to Hackensack before the British were able to arrive at this fortification.

On November 21, Hessians engaged Washington's rear guard at New Bridge. Washington abandoned Hackensack and began the long march to Saddle River, Acquackanonk Landing (Passaic), Newark, New Brunswick and across New Jersey and the Delaware River into Pennsylvania.

The Revolutionary War in Bergen County

The British set up military posts from New Bridge to Bordentown, including Hackensack, New Brunswick, Princeton and Trenton.

General Lee and his troops belatedly crossed the Hudson River from Westchester and marched down Valley Road (Ramapough, Mahwah) in early December to join Washington across the Delaware River. En route Lee, but not his troops, was captured by the British.

At that time General Horatio Gates and his army moved from Lake Champlain and also marched down Valley Road to join Washington's forces.

The Orange and Ulster County Militias sent three hundred men to Camp Ramapough (in the Clove north of Suffern) under General George Clinton on December 9.

General Heath sent troops from Haverstraw to Tappan for an attack on the British at Hackensack on December 14.

On December 19, General George Clinton moved from the Clove to Paramus and then attacked Colonel Abraham Van Buskirk's Loyalist troops at English Neighborhood (Leonia) and at Bergen Woods south of Fort Lee.

Clinton returned to Camp Ramapough and sent out patrols from Ringwood to Paramus.

Washington brought his troops across the Delaware River and successfully attacked fourteen hundred Hessian soldiers in Trenton on December 26.

The British in Bergen County attacked Rebel positions at Paramus and Hopperstown (Ho-Ho-Kus) on December 27.

1777

Washington moved his forces for a successful attack on a British position at Princeton on January 3.

The British vacated troops from exposed position at Hackensack on January 3 and from most other positions in New Jersey at this time to winter in New York City.

The Continentals wintered around Morristown.

Tories struck in Bergen County in the spring—at English Neighborhood (Leonia) on March 20, Closter on April 20, Allendale on April 23 and Paramus on May 12.

Washington sent a large contingent of New Jersey Militiamen into the territory between Pompton and Hackensack on April 26 to oppose the Tories.

An Essex County Militia moved into Bergen County and captured Loyalists in Lyndhurst, Harrington, English Neighborhood and Kinderkamack (Emerson).

General John Burgoyne in the early summer led a large English force out of Canada and captured Fort Ticonderoga on July 15. He was marching toward Albany.

Washington expected General William Howe to move with his English forces in New York City up the Hudson River Valley to meet Burgoyne's forces and cut the new nation in two. Thus Washington moved his eight thousand Continentals from Morristown northeast through Pompton Plains and camped at the Ponds (Oakland) on July 14.

The next day they marched down Valley Road in Ramapough (Mahwah) and Suffern.

General Howe put his troops on ships in New York. Instead of moving up the Hudson, he ordered his ships and troops south for a successful occupation of Philadelphia.

Military Actions in Bergen County and Vicinity, 1776–1781: A Timetable

Washington then marched the Continentals out of the Clove, camped at Ramapough and proceeded south to engage unsuccessfully Howe's forces in September at Brandywine and Germantown, outside Philadelphia.

Also in September, Washington put Lieutenant Colonel Aaron Burr in command of Colonel William Malcolm's regiment stationed in the Clove above Suffern.

On September 12, General Henry Clinton led British troops north out of New York City. They succeeded in capturing, in the Hudson Highlands, the important Rebel Fort Montgomery and Fort Clinton, and in Bergen County they attacked Hackensack and New Bridge.

Burr moved his regiment from the Clove to Paramus. On September 14, he attacked a British picket at Kinderkamack schoolhouse northwest of Hackensack and brought off prisoners to Paramus.

In mid-September, General Alexander McDougal was ordered to march his troops from Peekskill to Tappan, across Bergen County and then to join Washington outside Philadelphia.

Washington also ordered Burr and his troops to join him in Pennsylvania.

General George Clinton sent two hundred militia to Ramapough under Major Thomas Moffatt. They conducted forays against Loyalists around Suffern and in northern Bergen County.

When the British learned that General Burgoyne was defeated and forced to surrender his troops at Saratoga in northern New York State in mid-October, General Clinton pulled back his soldiers from the Hudson Highland forts and Bergen County and returned them to New York City.

1778

The Continental troops, including Lieutenant Colonel Burr and his soldiers, wintered at Valley Forge.

The Bergen County Courthouse moved from Hackensack to the Ponds (Oakland).

General Henry Clinton replaced General William Howe as British commander in Philadelphia in mid-spring. Clinton decided to evacuate Philadelphia in order to again concentrate the British forces in New York City.

When the British marched north through New Jersey, Washington had the Continentals cross the Delaware River and also move into this state.

The two armies met in a hard fought battle at Monmouth Courthouse (near Freehold) on June 28. There were many casualties on both sides, but neither army was destroyed.

The British continued on to New York City by way of Sandy Hook.

The Continental army marched to New Brunswick, the Great Falls of the Passaic (Paterson) and to Paramus and Hopperstown (Ho-Ho-Kus).

They encamped there for several days. Washington accepted the invitation of Theodosia Prevost to make the Hermitage his headquarters, July 11–14.

General Charles Lee's court-martial took place.

The Continentals then proceeded by way of Saddle River, Kakiat (Rockland County), Haverstraw and across the Hudson River to White Plains.

British troops moved into Bergen County to forage in late September—at New Bridge, Schraalenburgh (Bergenfield), Teaneck and the English Neighborhood.

At that time Colonel George Baylor and the Third Continental Virginia Dragoons were in Paramus. They moved to Overkill (River Vale). There they were attacked and massacred by the British on September 28. The British continued north to Tappan.

Two North Carolina regiments were posted at Ramapough in November. By December they had moved to Paramus for the winter.

1779

The Continental army moved across the Hudson River from Westchester and wintered at Middle Brook, New Jersey.

Through March and into May there were skirmishes at Closter, Little Ferry, Weehawken, Paramus and the English Neighborhood (Leonia).

In May, General Henry Clinton and British troops moved up the Hudson and took and strengthened fortifications at Stony Point.

Twice in May and again in June, British and Loyalist troops conducted foraging raids into the eastern part of Bergen County, including into Closter and the English Neighborhood.

In July, General Anthony Wayne led Rebel troops in an attack on and captured the British garrison at Stony Point.

In August, Colonel Henry Lee moved his troops from the Clove to an encampment at Paramus and then marched by way of New Bridge and the English Neighborhood to a successful surprise attack on the British fortification at Paulus Hook (Jersey City).

During the fall, Virginia troops who were posted in the Clove, together with General John Sullivan and his troops, marched south on Valley Road (Ramapough). They foraged as they moved through Bergen County.

In November, General Wayne and his troops foraged at Paramus, New Bridge and south of Fort Lee.

Washington moved the Continental army in November from West Point down Valley Road through Pompton to Morristown.

1780

The Continental army wintered at Morristown.

Colonel Levi Pawling commanded troops stationed in the Clove.

In March, the British launched a two-pronged attack into Bergen County. One unit landed at Weehawken, proceeded to Little Ferry and then to Hackensack, where they burned the courthouse and several other buildings and captured many Rebel sympathizers. The other unit landed at Closter, went through Pascack (Woodcliff

Military Actions in Bergen County and Vicinity, 1776–1781: A Timetable

Historic First Reformed Church in Hackensack. Many Patriots, including Brigadier General Enoch Poor, are buried in the adjacent cemetery. *Courtesy of Ira Lieblich.*

Lake) and Werimus (Saddle River) and approached Paramus, where a contingent of Pennsylvania troops was stationed. The British, with three hundred men, scattered the defending Pennsylvania unit. However, as the British were returning toward New York, the Pennsylvania soldiers harassed them along the route to New Bridge and to the crossing of the Hudson

In April, the British launched another attack into the same area. A cavalry unit landed at Bergen Point and marched north to meet in the English Neighborhood an infantry unit that had crossed the Hudson at Fort Lee. This seven-hundred-man combined force of British, German and Loyalist soldiers scattered a small Rebel militia unit at New Bridge. They then overran a picket of Continental soldiers stationed at the bridge over the Saddle River just below the Paramus Church. At Hopperstown, they beat back a Pennsylvania regiment after a sharp but short fight. They then plundered the area, but again were harassed by Patriot fighters on their march from Paramus to Fort Lee.

The posting of troops at Paramus, according to Washington, was primarily for intercepting trade with the enemy in New York City.

The British and Loyalists in May built a blockhouse at Bull's Ferry (Guttenberg) as a base for attacks by Loyalists into Bergen County—to Closter, New Bridge and Schraalenburgh.

In May, the Marquis de Lafayette rode through the Clove to Morristown to announce to Washington that a major French force would arrive at Newport, Rhode Island, to support the Patriot war effort.

Washington then decided to move his Continentals toward the Hudson for a possible assault on New York City. These troops proceeded to Whippany and on June 26 marched down Valley Road and camped in Ramapough. They remained there until July 1. This army then moved to Colonel Dey's in Preakness (Wayne).

A large force of French troops arrived in Newport on July 10. However, Washington and the French officers were unable to develop a joint military operation for 1780.

Through August and September, the Continentals kept on the move through Orange and Bergen Counties—including Liberty Pole (Englewood), English Neighborhood, Tenafly, New Bridge, Hackensack and Steenrapie (New Milford). During this time the soldiers foraged throughout the area for food.

General Wayne, with 1,800 troops on July 21, attacked the British blockhouse at Bull's Ferry (Guttenberg), but failed to dislodge the defenders. In late summer the British evacuated this fortification, burned it and moved to Fort DeLancey in Bergen Neck. Major André wrote "The Cow Chase" about this action.

During this time British officer Major John André was arranging for General Benedict Arnold to surrender West Point to the enemy. The plot was discovered in late September. Arnold escaped, but André was captured. He was tried and hanged at Tappan on October 2. The British did not get West Point.

1781

Washington wintered a large portion of his troops at New Windsor (just north of West Point).

Pennsylvania troops were stationed at Morristown and New Jersey troops at Pompton.

In January, the Pennsylvania and New Jersey troops mutinied because of poor living conditions. Both uprisings were quelled. In the latter case, Washington sent troops from West Point to Pompton, where they succeeded in restoring order.

In March, Loyalists attacked Closter and were driven off by local Patriot militiamen.

In another engagement, a British contingent sailed to Moonachie Point just south of Hackensack and they were routed by a local Patriot militia

Loyalists rebuilt a blockhouse at Fort Lee. After a number of attempts, Bergen County Militia forced the Loyalists to abandon the post.

Washington and French officers and military parties crossed and recrossed Bergen County during the summer appraising possibilities for an attack on New York City. When they learned that the French fleet was planning to sail to Chesapeake Bay to blockade the British army of General Charles Cornwallis in Virginia, Washington and the French General Comte de Rochambeau decided to support this effort by moving their armies to Virginia.

The allied armies crossed the Hudson at Kings Ferry and marched to Suffern. The Patriots then proceeded south by way of Ramapough, Paramus, New Brunswick and Princeton. The French went down Valley Road to the Ponds, Pompton, Morristown and met the Americans at Princeton. They then both proceeded to Virginia and to the decisive Battle of Yorktown.

Bibliography

Bill, Alfred Hoyt. *New Jersey and the Revolutionary War.* Princeton, NJ: D. Van Nostrand Company, Inc., 1964.

Bischoff, Henry. *Mahwah and the Ramapo Valley in the American Revolution.* Mahwah, NJ: Mahwah Tricentennial Committee, 2000.

———. *A Revolutionary Relationship: Theodosia Prevost, Aaron Burr and the Hermitage.* NJ: The Friends of the Hermitage, 2004.

Bischoff, Henry, and Kahn, Mitchell. *From Pioneer Settlement to Suburb: A History of Mahwah, New Jersey, 1700–1976.* South Brunswick, NJ, and New York: A.S. Barnes & Company, 1979.

Bogert, Frederick. *Bergen County, New Jersey History and Heritage, The Revolutionary Years 1776–1783.* NJ: Bergen County Board of Chosen Freeholders, 1983.

Clary, David. *Adopted Son: Washington, Lafayette and the Friendship that Saved the Revolution.* New York: Bantam, 2007.

Conway, William F. *Fort Lee—The Post at Burdett's Ferry.* Bergen County History Annual, 1975.

Dater, Joan. "Andrew Hopper Revisited. George Washington's Stays at the Andrew Hopper House during the Revolutionary War." Text of lecture presented at the Hermitage, Ho-Ho-Kus, November 30, 2005.

Dewy, William. "Defending the Lower Hudson River in 1776." *Sea History* 98. National Maritime Historical Society, 2001.

Diamant, Lincoln. *Chaining the Hudson: The Fight for the River in the American Revolution.* New York: Citadel Press, 1989.

Di Ionno, Mark. *A Guide to New Jersey's Revolutionary War Trail.* Camden, NJ: Rutgers University Press, 2000.

Ellis, Joseph J. *His Excellency George Washington.* New York: Alfred A. Knopf, 2004.

Eslwyth, Thane. *The Fighting Quaker: Nathanael Greene.* New York: Aeonian Press, 1972.

Ewald, Captain Johann. *Diary of the American War, A Hessian Journal.* Translated and edited by Joseph Tustin. New Haven, CT: Yale University Press, 1979.

Bibliography

Fischer, David Hackett. *Washington's Crossing*. New York: Oxford University Press, 2004.

Greene, Jerome A. *The Guns of Independence: The Siege of Yorktown, 1781*. New York: Savas Beatie, 2005.

Gruber, Ira D., ed. *John Peebles' American War: The Diary of a Scottish Grenadier, 1776–1782*. Mechanicsburg, PA: Stackpole Books, 1998, 221–22.

Hahn, Harold M. *Ships of the American Revolution and their Models*. England: Conway Maritime Press Ltd., 1988.

Hallahan, William H. *The Day the Revolution Ended: 19 October 1781*. New York: John Wiley & Sons, 2003.

Harvey, Robert. *A Few Bloody Noses: The Realities and Mythologies of the American Revolution*. New York: Overlook Press, 2002.

Hastings, Hugh, ed. *Public Papers of George Clinton*. Vols. I & II. New York: Wynkoop Hallenbeck Crawford Co., 1899 and 1900.

Hodges, Graham Russell, ed. *The Black Loyalist Directory: African Americans in Exile After the American Revolution*. New York and London: Garland Publishing, Inc., in Association with the New England Historic Genealogical Society, 1996.

Ketchum, Richard M. *Victory at Yorktown: The Campaign that Won the Revolution*. New York: Henry Holt & Company, 2004.

Kitman, Marvin. *The Making of the Prefident 1789*. New York: Grove Press, 1989.

Lefkowitz, Arthur S. *The Long Retreat, The Calamitous American Defense of New Jersey 1776*. NJ: Upland Press, 1998.

Leiby, Adrian. *The Revolutionary War in the Hackensack Valley*. Camden, NJ: Rutgers University Press, 1980.

Lodge, Henry Cabot, ed. *Major André's Journal*. 1903. Reprint of 1930 ed., New York: New York Times & Arno Press, 1968, 97–99.

Loh, Jules, *Treason: The Arnold-Andre Plot*. Tappantown Historical Society, 2005.

Lossing, Benjamin. *Pictorial Field-Book of the Revolution*. 2 vols. New York: Harper Brothers, 1850.

Ludlum, David M. *Early American Winters 1604–1820*. Boston: American Meteorologic Society, 1966.

Lundin, Leonard. *Cockpit of the Revolution*. Princeton, NJ: Princeton University Press, 1940.

Martin, Joseph Plumb. *Private Yankee Doodle*. Edited by George E. Scheer. New York: Eastern Acorn Press, 1995.

McCullough, David. *1776*. New York: Simon and Schuster, 2005.

Mitnick, Barbara, ed. *New Jersey in the American Revolution*. New Brunswick, NJ: Rivergate Books, 2005.

Morrissey, Brendan. *Yorktown 1781*. Oxford, UK: Osprey, 1999.

Murray, Stuart. *Eyewitness American Revolution*. New York: DK Publishing, 2005.

Newman, Debra Lynn. "An Inspection Roll Of Negroes Taken On Board Sundry Vessels At Staten Island Bound For Nova Scotia, 1783." *Journal of the Afro-American Historical and Genealogical Society* 1, no. 2.

Bibliography

Paine, Thomas. *American Crisis Papers.* Self published, 1776.

Pearson, Michael. *Those Damned Rebels: The American Revolution as Seen Through British Eyes*. New York: Da Capo Books, 1972.

Quarles, Benjamin. *The Negro in the American Revolution.* Chapel Hill, NC: University of North Carolina Press, 1961.

Rice, Howard C., Jr., and Anne S.K. Brown. *The American Campaigns of Rochambeau's Army 1780, 1781, 1782, 1783. Vol II: The Itineraries, Maps and Views.* Princeton, NJ and Providence, RI: Princeton University Press and Brown University Press, 1972.

Rose, Alexander. *Washington's Spies*. New York: Bantam Dell, 2006.

Royster, Charles. *A Revolutionary People at War: The Continental Army and American Character, 1775–1783*. Chapel Hill: University of North Carolina Press, 1979.

Rubel, David. *America's War of Independence 1763–1783*. New York: Silver Moon Press/Agincourt Press, 1992.

Schecter, Barnet. *The Battle for New York*. New York: Walker & Company, 2002.

Selig, Robert A. "The duc de Lauzun and his *Légion*, Rochambeau's most troublesome, colorful soldiers." *Colonial Williamsburg* 21, no. 6 (December/January 2000): 56–63.

———. "François Joseph Paul Comte de Grasse, the Battle off the Virginia Capes, and the American Victory at Yorktown." *Colonial Williamsburg* 21, no. 5. (October/November 1999): 26–32.

———. *March to Victory: Washington, Rochambeau, and the Yorktown Campaign of 1781*. Washington, D.C.: Center of Military History, 2007. Available for download at www.W3R-US.org.

———. *The Washington-Rochambeau Revolutionary Route in the State of New Jersey, 1781–1783*. 3 vols. Trenton: New Jersey Historic Trust, 2006. All three volumes of Dr. Selig's report are available for download at http://www.njht.org/dca/njht/publ/W3RReport.html.

Spring, John. *The 1776 British Landing at Closter.* Bergen County History Annual, 1975.

Unger, Harlow Giles. *Lafayette.* New York: Wiley and Sons, 2002.

Walker, James W. St. G. *The Black Loyalists.* New York: Africana Publishing Company, 1976.

Williams, George W. *History of the Negro Race in America 1619–1880*. Reprint. New York: Arno Press and the New York Times, 1968.

Wilson, Ellen Gibson. *The Loyal Blacks*. New York: G.P. Putnam's Sons/Capricorn Books, 1976.

Winfield, Charles. *The Blockhouse at Bulls Ferry.* New York: William Abbott, 1904.

MANUSCRIPTS

Adjutant General's Office, Loyalist Manuscripts. New Jersey State Archives.

Anthony Wayne Papers. Historical Society of Pennsylvania, Philadelphia.

Bibliography

Audit Office, Classes 12 & 13. The National Archives, Kew, Richmond, Surrey, United Kingdom.

Colonial Office, Class 5. The National Archives, Kew, Richmond, Surrey, United Kingdom.

Cornwallis Papers. The National Archives, Kew, Richmond, Surrey, United Kingdom.

Department of Defense, Military Records, Revolutionary War, Revolutionary Manuscripts Numbered. New Jersey State Archives, Washington, D.C.

"Diary of Joseph Clark, Attached to the Continental Army." May 1777 to November 1778. *Proceedings of the New Jersey Historical Society* 7 (1854): 108–09.

Frederick Mackenzie Papers. University of Michigan, William L. Clements Library, Ann Arbor.

George Washington Papers. Library of Congress, Washington, D.C.

Gilder Lehrman Collection. Pierpont Morgan Library, New York.

Headquarters Papers of the British army in America. The National Archives, Kew, Richmond, Surrey, United Kingdom.

Israel Shreve Papers, Buxton Collection, Prescott Memorial Library, Louisiana Tech University; and Alexander Library, New Jersey Room, Special Collections, Rutgers University, New Brunswick.

Josiah Harmar Papers. University of Michigan, William L. Clements Library, Ann Arbor.

Judd, Jacob. *Fort Lee on the Palisades: The Battle for the Hudson*. Bear Mountain, NY: Sleepy Hollow Restorations, Inc. for the Palisades Interstate Park Commission, 1963.

Lee, Francis B., ed. "Trenton, October 7 [1778]." *Documents Relating to the Revolutionary History of the State of New Jersey*, vol. II, Extracts from American Newspapers, 1778 (John L. Murphy Publishing Co., Trenton, NJ, 1903), 462–63.

Muster Rolls of the Fourth Battalion, New Jersey Volunteers. RG 8, "C" Series, Vols. 1858, 159 and 1900. National Archives of Canada, Ottawa, Ontario.

Papers of the Continental Congress, M247. National Archives and Records Administration, Washington, D.C.

Pension and Bounty Land Application Files, M804. National Archives and Records Administration, Washington, D.C.

Sir Henry Clinton Papers. University of Michigan, William L. Clements Library, Ann Arbor.

Treasury, Class 1. The National Archives, Kew, Richmond, Surrey, United Kingdom.

Various commanders' correspondence, George Washington Papers, Presidential Papers Microfilm. Washington, D.C.: Library of Congress, 1961. Series 4 (general Correspondence, 1697–1799).

War Office, Classes 42 and 71. The National Archives, Kew, Richmond, Surrey, United Kingdom.

William Livingston Papers. New York Public Library, New York.

Bibliography

NEWSPAPERS

The New Jersey Gazette (Trenton)
The New Jersey Journal (Chatham)
The New York Gazette and the Weekly Mercury
The Pennsylvania Gazette (Philadelphia)
The Pennsylvania Packet (Philadelphia)
The Royal American Gazette (New York)
The Royal Gazette (New York)

PUBLISHED SOURCES

Accounts, G. Washington with the United States, Commencing June 1775, and ending June 1783, Comprehending a Space of 8 Years. Library of Congress, Washington, D.C.

"Anecdotes of Charles Lee."

Collections of the New York Historical Society for 1875. *Official Letters of Major General James Pattison, Commandant of Artillery*, Printed for the Society (New York), 1876.

Collections of the New York Historical Society for 1883. *The Journals of Lt. Col. Stephen Kemble, 1773–1789.* Printed for the Society (New York), 1884.

The Diary of Frederick Mackenzie. Cambridge, MA: Harvard University Press, 1930.

Hester, Tom. *Star Ledger, Center of the Storm, NJ and American Revolution.* Edited by Len Meliswigo, Kean University, 2001.

Lydenberg, Harry Miller, ed. *Archibald Robertson: His Diaries and Sketches in America, 1762–1780.* New York: New York Public Library.

The Papers of the Continental Congress, 1774–89. "Inspection Roll of Negroes, New York City." National Archives, Washington, D.C. Roll 7 M 332 10-1-3.

Index

A
abatis 34, 133, 135
Acquackanonk 19, 67, 79, 115
Acquackanonk Bridge 114
Acquackanonk Landing 35, 67, 71, 175
African Americans 162–168
Aldington, John 26, 66
AMtY marchers 156–160
André, Major John 114, 116, 142, 143, 180
"Anecdotes of Charles Lee" 105, 110
Arnold, General Benedict 73, 101, 103, 124, 142, 143, 180

B
Babcock, David 132
Babcock, Ensign John 67
Banta, Aaron 132
Banta, Sergeant Samuel 73
Basking Ridge 109
Baumann, Major Sebastian 152
Bayard, John 66
Baylor's Dragoons 118–123
Baylor, Colonel George 114, 118, 178
Baylor Massacre 118–123, 178
Benson, Mathew 66
Berdan, Albert 70
Bergeneers 134
Bergenfield 178
Bergen Neck 66, 136, 139, 140
Bergen Point (modern Bayonne) 132, 136, 141, 179
Berry, John 134
Bertholf, John 155
Birch, Brigadier General Samuel 165, 166

Birchtown, Nova Scotia 166
Blackledge, Maria 84
Black Brigade 165
Black Loyalists 162–168
Black Pioneers. *See* Black Brigade
Black Watch 127
Blanch, Captain Thomas 82, 134, 137
Blauvelt, Private Harman 137
"Book of Negroes" 165–168
Brandywine, Battle of 87
British army 24, 31, 40, 42, 65, 67, 87, 97, 106, 107, 112, 130, 132, 139, 162–165, 176–180
British invasion 25–31, 172
Brooklyn, Battle of 32, 34, 124, 144
Browne, First Major Daniel Isaac 67
Bull's Ferry Blockhouse 27, 132–137, 179, 180
Bunker Hill, Battle of 156
Burgoyne, General John 176, 177
Burr, Lieutenant Colonel Aaron 92, 94, 96, 155, 156, 177
Buskirk, Lucas 132
Byles, Major Thomas Langhorne 129

C
Cameron, John 66
Camp Ramapough 175, 176
Carleton, Sir Guy 164, 165
Charleston 87, 92, 107, 165
Charlton, Samuel 164
Chesapeake 150, 151, 180
chevaux-de-frise 48, 49
Clinton, Governor George 90, 96, 99, 101, 176, 177
Clinton, Sir Henry 71, 127, 135, 137, 139, 140, 148, 163, 165

Index

Closter 27–30, 66, 73, 77, 78, 82, 84, 133, 137, 139, 140, 176–180
Clove, the 94, 132, 175–179
Coetus 55
Cole, Samuel 140
Combs, Moses N. 134
Common Sense 38, 42, 49
Communipaw 132
Conferentie 55
Continental army 30, 37, 40, 49, 70–75, 87–94, 97, 101–103, 107, 113, 115, 118, 127–138, 147, 148, 153, 156, 163, 175–180
Continental Congress 70, 97–99, 107, 118, 120, 155, 162
Cooper, Ensign Richard 72
Cornwallis, General Charles 17–25, 27, 28, 31, 49, 59, 84, 89, 112, 114, 120, 140, 150, 151, 180
Cortland Sugar House 70
Cresskill 27, 28, 30, 175
Crisis Papers, The 38, 40, 42, 44, 49
Crosbie, William 141
Cuyler, Abraham C. 132

D

Day, Elias 140
Dayton, Elias 115
Degraw, Casparus 75
DeHart, Lieutenant Jacob M. 135
DeLancey, Adjutant General Oliver, Jr. 139
Demarest 84
Demarest, Captain Samuel 84
Demarest, Peter 54
Demarest, Thomas 123
Devoe, Private John 137
DeWint, John 164
DeWint House 143, 144, 146
Dey, Colonel Theunis 79, 137
de Grasse, François Joseph Paul (French admiral) 149, 151, 156
De Kalb, General Baron Johann 101
dragoons 118–123
Drummond, Robert Major 75

E

Earle, Ensign Justus 67
Earle, Lieutenant Edward 67
Earl of Dunmore 162
Edgewater 138
Elizabethtown 79, 127
Emerson 176
English Neighborhood 19, 21, 22, 26, 32, 66, 72, 74, 85, 112, 129, 133, 137, 164, 167, 173, 176, 178–180

Erskine, Robert 27, 28, 153, 155
Ethiopian Regiment 162
ethnicity of Bergen County 54
Eutaw, Battle of 73
Everet, John 132
Ewald, Captain Johann 27, 30, 31
expense account of George Washington 169–174

F

Fell, John 70, 155
Ferguson, Major Patrick 72
First Pennsylvania Regiment 135
Fisher, Mary 75
Fisher, Private Lodewick 75
foraging 50, 71, 72, 93, 99, 101, 102, 112–118, 120, 125, 126, 178, 180
Fort DeLancey 139, 180
Fort Lee 19, 21, 22, 25, 27, 28, 30, 31, 32, 34, 35, 37, 38, 40, 44–52, 61, 65, 66, 78, 85, 107, 108, 125, 126, 129, 134, 137–139, 172, 175–180
Fort Montgomery 73, 175, 177
Fort Putnam 143
Fort Ticonderoga 70, 176
Fort Washington 20, 24, 25, 34, 35, 40, 46–52, 78, 107, 108
Fourth New Jersey Volunteers 127
Franklin, Benjamin 38, 147
Franklin, William 65, 67, 136
Fraunces, Samuel 144
Fraunces Tavern 165
French and Indian War 60, 105, 107, 147
French involvement 84–90, 97, 101, 139, 147–161, 180
Fyers, Lieutenant William 133

G

Garrison, Garret 155
Gates, General Horatio 101, 176
Germain, Lord George 20, 135
Goetschius, Major Mauritius 28, 73, 134
Great Awakening 55
Greene, General Nathanael 25, 27, 32–40, 42, 49, 87, 107, 143, 159, 175
Grey, General Charles 120

H

Hackensack 19, 27, 32, 34, 35, 37, 40, 59, 63, 65–67, 70–77, 82, 84, 94, 107, 112–115, 120, 123, 125, 127, 129, 134, 137, 156, 168, 175, 176, 177, 178, 180
Hackensack Courthouse 129, 178
Hackensack River 19, 27, 53, 58, 59, 107, 113, 115, 116, 120, 123, 127

Index

Hale, Nathan 144
Hamilton, Colonel Alexander 94, 143
Hammell, John 66
Harding, Captain William 139
Haring, Captain Abraham 77, 79, 84
Harlem Heights, Battle of 40, 143
Harrington 82, 137, 176
Harrington Township 82
Havemeyer Mansion 154
Haverstraw 96, 101, 126, 176, 178
Hayes, Major Samuel 61, 74
Hazen, General Moses 152
Heard, General Nathaniel 115
Heath, Major General William 19, 175, 176
Hermitage 91–96, 101–103, 155–156, 177
Hessians 17, 19, 22, 23, 27, 34, 35, 46, 49, 50, 51, 93, 114, 118, 124, 127, 129, 135, 139, 148, 176
Hoboken 26, 66, 132
Hopper, Andrew 90, 154
Hopper, Captain Jonathan 74
Hopper, John 129
Hopperstown 92, 93, 97, 176, 177, 179
Hopper Grist Mill Site 154
Hopper House 90, 129
Howe, General William 17, 20, 25, 26, 40, 59, 109, 165, 166, 175, 176, 177
Hudson (North) River 23, 82, 103, 112, 164
Hudson Highlands 94, 101, 102, 148, 177
Huguenots 55
Huyler, Captain John 28, 84
Huyler's Landing 27

I

Inglis, Reverend Charles 130
invasion of New Jersey 17–31

J

Jefferson, Thomas 42, 89, 125, 174
Jersey Dutch 50–57, 118, 120, 143
Jersey Dutch farmers 50, 118
Jockey Hollow 125

K

Kearney House 77, 83, 84
Kinderkamack Road 120
Kings Ferry 175, 180
King George III 32, 47, 66, 74, 86, 135, 147, 162
King Louis XVI 147, 148
Knox, Henry 143
Knyphausen, General Wilhelm 120, 127

L

Lafayette, General Marquis de 85–89, 94, 110, 149, 156, 179
Laroe–Hopper–Van Horn House 154
Laune, Peter 145
Laurens, Henry 98, 102
Lee, Colonel Henry 72, 178
Lee, Major General Charles 19, 87, 97, 99, 105–111, 175, 176
   court-martial 110, 177
Leonia 19, 26, 32, 35, 40, 85, 172, 176, 178
Lexington and Concord 32, 78
Liberty Pole 31, 35, 40, 49, 77–79, 82, 113, 114, 137, 174, 180
Lincoln, General Benjamin 90, 152
Little Ferry 35, 127, 178
Livingston, Governor William 65, 73, 96, 112
Long Pond Ironworks 153
Lord Rawdon 72
Lord Stirling 94, 99, 114–116, 126, 127
Loyalists 26, 56, 59, 65–76, 92–94, 120, 132–141, 165, 176–180
Lozier, John 73
Luke, Philip 132
Lutheran Church Mahwah 155
Lyndhurst 176

M

MacPherson, Duncan 127
Magaw, Colonel Robert 34, 49, 107
Mahwah 90, 153, 154–156, 159, 176
Malcolm's Regiment 132, 177
Manhattan 26, 34, 40, 46–49, 54, 61, 63, 70, 84, 112, 125, 127, 130, 175
Marcus, James 92, 95, 96
Marsh, Captain Lieutenant Hendrick 67
Maxwell, General William 112–115
May, John 155
McDougal, General Alexander 177
McHenry, James 94
Middle Brook 178
militia 50, 61, 67, 73, 74, 77, 113, 115, 118, 123, 134, 136, 137, 164
Miller, Captain Joshua 133
Moffatt, Major Thomas 177
Monmouth, Battle of 79, 94, 97–99, 110, 124, 177
Monroe, James 37, 94
Moonachie 180
Moore, Major James 73
Morristown 61, 72, 74, 90, 114, 125, 167, 171, 176–180
Mount Vernon 169, 172
Muhlenberg, Reverend Henry 58, 126
mutiny of New Jersey and Pennsylvania troops 180

Index

N

Napoleon 89
Narragansett Bay, Rhode Island 148
neutral ground 131
Newark 117
Newport, Rhode Island 88, 102, 103, 151, 165, 179, 180
New Bridge 19, 27, 31, 34, 35, 40, 53–67, 74, 78, 79, 82, 112, 115, 120, 129, 134, 175–180
New Bridge Landing 34, 53–64
New Brunswick 37, 75, 76, 79, 94, 97, 99, 125, 175, 176, 177, 180, 182, 184
New Jersey Brigade 115
New Jersey Journal 64, 141
New Jersey Volunteers 59, 66, 67, 70–75, 127, 139
New Milford 35, 55, 180
New Windsor, New York 138
New York City 24, 97, 101, 102, 118, 125, 127, 130, 132, 134, 138, 139, 140, 148–152, 158, 164, 165, 175–180
Noble, Isaac 67, 70
Nova Scotia 66, 75, 76, 141, 165

O

Oakland 155, 158, 176, 177
Old Paramus Reformed Church 91, 99, 110, 127, 156
Old Stone House, Ramsey 155
Old Tappan 123
Oradell 53
Orangetown 164
Orange and Ulster County Militias 176
Orange County 90, 132
Orange Rangers 66, 73
Outwater, Captain John 79

P

Paine, Thomas 30, 38–45, 49
Palisades 17, 25, 26, 28, 38, 47, 49, 51, 52, 65, 78, 82, 133
Paramus 28, 66, 70, 73, 91–99, 110, 114, 115, 126, 127, 129, 133, 152, 156, 176–180
Passaic County 27, 152, 153
Passy (suburb of Paris) 148
Paterson, Governor William 94, 96
Patriots 19, 26, 65, 82, 85, 102, 118, 120, 123, 124, 180
Pattison, Major General James 164
Paulus Hook 72, 79, 116, 126, 130, 132, 134, 136, 178
Paulus Hook Ferry 54
Pennsylvania troops 120, 134, 179, 180
Perth Amboy 172

Petersfield 155
Philadelphia 24, 34, 40, 42, 79, 86–89, 97, 101, 111, 125, 126, 151, 165, 172, 176, 177
Phoenix, English frigate 47–49
Pickering, Quartermaster General Timothy 117
pillaging and plundering 23, 70, 114, 127–129, 137
Pompton 90, 125, 152, 159, 176, 178, 180
Pompton Plains 176
Poor, Brigadier General Enoch 179
Prevost, Theodosia 92–96, 156, 177
Princeton 34, 35, 42, 79, 125, 176, 180, 182
Provincial corps 73, 75
Provincial forces 66, 67
Provisional Peace Agreement 164
Putnam, Rufus 47

R

Rall, Johann 19
Ramapough 53, 66, 67, 70, 75, 152, 159, 160, 174–180
Ramapough Mountains 53, 174
Ramapo Reformed Church 155
Ramapo Valley Road 90, 154, 156, 158, 159
Ramsey 90
Rebelmen statue in Fort Lee 44
Rebel Standard 164, 165
Rebel troops 20, 23, 32, 92–96, 162, 175, 178
Refugees 132–141
Regiment of Foot 19, 23, 132
Regiment of Horse 116
religion 55
retreat, the 27, 31–46, 49, 50, 67, 79, 88, 108, 110, 125, 135, 173, 174
Rhode Island 102, 148
Richards, John 73
Ridgewood 156
Ringwood 66, 152, 176
Ringwood Iron Mines 153
Ringwood Manor 153
Rivervale Road 120
River Edge 35, 55
River Vale 118–123, 178
Robertson, Major Archibald 139
Robinson, Lieutenant Colonel Thomas 135
Rochambeau, Comte de 88, 90, 91, 103, 145, 147–161, 180
Rockland County 164
Roebuck, the ship 20, 49, 50
Romaine, Sergeant Benjamin 73, 139
Rose, English frigate 47, 48
Rutan, Captain Peter 66, 67
Ryerson, Captain Samuel 67, 72, 76

Index

S

Saddle River 67, 175, 178, 179
Saratoga 79, 148, 177
Scammell, Alexander Colonel 138
Schraalenburgh 73, 134, 178, 179
Secaucus 74
Second Pennsylvania Regiment 135
Selig, Robert 159
Seven Years' War 85, 86
Shays' Rebellion 42
Shreve, Colonel Israel 114
Sixteenth Regiment of Light Dragoons 19
Skinner, Brigadier General Cortland 67, 70
skirmishes 31, 49, 82, 127, 129
slavery 162–168
South Carolina 66, 70, 72, 73, 87, 99, 127, 165
Spuyten Duyvil 17, 25, 47
Staten Island 70, 77, 78, 112, 113, 116, 125, 127, 129, 130, 136, 151, 175
Steuben House 53–64
Stewart, Captain Allan 165
Stony Point 143, 151, 178
Suffern 90, 94, 152, 153, 159, 175–180
Sullivan, Major General John 70
Sumter, Thomas 72
Symmes, John Cleves 103

T

Tallmadge, Major Benjamin 143
Tappan 46, 47, 49, 82, 114, 118, 120, 123, 139, 142–146, 166, 176, 177, 178, 180
Tappan Zee 46, 47
Tarleton, Banastre 109
Tarrytown 143
Tartar HMS 49
Taswell, Sergeant John 72
Teaneck 35, 54, 55, 67, 178
Terhune, Richard 75
Thatcher, Dr. James 125, 126, 127
Theodat, Charles Henri, Comte d'Estaing 101
Third Pennsylvania Regiment 129
Tilghman, Tench 52, 94
Timpany, Second Major Robert 67
Tomlinson, Jabez 142
Tories 37, 137, 176
Treaty of Alliance 148
Treaty of Amity and Commerce 148
Trenton 34, 37, 40, 42, 49, 79, 125, 153, 176, 183, 184, 185
Trenton, Battle of 88, 118
Trescott, Major Lemuel 133
Trumbull, Jonathan 101
Tryal 66

U

Upper Closter Dock 27

V

Valley Forge 87, 97, 124, 125, 171, 174, 177
Valley Road 176, 178, 180
Vanderbeck, Abraham 70
Vansciver, Daniel 77–84
Van Allen House 155
Van Buskirk, Captain Jacob 72
Van Buskirk, Dr. Abraham 58, 66, 67, 75, 127, 176
Van Buskirk, Lawrence 54, 58
Van Buskirk's battalion 70, 75
Van Cortland, Major Philip 75
Van Houten, John 75
Van Norden, John 75
Versailles (suburb of Paris) 88, 148
Virginia 72, 84, 89, 101, 103, 111, 115, 118, 125, 126, 140, 162, 172, 178, 180
Von Steuben, Baron 61–64, 74, 89, 110, 143, 156

W

W3R March 147, 154
Ward, General Joseph 73
Ward, Major General Artemus 107
Ward, Peter 82
Ward, Thomas 73, 131–143
Washington, General George 24, 27, 32, 35, 38, 40, 42, 45, 61, 65, 87, 90, 91, 94, 97–102, 107–110, 114, 116, 124, 135, 148, 164, 165, 169–174
Wayne, Brigadier General Anthony 27, 87, 120, 126, 134, 135, 178, 180, 184
weather conditions during war 124–130
Weehawken 132, 178
Westchester 19, 92, 103, 138, 175, 176, 178
West Point 127, 138, 142, 143, 178, 180
Whigs 56, 74, 92, 93, 94, 117, 129, 134, 137, 141
White Plains 40, 99, 143, 151, 178
witness sites 153–156
Woodford, Brigadier General William 115
Wyckoff, Polly (legend of) 30

Y

Yorktown, Virginia 89, 91, 140, 147, 151
Young, Mahonri 173

Z

Zabriskie, Albert 55
Zabriskie, John 37, 58, 59–61, 63, 64, 66, 74
Zabriskie, Peter 32, 37

Visit us at
www.historypress.net

www.ingramcontent.com/pod-product-compliance
Lightning Source LLC
Chambersburg PA
CBHW080925100426
42812CB00007B/2376